# We the Media

# We the Media

## A Citizens' Guide to Fighting for Media Democracy

Edited by Don Hazen and Julie Winokur

THE NEW PRESS

NEW YORK

The publisher is grateful for permission to reprint copyrighted material from the following:

*Columbia Journalism Review, Detroit Metro-Times, Extra!, L.A. Weekly, Los Alamos Monitor, Mother Jones, New York Observer, New York Times, San Francisco Chronicle, San Francisco Examiner, The Nation, Third Force, Utne Reader, Village Voice, Wired,* and *Z Magazine.* Edward Alwood, *Straight News* (New York: Columbia University Press, 1996). Farai Chideya, *Don't Believe the Hype: Fighting Cultural Misinformation About African Americans* (New York: Penguin Books, 1994). Susan Douglas, *Where the Girls Are: Growing Up Female With the Mass Media* (New York: Times Books, 1994). Seth Friedman, *The Zine Reader* (New York: Crown Books, 1997). Sut Jhally and Justin Lewis, *Enlightened Racism* (Boulder, Colorado: Westview Press, 1992). Jean Kilbourne, "Killing Us Softly: Gender Roles in Advertising," in *Adolescent Medicine* (Philadelphia: Hanley & Belfus, 1993). Mike Males, *The Scapegoat Generation* (Monroe, Maine: Common Courage Press, 1996). Robert W. McChesney, *Corporate Media and the Threat to Democracy* (New York: Seven Stories Press, 1995). Danny Schechter, *The More You Watch, The Less You Know* (New York: Seven Stories Press, 1997). John Stauber and Sheldon Rampton, *Toxic Sludge Is Good for You* (Monroe, Maine: Common Courage Books, 1995). Rodger Streitmatter, *Unspeakable: The Rise of the Gay and Lesbian Press in America* (Winchester, Massachusetts: Faber and Faber, 1995).

Published in the United States by The New Press, New York
Distributed by W.W. Norton & Company, Inc., New York

The New Press was established in 1990 as a not-for-profit alternative to the large, commercial publishing houses currently dominating the book publishing industry. The New Press operates in the public interest rather than for private gain, and is committed to publishing, in innovative ways, works of educational, cultural, and community value that might not normally be commercially viable.

Book design by BAD

Production management by Kim Waymer
Printed in the United States of America

9 8 7 6 5 4 3

*The mass media does not reveal reality; it masks it. It doesn't help bring about change; it helps avoid change. It doesn't encourage democratic participation; it induces passivity, resignation and selfishness. It doesn't generate creativity; it creates consumers.*

*— EDUARDO GALEANO*

# Contents

## I. Ownership & Concentration

# II. Commercialization

# III. Content

# IV. Access

# V. The Next Frontier

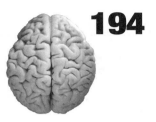

# Acknowledgments

We would not have been able to publish this book without the generous support of our contributors to whom we owe a debt of thanks.

This book was an outgrowth of the first Media & Democracy Congress held in San Francisco, February of 1996. Many of the ideas and some of the writings are a direct result of the creative interaction that took place during that event.

Much thanks to André Schiffrin, Matt Weiland, Hall Smyth, and Grace Farrell.

Special credit for creativity in weaving together the many pieces of the book and for tracking down the authors goes to coeditor Julie Winokur for her smarts, patience, and indispensibility; contributing editor Christine Triano for her wisdom and attention to detail; Nadya Tan for fact checking, computer wizardry, and ability to keep everything organized. Much thanks also to other hard working staff at IAJ/Alter-Net and our new Media Democracy Institute—particularly Clover Hale, who worked closely with cartoonists, and Christine Stavem, Viveca Greene, Robin Templeton, Robert Bray, Cynthia Sharpe, and Carina Mcleod.

Much thanks to the board of the Institute for Alternative Journalism, especially Katherine Fulton, who is truly an inspiration, Ron Williams, our committed and trusty president, and Mark Zusman for reviewing the manuscript and making valuable suggestions.

A special thanks to Janine Jackson and the staff of FAIR for rising above the call of duty to provide contacts, resources, and a wealth of material for reprint in the book.

Much appreciation to Katrina vanden Heuvel and *The Nation* for producing the "National Entertainment State" and "Book Publishing" issues and permission for the use of material from those and other issues of the magazine.

Kudos to Mark Crispin Miller for his passion and expertise in staking out the media issue and to his research partner Janine Jaquet for much of the information found in the maps of global media companies.

Acknowledgment to Ken Auletta for coining the term "synergy=poison."

Special thanks to Robert McChesney for his enthusiasm and integrity; Makani Themba for her wisdom and support; Ben Bagdikian for leading the way.

Special gratitude to longtime supporters of our work, especially Bill and John Moyers, Colin Greer, Harriet Barlow, Jane MacAlevey, Woody Wickham, Rob McKay, Carol Schwartz, Helen Brunner and many others.

Thanks also for wisdom and support to Danny Schechter, Jeff Cohen, Patrice O'Neill, Jeff Gillenkirk and especially to Vivian Dent for their editing skills and warm support.

# Navigation Tools

**B**ecause of the complex nature of the media system, there were countless ways to organize the material for this book. It is impossible to compartmentalize the information because it overlaps and interlocks in such an intricate weave. After great deliberation, we decided to divide the material along three main principles:

---

* **THE CHAPTERS** (Ownership, Commercialization, Content, Access, the Next Frontier) take a wide-angle approach to the major themes impacting the media;

---

* **THE COMPANIES** who control a major slice of the media pie (Time Warner, Disney, TCI, News Corp., Westinghouse) are represented through charts and interesting facts;

---

* **SECTIONS** titled "Incredible Shrinking Media" (for television, newspapers, books, and films) examine the paradox between these growing industries and their shrinking diversity.

**T**hroughout the book, you'll also notice a series of icons which denote different categories of information. The following key should help you wend your way through the media democracy maze.

---

 **MEDIA HEROES** are the beacons of light who defy corporate and commercial interests to provide information in the public interest

---

 **SYNERGY=POISON** is the skull-and-crossbones warning that corporations with holdings across various media serve their own interest when determining content

---

 **SCARY FACTS** are the concrete proof that something's wrong with the media picture

---

 **ACTION BOXES** denote things you can do to make a difference

# Introduction

**DON HAZEN**

Celebrity fluff. Talking hairdos. News you can't use, from sources you don't trust. American media is turning into a national entertainment state controlled by a dwindling handful of media moguls and global corporations. It has to stop.

When the media falls back on murder and mayhem, rather than investigating the roots of crime, it does the public a disservice. When it neglects labor's opinion on issues that affect our work lives, it has silenced a vital part of society. When self-censorship becomes a journalist's reflex because she assumes the story "will never get published," we know the media system is not serving us.

As I write these words I am conflicted. My instinct—my habit—when writing about the media is to dwell on gloom and doom. But that is not the job of this book. Not the main job, anyway. Along with the bad news I promise plenty of good news—media heroes who hold the system accountable and creative media makers who provide alternatives to the dumbed-down fare that dominates today's world of news and information. I also urge you, the reader, to join a very important movement. But more about that in a moment.

Before you delve into this book, ask yourself what happens when we have media monopoly and why you should care. You are committed to a better world, to fairness, human rights, environmental preservation, and other concerns. How often are your passions fully featured in the media, right up there with Disney World's birthday and the latest $100 million blockbuster film? So much of our social policy about welfare, crime, prisons, drugs, youth, and the allocation of our precious resources is based upon grossly distorted media images. Is this the way we want our decisions made? Do we want entire segments of the population missing from or severely misrepresented by the media, the so-called mirror of American life?

This book attempts to explain why the global media system dominates our lives, what it means to us and what we can do about it. We'll take you on a journey of discovery to understand how our media system has been transformed into a consumer-shaping machine and which mega-companies control its workings. We'll explore how powerful and seductive this machine is, and how it will affect your life in untold ways.

*We the Media* is about how the twin virtues of the press and democracy have been torn asunder. Today, instead of a communication system that enlightens the public and speaks truth to power, we have a media system that has become all-powerful itself and threatens to overwhelm democracy in the process. That is, unless we take a stand and insist that media and democracy go hand in hand. That's where you come in. This book has been constructed as a guide to navigating the enormous changes in the media system. But more importantly, it describes dozens of organizations and individuals who are fighting back and winning in the battle against media monopoly.

In some crucial ways, the big media companies have overplayed their hands. People instinctively fear huge concentrations of power and are disgusted with perverse TV violence. They're getting fed up with celebrity pontificators who make $25,000 giving speeches to organizations they cover as journalists. And they're burning up about rising cable rates and the diminishing quality of content.

It seems clear that the excesses of the media corporations will become a major issue for the millennium, and growing numbers of people will say no in various ways. The public is in the early stages of media rebellion. But we can't sit around and wait for the moguls to fall flat on their faces. We have to resist media which undermines our democracy and our soul and say yes to media which empowers us to participate in civic life and stimulates our active creativity. Some people are calling the growing effort of fighting the media powers a "Media and Democracy" movement. Others are calling it common sense. Whatever it is called, one basic step includes holding our elected officials and the media companies accountable. They have been awarded the public trust; we must insist that they produce a media that reflects America in all its diversity and provides information that people can use.

Simultaneously, we need to create a different—and renewed—independent media system that will celebrate public interest journalism and provide a stimulating and powerful alternative to the infotainment-oriented corporate media of today. Can we do that? Of course we can, and we must. This book will help you find the way, especially in the last chapter where some of the best "how to's" for participating in a media and democracy movement are presented. That's why, despite the doom and gloom, this is an optimistic book.

We want to ensure that future generations read a history that credits citizens—journalists, advocates, parents, philanthropists and policymakers—with democratizing the media in the face of commercial onslaught. If we don't act now, our children may not be able to discern a news story from a sneaker ad, and *Hard Copy* may come to represent the standard for investigative reporting for generations to come.

In March of 1996 in San Francisco, the Institute for Alternative Journalism hosted the first-ever Media and Democracy Congress. More than 600 journalists, mediamakers, critics and concerned citizens came together to collaborate and plan for the future. In October of 1997 in New York City, a larger and more ambitious gathering gave more impetus to the growing media rebellion.

This book in part is inspired by those gatherings and by the hope that fighting media monopoly can move to the top of many people's concerns. I urge you to join this embryonic Media and Democracy movement. It needs informed and effective grassroots organizing to fight in city councils and in legislatures against the growing concentration of media. It needs dynamic spokespeople making presentations for the cause of media democratization. It needs to learn specific lessons from the right wing's effective organizing, which not only uses grassroots groups, think tanks, publicists, and spokespeople, but creates and strengthens its own media and communication structure to keep important ideas in play.

Reading this book is one of the first steps. More than 150 informed commentators and activists on our global media system have combined efforts to cover the full media landscape. I hope you find the results stimulating and motivating.

*Don Hazen is the director of the Institute for Alternative Journalism.*

# Ownership & Concentration

Part **I**

**N**o longer can any serious executive regard TV, movies, magazines and radio as simple "entertainment"... For these are the economic dynamos of the new gilded age, the tools by which the public is informed of the latest offerings, enchanted by packaged bliss, instructed in the arcane pleasures of the new, taught to be good citizens and brought warmly into the consuming fold. Every leader of business now knows that the nation's health is measured not by production of cars and corn, but by the strength of its culture industry.

— TOM FRANK, The Baffler

**T**rue, our current moguls are in the hallowed tradition of media empire builders past, but the cultural landscape is alarmingly different. While Hearst built a vast newspaper chain, Luce a stable of powerful magazines, and Warner a movie studio, today's more powerful titans run conglomerates that encompass not just newspapers or magazines or movies or broadcast TV or cable — but all of the above, and more. Even as the dizzying proliferation of media outlets promises a greater variety of content, how much variety will there be if all the new "channels," from cable TV networks to the flashiest Internet sites, ultimately have the same few owners?

— FRANK RICH, New York Times

**W**hen I began putting the pieces together for the new, fifth edition of Media Monopoly, it quickly became apparent that we had an entire new game. The whole idea of the robber barons — who made their money in railroads or steel, or in the case of media monopoly in newspapers or television — is over. Now the big operators are in all the media industries and that picture, when pieced together, is very scary indeed. And worse, not only do we have much larger corporations, they are increasingly focused on controlling both the creation of content and its distribution. Some of the largest corporations in the country and the world — General Electric, Disney, Time Warner, Westinghouse — now own distribution and control what much of the American public sees. No longer do you look at a media and see who is dominant. When you do, you find the same companies through all the media. A big shot at Disney or Time Warner can say, "It doesn't make a difference whether it's movies, books, television, magazines or cable. Everybody has to come to us." It's a very explicit strategy. These corporations are larger and more powerful and control more media than ever.

— BEN BAGDIKIAN, Dean Emeritus
of University of California, Berkeley
and author of Media Monopoly

# 1. The Media Transformed

*Plus comments by* Ben Bagdikian, Walter Cronkite, and Max Frankel

*And profiles of* Media Access Project, Project Censored, and "Fear and Favor in the Newsroom"

# FREE THE MEDIA

## MARK CRISPIN MILLER

Four giant corporations now control the major TV news divisions: GE, Westinghouse, Disney, and Time Warner. Two of these four corporations are defense contractors (both involved in nuclear production), while the other two are mammoth manufacturers of fun 'n' games. Thus we are the subjects of a *national entertainment state*, in which the news and much of our amusement come to us directly from the two most powerful industries in the United States.

Glance at the ownership charts in this book, and see why, say, Tom Brokaw might find it difficult to introduce stories critical of nuclear power. Or why it is unlikely ABC News will ever again air an exposé of Disney's practices (as *PrimeTime Live* did in 1990); or, indeed, why CNN—or any of the others—will not touch the biggest story of them all: the media monopoly itself.

A few other titans are converging on the culture: Rupert Murdoch's News Corporation—parent of (among much else) Fox Television, Twentieth Century-Fox, *TV Guide*, HarperCollins and the *New York Post*, as well as many major dailies throughout Britain and Australia, and Asia's largest TV system—has started up an all-news channel to compete with CNN. Likewise, GE's NBC has joined with Microsoft to start the telejournalistic venture MSNBC, whereby Bill Gates's great software monopoly can now help set the national agenda. Likewise, such mammoth players as Viacom, Universal, Bertelsmann of Germany, and Sony of Japan are also variously gobbling up the airwaves and the newsstands, the movies and the music, the satellite feeds and the cable stuff—while the octopus that is S.I. Newhouse mainly glides within the world of print, darkening publishing houses, magazines and newspapers that, in one way or another, reach us all.

In short, the true cause of the enormous ills that now dismay so many Americans—the universal sleaze and "dumbing down," the flood-tide of corporate propaganda, the terminal inanity of United States politics—has arisen not from any grand decline in national character, nor from the plotting of some Hebrew cabal, but from the inevitable toxic influence of those few corporations that have monopolized our culture. The only way to solve the problem is to break their hold; and to that end the facts of media ownership must be made known to all.

Media concentration started getting very obvious in the spring of 1995, when the Federal Communications

Commission (FCC) summarily let Rupert Murdoch off the hook for having fudged the actual foreign ownership of his concern (an Australian outfit, which Murdoch had not made clear to the busy regulators). ABC was then sucked into Disney, CBS swallowed by Westinghouse, and Ted Turner's miniempire became part of Time Warner—a grand consolidation that the press, the White House, Congress, and the FCC all failed to question.

With the mergers came some hints of how the new proprietors would henceforth use their journalists: Disney's ABC News apologized to Philip Morris—a major TV advertiser, through Kraft Foods—for having told the truth, on a broadcast of *Day One*, about the company's manipulation of nicotine levels in its cigarettes; and CBS's in-house

counsel ordered the old newshounds at *60 Minutes* to bury an explosive interview with whistleblower Jeffrey Wigand about the addictive practices of tobacco producer, Brown & Williamson.

Such moves foretold the death of broadcast journalism, as did the radical cost-cutting now being dictated by the networks' owners. And yet some good seems also to havecome out of that *annus horribilis* of big waivers, big mergers, big layoffs, and big lies. The risks of media monopoly were suddenly apparent not just to the usual uptight minority of activists and scholars but, more and more, to everyone. People wanted to know just what was happening and what to do about it. The time has therefore come to free the media by creating a new, broad-based Media Democracy movement dedicated to this crucial civic mission.

This movement must begin by getting out the word—and there's the rub. Our problem has no precedent, for what's monopolized today is no mere staple such as beef or oil but the very media whereby the problem could be solved. Today's media democracy campaign will therefore have to be a

*continued on page 6*

## COMMENT

*The joint venture is another thing that is generally frightening. I call it the "communications cartel." A cartel, of course, is a formal arrangement among corporations to arrange prices and all the other terms of delivery. What you have now are joint ventures and stock sharing among the big media companies who are supposedly the big competitors. Over and over again you get a close knit set of relationships among the biggest companies supposedly deregulated to provoke more competition. For example, Time Warner and TCI are the two biggest cable companies — together they have more than 47 percent of the 13,000 cable systems in the country. TCI had a piece of Time Warner and they both owned a piece of Turner. They get that kind of interlock where nobody moves independently or they move independently with great reluctance because they are in each other's pocket.*

— *Ben Bagdikian, author of* Media Monopoly

*continued from page 5*

thoroughly grass-roots effort—one that will work around the mainstream entities. It will depend on those idealists who still work within the media: those who would do a good job if they could, but who've been forced to compromise, and those working on the margins—the stalwarts of the alternative press and of groups like Fairness & Accuracy In Reporting. All should henceforth pay attention to developments within the different culture industries.

This movement must devote itself to antitrust—the enforcement of the present laws, and the design of new legislation. The American Booksellers Association, for instance, filed an antitrust suit against Random House for illegally providing discounts to the nationwide bookstore chains and retailers. Those in other industries should likewise make a fuss, so as to reclaim their debased profession.

The public, furthermore, must be reminded that it owns the airwaves—a fact of vast importance, now that the triumphant giants don't even pretend to compensate us with programs "in

the public interest." Likewise, we should start discussing taxes on mass advertising. Such a tax, and the tolls on usage of the airwaves, would yield enough annual revenues at least to pay for public broadcasting.

The Media Democracy movement must acknowledge and explain the cultural consequences of monopoly. Our aim is certainly not censorship, which is the tacit goal of rightist demagogues like Ralph Reed and the Rev. Donald Wildmon. The purpose, rather, is a solution wholly constitutional—and, for that matter, sanely capitalistic. We would reintroduce a pleasurable diversity into the corporate monoculture.

There is no substitute for actual democracy—which cannot work unless the people know what's going on. And so, before we raise the proper legal questions and debate the legislative possibilities, we need simply to teach everyone, ourselves included, that this whole failing culture is an oversold dead end, and that there might be a way out of it. (A version of this article first appeared in *The Nation*)

*Mark Crispin Miller, chairman of the*

## Media Access Project

 In the words of the Supreme Court, "It is the purpose of the First Amendment to preserve an uninhibited market-place of ideas in which truth will ultimately prevail....It is the right of the public to receive suitable access to social, political, esthetic, moral and other ideas which is crucial here."

The Media Access Project (MAP), a 24-year-old nonprofit telecommunications law firm, works to promote the public's First Amendment right to hear and be heard via electronic media. The project provides legal council and informal advice to nonprofit groups, and members of the staff often testify at Congressional and FCC hearings on telecommunications issues. The group is dedicated to helping enforce FCC rules that promote minority and female ownership and employment in broadcasting, cable TV, and telecommunications.

*Contact: Media Access Project, 1707 L St., NW, Suite 400, Washington, DC 20036; Tel: (202) 232-4300; Fax: (202) 466-7656.*

---

COMMENT

COMMENT

*Bill Gates is the 2,000-pound gorilla. He moves in wherever he wants. Every time someone buys a PC, he gets money. He's limitless in his power. Everyone wants to join ventures with him.*

*— Ben Bagdikian, author of* Media Monopoly

*The deeper danger of the concentration of media ownership comes in matters that much more deeply concern us than whether Murdoch gets on the local cable system in New York: The matters of great national policy, matters of local policy. When they control all the sources of media within a community, this is a very danger-*

*ous situation. They can declare their own blackout of news they don't want the public to share. Or they can twist the news any way they please. And there's no monitor. There's nobody to say "don't." Nobody to say, "Hey, wait a minute, folks, you're not getting the truth."*

*— Walter Cronkite*

# SETTING THE TERMS: THE ESSENTIAL GLOSSARY OF MEDIA LINGO

*In today's highly concentrated media environment, large corporations are writing their own rules of conduct. Accordingly, they put forth jargon that conceals true meaning. To read between the lines, we need a glossary to make sure we all speak the same language.*

| What They Say | | What We Say |
|---|---|---|
| The corporate profiteer's dream of boosting sales by promoting products across media, so for every *Lion King* movie there's a TV special, pajama set, and plastic mug to match, as well as sound tracks, television, magazine coverage, and on and on | **SYNERGY** | The use of media to market unnecessary goods with unprecedented scope so cartoon characters take precedence over real news; antithetical to the idea of supply and demand; denies "consumer choice" in an avalanche of products that no one asked for |
| A choice opportunity to corner a market by owning complete control of an industry | **MONOPOLY** | The hazardous concentration of power into select hands so the public is denied choice; this destroys free markets |
| The reduction of government controls to allow the market to determine its own limits | **DEREGULATION** | The means by which large corporations swallow smaller competitors and belch out their remains *(see monopoly)* |
| Maximizing public awareness for any goods that will sell | **COMMERCIALIZATION** | Using any venue possible to create markets for goods; filling public space with advertisements; injecting news coverage with commercial content |
| A term which should be relegated to small neighborhood parks | **PUBLIC SPACE** | Our surrounding environment and the surfaces of public-owned property—which are increasingly being plastered over with ads—as well as the TV airwaves, libraries, museums, etc. |
| The corporate profiteer's notion of media welfare | **PUBLIC MEDIA** | Taxpayer-funded media established to ensure non-commercial media |
| Legally sanctioned near-monopoly when corporations acquire large holdings across various media to increase profits; a system that enables synergy (see above) | **MEDIA CONCENTRATION** | A situation where a handful of companies own a majority of the market thereby creating an illusion of choice but no true diversity (100 stations and nothing on) |
| An attractive arrangement where several companies invest together in order to lessen financial risk to any one company and they jointly set the terms of business | **JOINT VENTURE CARTEL** | A gentleman's club of large corporations with close knit relationships that blurs the distinction between competition and partnership |

## CHAIRMAN AND CEO: GERALD LEVIN

The largest media company in the world, with a 1997 projected revenue at around $25 billion, according to the *Wall Street Journal*, Time Warner owns one of the two largest cable systems in the United States, one of the biggest record companies in the world, a movie studio, theme parks, retail stores, HBO, and its own TV network. It is also the biggest publisher of magazines in the United States and in 1996 acquired Turner Broadcasting and its news channel, CNN.

**A Short List of Time Warner's Holdings** *Time Warner is a major force in virtually every medium and on every continent. Its holdings include:* * The second-largest book publishing business in the world, including Time Life Books (42 percent of sales outside the United States) and the Book-of-the-Month Club * Warner Music Group, one of the largest global music businesses, with nearly 60 percent of revenues from outside the United States * Leading global motion picture theater company, with over 1,000 screens outside the United States * Retail stores, including over 100 Warner Bros. stores and Turner Retail Group * The second-largest cable system in the United States after TCI, controlling 22 of the largest 100 markets * A library of over 6,000 films, 25,000 television programs, books, music, and thousands of cartoons * CNN, TNT, and the Cartoon Network * 24 magazines, including *Time*, *Fortune*, and *Sports Illustrated*

**Sega Channel (33%)**

**NBC owns 25-50% of the following:**
History Channel (with ABC and Hearst)
Independent Film Channel (with Rainbow)
News Sport
Prime
Prism (with Rainbow and Liberty Media, a subsidiary of TCI)
Romance Classics
+7 regional sports channels:
Sports Channel
Cincinnati,
Chicago, Florida,
New England, Pacific,
Ohio, Philadelphia

**Time Warner Entertainment**
(US West owns 25%;
Part of HBO falls under this division)
Cable franchises (11.7 million subscribers)
Six Flags

**CNBC**
Court TV (33% with Time Warner)
Bravo (50% with Rainbow, a subsidiary of Cablevision)
American Movie Classics (25% with Rainbow)
America's Talking (50% with Microsoft. Will become MS/NBC, a 24-hr. interactive news service)
A&E (25% with Disney and Hearst)

**E! (49% with others)**

**Music:**
Warner/Chappell Publishing
The Atlantic Group
Time Warner Audio Books
Elektra Entertainment Group
Warner Bros. Records
Warner Music Int'l.
SubPop (40% ownership)
Columbia House (50% ownership)

**Forming CNN/SI,**
a 24hr sports network

**Atlanta Hawks**
**Atlanta Braves**

**Retail:**
Turner Retail Group (Hanna-Barbera store at Universal Studios/ The Turner Store, Braves Clubhouse and the Medalist)
Turner Home Entertainment Licensing and Merchandising

**Programming/production:**
World Championship Wrestling
Hanna-Barbera Cartoons
New Line Cinema
Castle Rock Entertainment
Turner Entertainment Co. (MGM, RKO and pre-1950 Warner Bros. films)
Turner Original Productions
Turner Pictures

*"The Disney purchase is the latest manifestation of irresistible global and economic forces demanding integration and conformity. The fashionable term for all this vertical and lateral corporate integration is synergy, but synergy turns out to be just another word for monopoly.... Do Americans simply want to be spectators and consumers of the synergy frenzy that is turning entertainment and media into a subsidiary of conglomerates like Disney?"*
**—BENJAMIN BARBER, NEW YORK TIMES**

*In an era in which entertainment is conveyed by T-shirts and theme parks as well as by print, films and broadcasting, Time Warner has the further advantage of owning many of the means for transmitting the stories and tunes and symbols it owns.*
**—FORBES**

*[Media concentration] is a frightening thing. It's owned more and more by Disney, General Electric...Westinghouse, which now owns CBS. You have two of the four major networks owned by people that have huge investments in nuclear power and nuclear weapons: Both GE and Westinghouse. What kind of balanced story are they going to give you on the news about the nuclear issues?*
**—TED TURNER IN A SPEECH TO HARVARD LAW SCHOOL GRADUATES**

**Seagram's (14.5% owners)**

**Capital Group Companies Inc.**
institutional investment managers (9% owners)

If merger goes through, TCI will be third-largest shareholder in Time Warner/Turner conglomerate

**Houston Industries Inc.** (electric utilities, coal, cable franchises)

# Time Warner

**Retail:**
Warner Bros. stores (100+)

**Motion pictures:**
Warner Brothers
Warner Brothers Animated

**Home video:**
Time-Life Video
HBO Home Video
Warner Home Video

**TV programming:**
Warner Brothers Television
*(ER, Murphy Brown)*
Witt Thomas Productions
*(John Larroquette Show)*

**Book publishing**
Oxmoor House
Sunset Books
Little, Brown & Co.
Time-Life Books
Warner Books
Book-of-the-Month

**Cable**    **Cinemax**

**Comedy Central**
(50% with Viacom)

**Magazines:**
*Time*
*Fortune*
*Life*
*Vibe*
*People*
*Money*

*Sports Illustrated*
*In Style*
*Sports Illustrated for Kids*
*Martha Stewart Living*
*Parenting*

**Turner Broadcasting**

**HBO**
HBO Direct Broadcast

**Goodwill Games**

**Book Publishing:**
Turner Publishing

**Multimedia:**
CNN Interactive (Web Site)
Turner New Media (CD ROMS)

*Baby Talk*     *Health*
*Sunset*        *Hippocrates*
                *Entertainment Weekly*
                *Asia Week*
                *President*
                *DC Comics (50%)*
                *Dancyu*

**Home entertainmentt**
Turner Home Entertainment
Domestic Home Video
Turner Home Satellite

**Cable**

**TBS Superstation**

**Turner Classic Movies**

*Who*
*Cooking Light*
*Southern Living*
*American Lawyer*
*(83.25%)*

**Cartoon Network**

**TED TURNER:** Founder and former chairman, Turner Broadcasting. Built up media conglomerate from his father's billboard business. Founded CNN. Company acquired by Time Warner in 1996 for $7.5 billion. In return, Turner gained the vice-chairman seat at Time Warner and is the corporation's leading shareholder.

**CNN**

CNN          **CNN Airport Network**

Headline News     CNN International     CNNfn (financial network)

Sportsouth             CNNRadio
(regional Sports network)

## Synergy = Poison When...

**1** Ted Turner's TNT delayed production of *Strange Justice*, a TV-movie adaptation of the best-selling book about the Clarence Thomas hearings, for fear of offending Justice Thomas during the Supreme Court's ongoing deliberations over a cable regulation case whose outcome could enrich Time Warner by zillions of dollars. *(Variety)*

**2** Henry Kravis, whose leverage buyout firm Kohlberg Kravis Roberts (KKR) owns K-III Communications, doesn't exactly appreciate independent-minded editors. In March 1996, Kravis suggested that *New York* magazine editor Kurt Anderson kill a story about the rivalry between two of Wall Street's most powerful investment bankers. Over a civilized breakfast, Kravis told his star editor that "K-III and KKR need relations with the investment banking community to be untroubled and robust." When Anderson went ahead and ran the story anyway, the message from the top came loud and clear; within six months Anderson was looking for a new job. *(New York Times)*

**3** Censorship is a Rupert Murdoch stock-in-trade. He took the BBC off his satellite programming to Asia because it sometimes ran stories critical of the Chinese government—which controlled a lucrative market for Murdoch. "The BBC was driving them nuts," Murdoch told *The New Yorker*. "It's not worth it." *(EXTRA!)*

copy, including date and source, to Nominations at this address.

*Media moguls normally resist antitrust policing on the ground that costly cable-laying makes them "natural monopolies." Yet when faced with the regulation that is appropriate for monopolies — regulation bearing on prices and program requirements — they claim the free-speech protections of the First Amendment. The absurdity of that paradox is never argued. It is simply buried beneath tons of political campaign contributions and mountains of costly legal argument.*

*The best way to resolve the paradox is to separate cable from content. . .to make all media companies (the phones included) choose between owning wire or traveling on it. Those owning a cable can then be regulated, as a monopoly.... Those choosing to be transmitters of information and services*

# 20 LEADING COMPANIES BY MEDIA REVENUE

| Rank | Company | Headquarter | 1996 Total revenue (In $ Millions) |
|------|---------|-------------|------------------------------------|
| 1 | **Time Warner Group** | New York | 24,000 |
| 2 | **Disney Capitol Cities/ABC** | Burbank, Calif./New York | 24,000 |
| 3 | **Bertelsmann** | Guttersloh, Germany | 15,000 |
| 4 | **Viacom** | New York | 13,500 |
| 5 | **News Corp.** | Sydney | 10,500 |
| 6 | **Sony Corp.** | Tokyo | 8,000 |
| 7 | **Tele-Communications Inc.** | Denver | 7,000 |
| 8 | **Thomson Corp.** | Toronto | 6,700 |
| 9 | **NBC TV (General Electric)** | New York (Fairfield, Conn.) | 5,000 |
| 10 | **Advance Publications** | Newark, N.J. | 4,900 |
| 11 | **CBS (Westinghouse)** | New York (Pittsburgh) | 4,500 |
| 12 | **Gannett Co.** | Arlington, Va | 4,500 |
| 13 | **Cox Enterprises** | Atlanta | 3,800 |
| 14 | **Times Mirror Co.** | Los Angeles | 3,500 |
| 15 | **Comcast Corp.** | Bala Cynwyd, Pa | 3,400 |
| 16 | **Reader's Digest** | New York | 3,200 |
| 17 | **McGraw-Hill** | New York | 3,000 |
| 18 | **Knight-Ridder** | Miami | 2,900 |
| 19 | **New York Times Co.** | New York | 2,500 |
| 20 | **Dow Jones & Co.** | New York | 2,500 |

Source: *The Global Media: The New Missionaries of Corporate Capitalism* (London: Cassell, 1997) by Edward S. Herman and Robert W. McChesney

*writing seminars at Johns Hopkins University, is the author of* Mad Scientists *.*

**Project Censored**

# 120 BILLION FISH DINNERS WASTED ANNUALLY
# AMERICA'S DEADLY DOCTORS
# DEFENSE DEPT. PAYS GIANT CORPORATIONS TO MERGE

Remember these headlines? Probably not, as they were never written. The stories they portray, however, are quite real—and are but a handful of the dozens of stories Project Censored has singled out for its annual "top-10 censored" stories list over the past 22 years.

Founded by Sonoma State University communications professor Carl Jensen in 1976, Project Censored operates under the principle that since the mass media is the public's primary source of information, any suppression of information—via bias, omission, underreporting, or self-censorship—rates as "censorship." Each year, a panel of esteemed media watchers—from the likes of Susan Faludi to Nicolas Johnson—select 10 "winners" from 25 stories, culled from hundreds the project receives each year.

*Contact: Project Censored, Sonoma State University, Rohnert Park, CA 94928; (707) 664-2893; http://zippy.sonoma.edu/ Project Censored. To submit a story you think deserves greater media attention, send a*

## Fear and Favor in the Newsroom

Some of the best media criticism comes from those who have witnessed the production of news firsthand. *Fear and Favor in the Newsroom*, a video produced by Beth Sanders and Randy Baker and distributed by California Newsreel, gathers some of the United States's foremost journalist/critics to answer the question posed by narrator Studs Terkel: "How do journalists report on the environment, business, issues of war and peace when these same issues touch on the interests of the people they work for?"

The documentary gives insight into how the bounds of acceptable reporting are implicitly defined. "If you know that they really don't want certain kinds of stories at the top, you're not going to do those kinds of stories," Richard Cohen, a former top CBS producer, explains.

Much of the video explores what happens to those who ignore the unwritten rules, like John Alpert, who was blacklisted as a stringer for NBC after he submitted footage showing United States bomb damage to civilians in Iraq. Or consumer reporter Frances Cerra, who was yanked from her beat after she wrote a story on the LILCO utility company's financial difficulties; she was told by her editor, "We can't print a story like that—it would affect LILCO stock." (*EXTRA!*)

*Contact: California Newsreel, (415) 621-6196.*

# 2. The Media Goes Global

# GLOBAL MEDIA FOR THE GLOBAL ECONOMY

**ROBERT W. MCCHESNEY**

We are in the midst of a sea change in the history of media. Before the 1990s media systems had been primarily national in scope, with varying amounts of international trade in books, films, music, and television programs. These media sectors have traditionally been the province of a handful of Western, mostly United States, firms. The decisive new development has been the rapid emergence of a historically unprecedented integrated global commercial media market, dominated effectively by fewer than 50 transnational corporations. The past decade has experienced the greatest wave of media mergers on both the national and global scale in history.

United States–based firms—though not necessarily owned by Americans—dominate the global media market, and by all accounts they will do so for a long time to come. In global media markets, United States firms can capitalize on their competitive advantage of having by far the largest and most lucrative domestic audience to use as a testing ground and to yield large profits. United States–based firms can also take advantage of the widespread and growing international use of English, especially among the middle and upper classes.

By any known theory of political democracy, such a concentration of power in so few mostly unaccountable firms is nothing short of a severe crisis. When this concentration is fused with the overriding commercialism of the system, the implications for politics and culture are that much more alarming.

\* \* \*

What is emerging is a tiered global media market. In the first tier are around 10 colossal, vertically integrated media conglomerates. The six largest and most integrated firms are Time Warner, Disney, Bertelsmann, Viacom, News Corporation, and TCI. These firms are major producers of entertainment and media software and have global distributions networks.

Although the firms in the first tier are quite large—with annual sales in the $10–25 billion range—they are a notch or two below the largest global corporate giants, although all of them rank among the 500 largest global firms in annual sales. Other firms that round out this first group include PolyGram (owned by Philips), NBC (owned by General Electric), MCA (owned by Seagram), and Sony, all four of which are conglomerates with nonmedia interests, and three of which (Sony, GE, and Philips) are huge electronics concerns that at least double the annual sales of any first-tier media firm. None of them are as fully integrated as the first six firms, but they have the resources to be so if they wish.

There is a second tier comprising approximately three dozen quite large media firms—with annual sales generally in the $2–10 billion range—that fill regional or niche markets within the global system. Most of these firms rank among the 1,000 largest global firms in terms of market valuation. Nearly half of the second-tier firms are based in the United States and around the same number are based in Europe. The system is rounded out by a handful of powerful firms—like Mexico's Televisa and Brazil's Globo—that dominate nations and regions in the Third World. These second-tier firms will tend to have working agreements and/or joint ventures with one or

continued on page 14

# ATTACK OF THE MEDIA GIANTS ON CANADA

### MAUDE BARLOW

Canada has the greatest concentration of newspaper ownership of any Western nation, perhaps more than any country in the world outside dictatorships. Three large chains control three quarters of the print media—up from 25 percent in 1960. The biggest is Hollinger Inc., owned by financier Conrad Black, which now owns 58 of Canada's 104 daily newspapers. Hollinger runs all the dailies in the provinces of Newfoundland, Prince Edward Island and Saskatchewan, and almost every paper in Ontario outside of Toronto.

But Hollinger hasn't just cornered the Canadian market. It has become, with incredible speed, the world's third-largest newspaper chain, behind only Gannett and Rupert Murdoch's News Corp. Hollinger controls the *Daily Telegraph* in London, and the *Jerusalem Post* and has extensive holdings in the United States—102 dailies, including the *Chicago Sun Times*.

Black and his CEO, David Radler, are infamous both for their strong right-wing views and for their editorial power to promote their political ideology. Radler has warned, "I am ultimately the publisher of all these papers, and if the editors disagree with us, they should disagree when they're no longer in our employ." They invariably lay off staff when they take over, fire the educational, environment, and social reporters, and replace

local, progressive columnists with right-wing columnists from the head office.

The insidious impact of Black is a global phenomenon. He is of great concern already on Fleet Street in London, and in Israel where he turned the *Post* into an extremist right-wing paper. Without a concerted effort to stem the tide, Conrad Black might be coming to a paper near you.

*Maude Barlow is national chairperson of the Council of Canadians.*

**Scary but true....**

 Press baron Conrad Black, who acquired Southam's 17 daily and 33 weekly Canadian newspapers, now controls 42 percent (and counting) of all Canadian daily newspapers. *(Adbusters)*

*continued from page 13*

more of the giants in the first tier and with each other; none will attempt to "go it alone." As the head of Norway's largest media company stated, "We want to position ourselves so if Kirch or Murdoch wants to sell in Scandinavia, they'll come to us first."

Global advertising is dominated by the 200 or so largest corporations and is conducted mainly by a handful of global advertising agencies based in New York, London, Paris, and Tokyo. In constant dollars, annual global advertising expenditures have risen by 30 percent in the past decade, and forecasts call for spending to increase at rates in excess of economic growth beyond the year 2000. One industry analyst predicts global advertising will increase from the 1995 total of $335 billion to $2 trillion in 2020. The North American share of global advertising has fallen from 60 percent in 1970 to 47 percent in 1995. Although United States advertising will continue to increase at the pace of United States gross domestic production growth, the North American portion of global advertising is projected to continue to decline.

*Robert W. McChesney, Associate Professor, School of Journalism and Mass Communication, University of Wisconsin — Madison*

## Synergy = Poison When...

*TV Guide* published a cover story, "The Best Show You're Not Watching," that referred to a low-rated TV program, *Party of Five*. *TV Guide* is owned by Rupert Murdoch. He also owns the Fox Network, which shows *Party of Five*. The same week of the cover story, the *New York Post* and WNYW-TV, both owned by Murdoch, ran news stories that trumpeted actor Carroll O'Connor's joining the cast of *Party of Five*.

Last year, NBC's CNBC cable channel was excluded from *TV Guide's* listings, even though it had greater than 50 million subscribers, while Murdoch's Fox channel, with fewer than half as many subscribers, was listed. —David Morris, *AlterNet*

## Campaign for Press & Broadcasting Freedom

The Campaign for Press & Broadcasting Freedom, sponsored by the Council of Canadians and the Communications, Energy and Paperworkers Union, has organized to oppose the concentration of ownership in the media, particularly newspapers. The group's major goal is government legislation to curtail the power of the big media monopolies. The long-term goal of the campaign is to ensure the neutrality of the press and a diversity of political opinions within it.

*Contact: The Council of Canadians at 904-251 Laurier West, Ottawa, Ontario K1P 5I6; Tel: (613) 233-2773; E-mail: coc@web.net; http://wwwweb.net/coc*

# THE CHANGING MEDIA MAP

### HYE JUNG PARK

Multinational media corporations market monoculture through the single, homogenizing medium of global television networks and advertisers—leading many national, ethnic, and cultural groups to become concerned about maintaining their cultural and economic independence. People generally feel confused as to who they are and where they belong—feelings exacerbated by the changing global media map.

One result of the changing face of media has been the creation of many specialty channels, made possible in part by new satellite technology. Though these emergent channels generally begin with innovative ideas, the need for corporate sponsorship often drives them into serving niche markets, losing sight of their original goals. Even though new local, regional, independent channels and programs hold exciting potential, they are up against formidable forces, and face being overwhelmed, if not subsumed, by a handful of United States corporations.

Consider the reach of just a few mega-media companies worldwide:

* CNN International is transmitted to more than 210 countries and territories worldwide via a network of 12 satellites. Available in Spanish, Japanese, Russian, and Polish, the network has distribution agreements in over 143 countries, representing over 78 million households outside the United States, as well as 66 million households in the United States.

* Since 1981, MTV has created over 113,000 hours of programming. The network and its affiliates, MTV Europe, MTV Brazil, MTV Japan, MTV Asia, and MTV Latino, reach over 250 million homes, in 64 countries, spanning four continents. Each affiliate adheres to English-language programs while drawing from local talent and programming to fit local tastes.

* With 185 offices in 65 countries, Backer Spielvogel Bates World, Inc. (BSB) is a worldwide advertising megaagency. The company claims that the implications of globalization for advertising agencies are simple: globalize or die. The agency decided to change its name to Bates Worldwide in 1994, and its companies throughout the world adopted the Bates name followed by that of the county in which it is located.

*Hye Jung Park is program director at Downtown Community TV Center.*

---

**Cultural Environment Movement**

 For the past 25 years, George Gerbner, dean emeritus of the Annenberg School for Communication at the University of Pennsylvania, has led the Cultural Indicators Project, which examines the way the mass media portrays our culture. Troubled by the results of his research, Gerbner founded the Cultural Environment Movement (CEM), a coalition of more than 150 individuals and organizations dedicated to reclaiming control of world media, which he says has "drifted out of democratic reach" because of global consolidation. The CEM, explains the Hungarian-born septuagenarian, aims to "introduce a public voice into cultural decision making, which is now conducted behind closed doors and is accountable to no one."

"Most of what we see and what our children see on television and in the movies is not produced for us; it is produced for the global market," says Gerbner. "The reason other countries import it is because our syndicators present them with an irresistible deal. They say, "We can sell you an hour's worth of this television show or motion picture for less money than it would cost you to produce one minute of your own programming." That's destroying their own industries, their own creative people, the integrity of their own culture. Most people in many of these countries resent our syndicators for dumping action-packed, cheaply produced violent material on them."

*Contact: CEM, P.O. Box 31847, Philadelphia, PA 19104; Tel: (215) 387-8034; Fax: (215) 387-1560; E-mail: cemad@libertynet.org*

## ADELAIDE

**Adelaide Advertiser:** Daily, Circulation 220,477
**Mercury:** Daily, Circulation 54,047
**Sunday Mail:** Circulation 319,979

## MELBOURNE

**Ansett Airlines:** The no. 1 domestic carrier in Australia
**Computer Power**
**Herald-Sun:** Circulation 569,668. The largest daily paper in Australia.
**Sunday Herald-Sun:** Circulation 478,873
**Northern Territory News:** Circulation 21,550

## PERTH

**Sunday Times:** circulation 340,222
**Sunday Mail:** circulation 570,475

## NEW ZEALAND

**Independent Newspapers:** New Zealand's largest newspaper conglomerate.

## HONG KONG

**Star TV:** available in 53.7 million homes.
**Star Movies:** A pay-TV movie channel.
**JSkyB**
**Golden Harvest & Golden Princess:** Movie libraries containing 571 Indian movies.
**AsiaSat2:** A two-beam Moscow-to-Indonesia satellite.
**Star Radio**
**Pacific Magazines and Printing Limited:** Magazine printer, distributor and publisher.
**TV Asahi**

## INDIA

**ZEE TV**

## SYDNEY

**News Corporation Headquarters**
Ranks fourth in sales, following Warner, Disney and Bertelsmann
**The Australian:** Circulation 147,764
**Daily Telegraph Mirror:** Circulation 434,225
**Sunday Telegraph:** Circulation 685,430
**TV Week:** Similar to TV Guide
**Ansett Worldwide Aviation Services:** Leases airplanes to airlines.
**Seven Television Network**
**Festival Records**
**Cumberland Newspapers:** Suburban newspapers, weeklies.

## LONDON

**News International:** Murdoch owns approximately one-third of all national newspapers sold in Britain.
**The Sun:** circulation 4,160,935
**The Times:** circulation 524,270
**News of the World:** 4,758,888 Sundays, the largest-selling English-language paper in the world.
**The Sunday Times:** 1,201,768 Sundays
**Today:** Circulation 583, 845
**Harper Collins U.K.:** World's largest English language publisher. Home to Tom Clancy, Margaret Thatcher and C.S. Lewis.
**BSkyB:** (British Sky Broadcasting), reaches 5.3 million homes with a potential audience of 12.9 million.
**Sky News:** Carried over BSkyB, also broadcasts in Europe, Asia and Africa
**News Datacom:** News Corp's technology subsidary.

## ITALY

**Prego!:** Includes three of Italy's major TV networks, as well as the Pubblitalia advertising agency.

## GERMANY

**Vox:** a cable channel in Cologne, originally designed for the "highly educated."

**WASHINGTON, D.C.**
*The Standard*
**WTTG, Channel 5**
**MCI:** Gave Mr. Murdoch $2 billion for
13 percent of News Corporation.

**SALT LAKE CITY**
**KSTU, Channel 13**

**CHICAGO**
**WFLD, Channel 32**

# News Corp.

**SOUTH AMERICA**
**Canal Fox:** 3.8 million subscribers
in 18 Latin American Countries.

**NEW YORK CITY**
**Sydney-based News Corporation's U.S. headquarters.**
69% of News Corporation's 10 billion worldwide revenues
come from the U.S.
**FOX Television Stations**
**WNYW, Channel 5 (FOX 5)**
*Good Day New York*
**New World Communications Group**
**fX**
*A Current Affair*
**ASkyB**
**Echostar Alliance** (500 Channels)
**News Technology Group:** Includes ETAK, which makes
digital maps for your car's dashboard.
**Delphi Internet Services**
*New York Post*:
daily circulation 408,204.
*TV Guide*
**Fox News**
**Harper Collins**
*NYPD Blue*
**World League Football:** Joint venture between FOX
and the National Football League to create an international
league, including teams from London, Barcelona and Frankfurt.
**News America FSI:** Second largest publisher of those
"free-standing" inserts in your Sunday paper.
**The Weekly Standard**

**LOS ANGELES**
**Twentieth Century Fox Film Corporation**
**Fox Interactive:** Creates CD-ROMs and
video games from Fox productions.
**Twentieth Century Fox Television:**
*Picket Fences, Chicago Hope, The X-Files*
**Fox broadcasting Company:**
More than 200 affiliates. *The Simpsons,
Married With Children.*
**Fox Video**
**Savoy Pictures Entertainment**
**24-Hour Fox News Channel**

**DALLAS**
**KDAF, Channel 33**
 **Heritage Media**

**HOUSTON**
**KRIV, Channel 26**

Carl Swanson, *New York Observer*, June, 1995

# 3. Privatization Madness

## COMMENT

*Call it a perpetual-feedback loop: media conglomerates amass such power that they cow politicians and regulators into allowing them to become even more powerful, which in turn leads to another round of favorable treatment at the hands of government.* — *Dan Kennedy,* Boston Phoenix

## COMMENT

*The corporate drive to deregulate has led to a hostile ideological war on all things public — public health, public schools, public libraries, public land, public broadcasting, and, no doubt at this moment, even public toilets.* — *Bill Moyers*

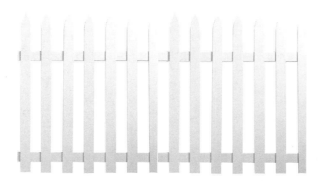

# THE TELECOMMUNICATIONS ACT IN OVERVIEW

### Compiled by CHRISTINE TRIANO

The Telecommunications Act of 1996 was signed by President Bill Clinton on February 8, 1996. The measure is the first significant revision of telecommunications law since 1934, when Congress passed the Communications Act, which, among other things, required broadcasters to serve "the public interest, convenience, and necessity" as a prerequisite to being given trusteeship of the airwaves. In place of the many tiers of regulation that have evolved in the past 60 years, the Telecommunications Act of 1996 opens up the industry to an essentially unfettered free market.

Communications is the fastest-growing industry in the United States, a $700-plus billion annual business comprising broadcasting, cable, telephone services, movies, records, publishing, computers, consumer electronics, wireless services, and satellite communications.

Issues affected by the Act include:

*Media concentration.* Any one network or company can now own TV stations that reach as many as 35 percent of the nation's households (previously, the limit was 25 percent). In areas with fewer than 35,000 people, the local phone company can completely buy out the local cable company. For the first time, television networks can also own cable systems; and existing networks can begin new affiliate networks. All national limits on radio station ownership have been lifted as well. Locally, one company can own up to eight stations in a market with 45 or more radio outlets, with a maximum of five in the same service (AM or FM).

*Deregulation.* The act eliminates legal barriers to competition across markets. This means, for example, that local phone companies can offer cable services, long-distance carriers can offer local phone service, a cable company could offer phone services, or one company could offer all three. With high barriers to competition—namely, the expense of getting into new businesses like phone service or cable—these interests are more likely to merge than compete.

*Universal service.* In one of its few bright spots, the Telecommunications Act outlines a plan for continued subsidization of phone service for rural and low-income people and for helping schools and libraries gain access to new telecommunications technologies.

*V-Chip.* Television manufacturers must equip all new TVs with a "V-chip," a plan that goes hand-in-hand with the requirement that broadcasters establish a ratings system for objectionable programming. Hollywood magnate Jack Valenti was put in charge of this effort.

*Ratings.* In November 1996, broadcasters unveiled—to the protest of parents and educators—a system of ratings akin to the movie system but with no descriptions of content. Content-based ratings are favored by 80 percent of American parents, according to a study of the National PTA.

*Broadcast licenses.* The act extends the terms of broadcast licenses and relaxes

---

### COMMENT

*"The bill has numerous terrible, onerous provisions, from allowing individuals to own more TV stations than ever before to deregulating the cable bill that was passed only a couple of years ago, so that cable rates will be able to go up, cable companies will be able to buy your local phone company, your local phone company will be able to buy your local cable company in many smaller cities under 50,000, so there'll be one voice there, and try to get lower rates when you're dealing with the same company, whether it's cable or phone."*
— *Tom Shales,* Washington Post

---

### COMMENT

*"It's possibly the most important communications bill in history, and here's what the networks had to say about it. NBC said, 'No comment.' ABC suggested that we talk to CBS, who also told us 'No comment.' And Fox? They said, 'No comment.'"*
— *Ted Koppel, introducing a* Nightline *segment on the telecommunications bill*

---

the procedure for renewal. In May 1996, the Center for Media Education and the Media Access Project filed a complaint with the FCC, arguing that the "public interest will be harmed by an increase in license terms unless there are corresponding requirements to insure that broadcasters meet their public interest trustee obligations."

*continued on page 20*

### Synergy = Poison When...

When Congress passed the Telecommunications Act, which allows for the most concentrated ownership of media in American history, most of the public was uninformed about the radical nature of the bill. Why the media blackout? "It's self-censorship," said Edward Fouhy, veteran senior news producer and executive who has worked at CBS, NBC, and ABC. It appears that finally the major media have become mere tunesters, and he who pays, plays.
—David Morris, Alternet

---

### COMMENT

*"Those of us in office should be acting in the public good, and the public good is competition, deregulation, and that's the pattern of the future."*
— *Senator Larry Pressler (Rep. S. Dak.), chair of the Senate Commerce, Science and Transportation Committee, commenting on the bill*

*Cable rates.* The act repeals most of a 1992 law—passed by Congress over the veto of then-President George Bush—subjecting cable systems to rate regulation and a host of other requirements. Congress passed the 1992 law after rates increased at an average of three times the rate of inflation. Under the act, rates will be completely deregulated by 1999.

*Spectrum.* The act allows the FCC to double the spectrum allotted to television broadcasters to allow for digital television which offers a sharper picture resolution and higher-quality sound, using a fraction of the spectrum taken up by standard TV. In essence, this allowance grants each network a second channel over which to broadcast digital TV in addition to each existing channel they already have. Broadcast spectrum is in great demand, since it is used by television, radio, satellite, wireless phones, Internet services, and wireless data services.

For the complete text of the Telecommunications Act, visit the FCC's telecom page (www.fcc.gov/telecom.html) or the Benton Foundation's useful look at the act and related resources (www.benton.org).

*Christine Triano is founder of VoxPop, a progressive public relations firm.*

### Ideas in Action...
Under the Telecommunications Act, broadcast licenses will be automatically renewed, barring a "serious violation." The good news is that broadcasters must now include a summary of all public complaints about, for example, violent programming—meaning letters and phone calls count.

# INFO-BANDITS

## JIM NAURECKAS

There's a Latin phrase—*cui bono*—which translates as "for whose good?" It means that you can figure out who is responsible for a situation by looking at who benefits from it. Sometimes, though, it's easier to figure out who benefits by looking at who is responsible.

This rule greatly simplifies the task of comprehending the sweeping Telecommunications Act of 1996. Supporters widely praised the bill as beneficial to the public at large. It would lower prices and improve service, they claimed, by allowing the giant conglomerates of the telecommunications industry to compete with one another. Vice President Al Gore went so far as to call it an "early Christmas present for the consumer."

But the law was not created with consumers in mind. In effect, the bill was bought and paid for by the very telecommunications conglomerates it is supposed to bring under the discipline of the market.

Far from mandating competition among telecommunications companies, the act encourages already-mammoth corporations to pursue further mergers and allows businesses to form alliances with their supposed rivals in other sec-

tors, greatly reducing the risk that new technologies will provide consumers with meaningful choice.

Special-interest lawmaking has often been the norm in Washington, but the Congressional class of 1994 seems to have scaled new heights in eliminating the awkwardness of public discussion from the legislative process. "A lot of the public-interest sector felt totally shut out," says Kevin Taglang, who monitored the process for the Benton Foundation, which promotes public-interest media.

The law is filled with provisions that make no sense from a public-interest point of view but make perfect sense for the industries involved. Consider the deregulation of broadcasting. In the name of "competition," limits on TV station ownership are being raised so much that networks like ABC and NBC will be able to buy twice as many stations. (CBS, whose new owner, Westinghouse, already had stations of its own, needed the limit raised just to avoid having to sell off stations.)

If the broadcast provisions of the Telecommunications Act aim to preserve and expand the dominant positions of TV and radio networks, the sections of the bill that deal with cable have an even more perverse purpose: They allow cable companies to take full advantage of their local monopolies, and encourage them to make financial alliances with potential competitors from other telecommunications sectors. The chimera of cable-telephone competition was used to justify granting the cable industry its heart's desire: total deregulation of cable prices, starting in 1999. As Anthony Wright of the Center for Media Education, a public interest watchdog, points out, "A deregulated monopoly is the worst of both worlds."

The bill's most contentious dispute—and the most expensive, in terms of influence-peddling—pitted regional Bell telephone companies against long-distance carriers. The Baby Bells wanted access to the long-distance market. The long-distance companies wanted to keep the Baby Bells out of their business, unless the Baby Bells gave up a significant share of the local market.

Owning the phone wires leading to individual homes has given local phone companies a great deal of power over

*continued on page 22*

## COMMENT

*One of the things I had in the first edition of* The Media Monopoly *(1983) was the power companies had in politics. As a reporter and a Washington correspondent, I knew that all corporate leaders get special attention in Washington. But the ones who are the most feared are media corporations, because they control the way politicians can reach or not reach the home fronts. Not only do media companies have the biggest lobbies and the biggest law firms, but they can make or break a politician. They can simply not give a politician much space in magazines or on TV or talk shows. Or they can play up every negative thing they can find out. And politicians are nervous. So media power is political power.*

*In 1994, the Republicans came into office — the Gingrich revolution. They invited telecommunications corporate heads to Washington, sat with them and said, according to the* Wall Street Journal, *"What do you want?" And they gave it to them in the 1996 bill, which was billed, of course, as "opening up the whole field of communications to competition." In the month after the passage of that bill, there was a huge batch of joint ventures between telephone companies and cable companies and that was predictable. For example, it costs, for the average city, $220,000 a mile to lay fiber optic cable in the city street. When you say that the telephone companies and the cable companies are going to* compete *that means that they are going to be digging trenches side by side, $220,000 a mile. Do we think they're not going to look at each other and say, "Wait a minute. I got a great idea"? That's what happened. There's a whole list of joint ventures between the biggest telephone companies — Pacific Bell, Southern Bell — and cable companies and other companies, so that the supposed competitors are now in joint ventures and partnerships. That is very scary These are big, big companies, powerful companies, and the telephone companies are especially cash rich. You pay your telephone bill every month.*
*— Ben Bagdikian, author of* Media Monopoly

*continued from page 21*

consumers. Up to now, they've switched customers from one long-distance service to another with a minimum of bother. But once they've entered the long-distance market themselves, they may not act so obligingly when customers seek to switch to their competitors.

If the public-interest point of view was lost in the debate over the Tele-communications Act, it was because the bill's primary beneficiaries included media corporations—the same institutions that, in theory, are supposed to inform the public about what its elected representatives are up to. "The broadcasters made no effort whatsoever to cover the huge giveaways they were getting under the legislation," notes Andy Schwartzman of the Media Access Project, which advocates for public-interest communications reform. Print media covered the story little better—in large part because nearly every major newspaper group owns a stake in broadcast media, cable, or both. (*In These Times*)

*Jim Naureckas is editor of* Extra!, *the magazine of FAIR (Fairness & Accuracy In Reporting), with research assistance from Michael Dolny.*

## Scary but True...

The telecom industry contributed more than $2 million in PAC money during the six-month negotiation period for the Telecommunications Act, nearly three quarters of which went to the newly ascendant Republicans. By contrast, consumer groups contributed little, if anything. This figure does not include individual contributions given by telecommunications industry executives or investors, which may amount to as much or more than the institutional PAC money. Not coincidentally, members of Congress were rewarded in proportion to their power over the telecom bill, and to their enthusiasm for advancing industry goals:

* Senator Larry Pressler (Rep.-S. Dak.), chair of the Senate Commerce, Science and Transportation Committee, took in more than $103,000 in telecom PAC contributions alone in the first half of 1995.

* Representative Jack Fields (Rep.-Texas), chair of the House Telecommunications and Finance Subcommittee, followed closely with almost $98,000.

* Representative Thomas Bliley (Rep.-Va.), who chairs the committee that oversees Fields' subcommittee, received $31,000.

* On December 21, 1995, the day after lawmakers reached a compromise on the telecommunications bill that included several provisions beneficial to long-distance companies, AT&T's PAC distributed $166,500 to federal candidates in a single day. This was the *highest* amount the PAC gave on any day during the election cycle.

Faux "consumer" groups have sprung up in the wake of the bill with the ostensible goal of ensuring competition in the telecommunications industry. In reality, most are fronts for industry groups like the Consumer Policy Institute, which is funded by long-distance companies such as AT&T, MCI, and others, including the National Cable Television Association.
Source: Center for Responsive Politics

The Telecommunications Act of 1996 gave cable companies greater flexibility in setting rates, partially repealing a 1992 cable law passed to rein in soaring cable prices. As a result, cable television bills rose 10.4 percent during the first half of 1996, according to the *Wall Street Journal.*

In the first six months after passage of the Telecommunications Act of 1996, there were $50 billion of mergers and acquisitions, double the total of any previous 12-month period. Four of those deals exceeded $10 billion.

According to the *Tyndall Report*, a newsletter that tracks the amount of time nightly network newscasts devote to various issues, neither the passage nor the signing of the most sweeping telecommunications legislation in 60 years made the top 10 stories in their respective weeks.

# HOW ONE SMALL CHIP SWALLOWED THE WHOLE COOKIE

### TODD GITLIN

On the great media scoreboard for the Telecommunications Act of 1996, the V-chip stole the day. Just one fragment of the most consequential communications bill in more than 60 years concerns the V-chip, "V" for violence or veto, that little built-in device designed to help parents reclaim some control over the so-called culture in which their children are daily marinated. The president derived much satisfaction from outflanking Bob Dole on the media morality front and jawboning media executives into sounding a couple of cheers for the V-chip, about which we've heard so much no doubt an entry is being prepared for the next edition of *Webster's*.

Congratulations, reader, if you know anything of the bill's other provisions. Granted, deregulation and license renewals are pretty, well, *heavy* stuff for today's papers, but according to Nexis, major papers mentioned the V-chip 1,391 times in the first half of 1996; broadcast license terms—zero times.

How bad are the consequences of media mergers? Bad enough. Newspaper conglomerates are brisker dumbersdown than single-ownership organs. They care more about profits. The more newspapers in a chain, the fewer the column inches devoted to news, the shorter the articles, and the higher the proportion that goes to soft stuff. (In television, it's hard to find stations that *don't* belong to conglomerates, so the comparison doesn't even make much sense.)

The worst hasn't happened (yet), but then again some critics have been looking for dangers in the wrong dystopian places. Big Brother isn't looming, Brave New World is. Conglomerates with considerable capacity for overbearing power are being merged and acquired into existence as if there were nothing at stake but stock values. The point is not that the media were once fearless and are suddenly in danger of becoming fearful; or that entertainment was once brilliant and is suddenly in danger of dumbing down. (Network television in the fabled '60s, for example, was largely braindead.) No one who worries about trusts proposes a return to the narrow pipeline of yesteryear. The question is, What brand of diversity will the titans indulge? Most likely, immense varieties of segmented entertainment. Serious art is at a premium, and ideas are scarce unless they can be channeled into "You're-a-jerk-no-*you're*-a-jerk" McLaughlin-goof type crossfires.

The buzz about the media biz has everything to do with the sort of Happiness Lite that comes from entertainment, and almost nothing about virtue (unless of the cheap V-chipped sort).

While so-called conservatives in full campaign voice fulminate on behalf of the virtue of virtue, in office they preside over the deregulation chorus celebrating purely and simply the virtue of "the market," that God to which prayer is daily delivered. It suits the parties in power to collect impressive sums from the titans while proclaiming the virtues of self-regulation. Follow the money from media and you see a lot of it flowing to both parties in Washington. Now there's a nonstory in today's big-deal media. (Excerpted from the *New York Observer*.)

*Todd Gitlin teaches in the Department of Culture and Communication at New York University.*

---

### Libraries for the Future

Although much of the Telecommunications Act caters to the interests of big business, the universal access provisions could be a boon for the public interest. The Telecom Toolbox, produced by Libraries for the Future, a national organization of library advocates, includes an overview of the Telecom Act and valuable advice for citizen activism. It explains how to access up-to-the-minute information on policy issues in your area and how to identify the key players in universal access negotiations.

*Contact: Libraries for the Future, 121 W. 27th St., Suite 1102, New York, NY 10001; Tel: (212)352-2330 or (800)542-1918; E-mail: lff@lff.org.*

# UNIVERSAL ACCESS

**JULIE WINOKUR**

When the telephone was first invented, it quickly became apparent that if only one person had a phone, it was useless. If two people had phones, a novel exercise was underway. If the entire country had access, there was a communication revolution. The same can be said today of computers.

The telephone wires have become more than a pipeline for two-way conversations, they mainline infinite voices into a single box, be it a television, computer, or whatever new gadgets the wizards at Intel have in store for us. Computers are already a primary tool for communication but given the expense of new technology, not everybody is assured a place at the table.

That's why guaranteeing telecommunications access is as important as democracy itself. Without computers, and the phone lines that carry their coded messages, rural communities are in danger of being cut off from vital information, and poor urban neighborhoods are destined to sink even deeper into the social divide. Students without computer training leave the professional starting gate with cement shoes on their feet.

This is where "universal access" comes in. Perhaps the most positive provision (from the consumers' point of view) of the Telecommunications Act of 1996 is its attempt to redefine universal access and make provisions that guarantee telecommunication service to poor and rural areas as well as nonprofit entities such as libraries and schools. It firmly establishes a set of goals to ensure affordable access not only to basic phone service but, if we make our voices heard, also to more advanced communication services, which may eventually include e-mail, a modem-ready line, and video.

The Telecommunications Act requires all carriers to pay into a fund or develop a funding system to support universal access. The idea is that if a future telecommunication service, such as touch tone or ISDN, becomes standard around the country, then a person in rural Idaho should be able to have it at a similar price as a person in New York City, even though it will be more expensive to provide the service in rural areas.

Based on the recommendation of a joint federal-state board the FCC decided to ensure schools, libraries, and health centers special access to certain services at a discount. Schools and libraries were granted a 20-90 percent discount on the cost of telephone lines, internet service provisions, internal wiring, and network components such as hubs, routers, and ethernet. The caveat: the FCC only has jurisdiction over out-of-state calls. While the ruling provides an overarching policy, each stae must now determine how to apply its own interpretation. Citizen activism will play a large role in shaping universal provisions at a state level.

*Julie Winokur is a freelance writer.*

## Ideas in Action...

At the national and state levels, the Center for Media Education (CME) is working with education, library, and child-advocacy organizations to expand the access of poor and minority children to new educational technologies at school and at home and to promote telecommunications policies on behalf of children. Key to this are universal service provisions now being worked out, especially on the state level.

According to CME, universal service is an area where citizen involvement is critical to help determine:

* Whether all students will have equal access to the Internet and the vast educational resources it provides, or whether only students in the most affluent schools will reap these benefits;

* Whether basic telephone service will be affordable to poor families or whether they will find themselves cut off from the communications system;

* Whether libraries and community centers will be equipped to serve all citizens in the digital age, or whether some communities will be woefully unprepared to meet the challenges of this new era.

# SPECTRUM, LIES, AND DIGITAL TV

### CHRISTINE TRIANO

It had all the drama of a miniseries. Armies of influence are arrayed against each other, the White House, TV networks, the FCC, consumer activist groups, and, until he left office, Bob Dole.

It's the battle over public-broadcast spectrum and, as the dismal news coverage has shown, it's *not* coming soon to a TV near you.

What's involved is a fundamental alteration in the way television signals are transmitted and received, a change that will eventually render your current TV and VCR obsolete. It's called high-definition television, or HDTV, and it relies on *digital* signals, rather than traditional analog, to send sharper-quality pictures and CD-quality sound. It also takes up a *fraction* of the space used by analog signals, meaning that where there is now one channel, there will be room for as many as *six* using digital signals.

The Telecommunications Act of 1996 mandated that the FCC can give each of the networks an extra channel to begin broadcasting digital TV, in addition to standard transmissions. Under a provision known as "spectrum flexibility," it also stipulated that broadcasters are not restricted to using the extra spectrum for HDTV. That means networks could use it for cell phones, pagers, wireless data— any lucrative enterprise they choose.

It left it up to Congress, however, to figure out what, if any, financial or other obligations to require of broadcasters in return for their respective chunks of spectrum. Naturally, broadcasters lobbied for a total giveaway—free spectrum, no strings attached. On April 1, 1997, the spectrum giveaway began. In return, broadcasters were told they might be asked to make some contribution in the public interest at some point in the future.

The size of this giveaway is formidable. In auctions of nonbroadcast spectrum to wireless companies, the FCC has already brought in upward of $19 billion. Similar sales of broadcast spectrum, could not only go toward the deficit, some argue, but toward supporting public broadcasting and children's programming. Consumer activists and former FCC chair Reed Hundt proposed another kind of deal: Give away the spectrum free, but require broadcasters to meet new public-interest standards—worth an estimated $20-50 billion—for noncommercial and children's TV.

*Christine Triano is founder of VoxPop, a progressive public relations firm.*

# 4. Incredible Shrinking Media: Television & Cable

Plus comments by Randall Rothenberg, Steve Behrens, George Gerbner, Barry Diller, Dan Kennedy, John Malone, Andrew Neil, and Tom Shales

And profiles of Free Speech TV, Paper Tiger Television, Globalvision, Independent Television Service, and Livelyhood

## COMMENT

Research conducted over several decades by Andrew Ehrenberg, a British marketing professor, has shown that, whatever the category, consumers make their choices from among seven or so interchangeable brands, while ignoring the others.

Recognizing this, makers of household products have long crowded supermarket shelves with an ever-increasing number of their own brands. They want to make sure that consumers have little opportunity to consider a competitor's product. Over time,

this strategy works; whether you buy Tide or Cheer or Omo, you will end up giving your money to Procter & Gamble or Unilever.

Giant media companies are now following the same script, cranking out as many channels as possible — all to ensure that they remain preeminent when the million-channel pipeline reaches your door.

— Randall Rothenberg, New York Times

## COMMENT

In 1996, a federal appeals court upheld a little noticed 1992 law setting aside four to seven percent of direct broadcast satellite (DBS) capacity for non-commercial programming of an educational or informational nature. DBS operators had previously claimed their First Amendment rights were violated by the law and won a district court decision to that effect. Pub-

lic broadcasting stations as well as PBS intervened to support the set-aside.

If the Supreme Court doesn't overrule, it means that a DBS operator with 175 channels (what many claim) will have to offer 7–12 channels of non-commercial fare. Gigi Sohn, of the Media Access Project, who represented the Center for Media Education and the Consumer Federation

of America in court, says the ruling provides a "great basis" for arguing that broadcasters airing multiple channels over their new digital TV frequencies should be required to provide some non-commercial programming.

— Steve Behrens, Current

# DEFINING THE PARADOX

**DON HAZEN**

If you feel totally confused trying to understand the changes in today's media system, you're not alone. The mass media has gone schizoid. If you pay attention, there is a definite contradiction between shrinking and growing in the media, and in the current landscape they're both happening at once.

With the help of the Telecommunications Act, the major media companies are on the growth end of the spectrum. More and more media conglomerates are gaining control of both the content —(what you see and hear, such as movies, videos, cable channels, televisions shows)—and the conduit, which is how the images get to you—(television stations, cable franchises, movie houses and so on). These changes have a direct

affect on the diversity of programming that's available, as, for example, more and more cable companies fill their lineups with their own shows.

Simultaneously, there is some new decentralization and fragmentation in the media system as the World Wide Web attracts some attention and direct broadcast satellite begins to make its presence felt.

But let's face the facts. The big audiences and the huge bucks are being made by the same handful of colossal media companies that control the networks, the cable franchises, and the movie houses— the same media companies that increasingly own the content as well. Add to that the exponential factor of global franchising as well as technological advances such as digital compression, which will make significantly more channels available to

the same media companies.

So, as Bruce Springstein sings, "Fifty-seven channels and nothing's on." While the channels multiply, the number of information providers dwindles and so does the diversity of offerings. Therein lies the paradox. This is the story of the Incredible Shrinking Media.

Major shrinkage can be seen in almost every arena: in cable, Time Warner and TCI control 47.4 percent of all subscribers; in radio, Westinghouse, in addition to owning the CBS Television network, now owns 82 radio stations; in books, Barnes & Noble and Borders sell 45 percent of all books in the United States; despite the proliferation of movie houses, three studios share 57 percent of the overall market.

*continued on page 28*

---

## COMMENT

*Television programming is getting worse very rapidly because with every merger staffs are reduced and new entries are denied. Homogenizing formulas are spreading wider and wider. It's very peculiar, because people say we have all these channels now. But today, more channels are owned by fewer companies, and you get pretty much the same representation of men and women, rich and poor, young and old. We're faced with the imposition of a marketing formula on journalists and*

*creative people, which is then foisted on the children of the world. That is not an expression of freedom. What we want is greater freedom for the journalists and the creative people, a loosening of the noose on the market formula, and a greater diversity of perspectives. The First Amendment has been perverted to shield monopolies as censors, and that's unacceptable.*
*— George Gerbner, Dean Emeritus of the Annenberg School of Communication, University of Pennsylvania*

## COMMENT

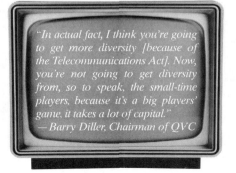

*"In actual fact, I think you're going to get more diversity [because of the Telecommunications Act]. Now, you're not going to get diversity from, so to speak, the small-time players, because it's a big players' game, it takes a lot of capital."*
*— Barry Diller, Chairman of QVC*

*continued from page 27*

In newspapers, 50 years ago approximately 400 cities supported two or more daily papers. Today the same can be said of a mere 24 cities, and some of them have joint operating agreements. In this and the next three chapters, we'll cover these industries and demonstrate the reach of the leading conglomerates.

What's the alternative, you ask? Throughout this book are exemplary examples of high-quality independent journalism and media. In the case of television, there are groups and leaders working with top-notch people at stations across the land, fighting to keep public television from becoming another commercial network. Meanwhile, independent media makers are seeking to broaden audiences and break out of the margins, while grassroots media thrives in many pockets around the country.

*Don Hazen is the director of the Institute for Alternative Journalism.*

## COMMENT

*On October 31, 1995, The 90's Channel withdrew from seven cable systems operated by TCI after the FCC refused to reject a 3,000 percent rate increase the channel president, John Schwartz, charged was improperly aimed at forcing his channel off the air.*

*"Our problem at the moment," says Schwartz, "is not how big TCI is, but the particular degree of control that it exercises over its facilities, which is absolute control."*

*Indeed, a number of reformers say one of the principal impediments to diversity is that cable operators are allowed to control both the distribution system and what is carried on it. By contrast, telephone companies by law must act as "common carriers," allowing full, equal access to the phone lines. It is common-carrier status, as much as anything, that has fueled the growth of the Internet.*
*— Dan Kennedy,* Boston Phoenix

**Scary but True...**

 The History Channel—co-owned by Disney/ABC, GE, and Hearst—offered corporations a chance to buy history. Companies like DuPont, Boeing, AT&T, and Anheuser-Busch agreed to pay to be profiled in the channel's *Spirit of Enterprise* series—and have veto power over how they were portrayed. The documentaries would be "balanced," claimed History Channel Vice President Whitney Goit. "But will they be positive stories? I hope so. TV, generally, is hard on business." After receiving criticism from the Center for Media Education and other observers, the History Channel decided to scuttle this plan to auction off history. *(Extra!)*

 Television news is in trouble with the American public. Fewer adults are regularly watching it these days. Fewer than half the public (42 percent) now says it regularly watches one of the three nightly network broadcasts—down from 48 percent in 1995 and 60 percent in 1993. Opinion of the network news has also eroded.

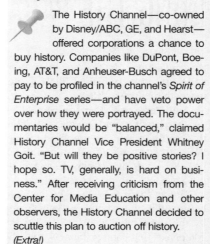 Nightly network news shows are viewed regularly by 64 percent of people 65 years old or older compared to only 22 percent among those under 30. Democrats are more likely than Republicans to tune in (47 percent vs. 39 percent), as are noncomputer users versus users (50 percent vs. 35 percent)

 Tabloid TV viewers are by far the least informed on strictly political questions (19 percent knew Rep. Newt Gingrich is Speaker of the House vs. 50 percent of the public at large), but were just as informed as the general public about the current minimum wage.

Americans continue to rely overwhelmingly on television for news about presidential election campaigns. Asked how they get "most" of such news (with two answers permitted), 81 percent said television, 48 percent said newspapers, and 21 percent said radio.

• Crime, the local community, and health are the subjects that most interest the American public. Culture and the arts, news about famous people, and business and financial news are the least interesting of 14 subjects tested in the survey.

• MTV viewers are least critical of the federal government.

(Pew Research Center for the People & the Press)

# CABLE CONTROL

We all know about the dream of cable television, a technological breakthrough that was going to bring wide viewing diversity to consumers. What many didn't anticipate is how few companies would end up controlling the vast cable network, and in turn dictating what people get to see. At this point, as Andy Schwartzman, director of Media Access Project, asserts, "For a cable channel to be viable, you need to reach a certain percentage of TV households. To get that number without Time Warner and TCI is basically impossible."

Furthermore, unless the cable company is able to buy into a new channel, it's quite unlikely that the channel will get on the air. The result is an interlocking directorate of cable systems dealing with or blocking channels to support their business interests, while the consumer sits, virtually helpless.

## COMMENT

*"You'd have to be an ostrich not to know that my politics are conservative, and I really do think there's a bias to the left [in the news media], so when Rupert says, 'Hey, don't you want to do something about that,' my instincts say that would be a good thing to do."*
—*John Malone, chairman, TCI*

# CABLE TV INDUSTRY CONCENTRATION AFTER MERGERS (1995)

| Rank | Company | Subscribers (%) | Cumulative (%) |
|------|---------|-----------------|----------------|
| 1 | TCI | 29.0 | 29.0 |
| 2 | Time Warner | 18.4 | 47.4 |
| 3 | United States Media Group/Continental Cablevision | 7.1 | 54.4 |
| 4 | Comcast | 6.9 | 61.3 |
| 5 | Cox Cable | 5.3 | 66.6 |

The "cumulative" column shows the overall amount of cable industry revenue when you combine the companies, e.g., the first five companies control 66.6 percent of the market.

Source: Annual Assessment of the Status of Competition in the Market For the Delivery of Video Programming, Appendix G, Table 3, (CS Docket No. 95-61)

**Scary but True...**

TCI is probably familiar to many households as the nation's largest cable company. Chairman John Malone, widely nicknamed the Darth Vader of the communications industry, is known as an astute businessman with close ties to Ted Turner. He's also known for his conservative political views. After Time Warner's merger with Turner Broadcasting, Malone converted his 21 percent stake in Turner into a 9 percent stake in Time Warner—and gained a lot more power. Together, TCI and Time Warner control access to 47 percent of the nation's cable customers, and own a bunch of programs to boot. The Federal Trade Commission held up the merger due to its grand scale and implications for monopoly, but in the end rolled over by imposing some limited conditions on the deal.

# TROUBLETOWN

BY LLOYD DANGLE

WELOME TO TNN'S CORPORATE APOLOGY NEWS.

TONIGHT WE APOLOGIZE FOR A PIECE OF NONSENSE WE AIRED IN JUNE.

IT WAS THE STORY OF KIDS WHO GOT LUNG CANCER—PRESUMABLY FROM SMOKING CIGARETTES.

TNN NEWS HAS LEARNED FIRST HAND FROM A CIGARETTE C.E.O. WHO'S ALSO A MAJOR TNN SHAREHOLDER WITH A CO-INTEREST IN A TECHNOLOGY VENTURE, THAT THERE'S NO SCIENTIFIC EVIDENCE TO SUPPORT OUR STORY!

WE'RE SO SORRY.

NEEDLESS TO SAY, THE OVERZEALOUS JOURNALISTS RESPONSIBLE NO LONGER WORK FOR TNN...

ONE OF THEM ALSO DID A STORY ON EXPLODING CARS WE HAD TO APOLOGIZE FOR!

WE'RE SORRY!

A SPOKESPERSON FROM OUR PUBLISHING DIVISION CALLS HIS CHARGES OF CORPORATE COVER-UP, "ABSURD.."

THE DECISION TO SHOVEL 22,000,000 FRESHLY-PRINTED COPIES OF THE JOURNALIST'S BOOK INTO A CLAY-LINED PIT WAS BASED ENTIRELY ON MARKETING CONSIDERATIONS!

COMING UP: THE MEDIA MERGER STORY YOU'VE BEEN WAITING FOR!

WHAT HAPPENS WHEN TWO SWASHBUCKLING MEDIA TITANS JOIN FORCES?!

IT'S BOUND TO BE A CLASH OF TITANIC EGOS!!

HA HA! HA!

HA

HA HA!

BUT FIRST, MICHAEL OVITZ IS TAKING ONE OF OUR CORPORATE BOARD MEMBERS TO TASK OVER OUR REPORTING...

WE'LL APOLOGIZE TO THE DISNEY CORPORATION **LIVE** AT A DINNER PARTY IN MALIBU.

©1995

# THE ILLIBERAL MEDIA

### EDWARD S. HERMAN

Claims of pervasive "liberal" or "left" media bias are heard repeatedly in the allegedly liberal/left media, but counterclaims of exceptional "illiberal" or "conservative" bias and power in the media are exceedingly rare. This is hardly a reflection of reality: there is a huge right-wing Christian radio and TV system; the right-wing Rupert Murdoch and Rush Limbaugh-admirer John Malone own two of the largest media companies in the world; the *Wall Street Journal*'s editorial page is aggressively reactionary; talk shows on radio and TV are dominated by the likes of Robert Novak (*Crossfire*), the *McLaughlin Group,* and Rush Limbaugh and his clones; even PBS is saturated with right-wing regulars (Buckley, Brown, McLaughlin, Wattenberg).

Murdoch and Malone vowed a year ago that they were jointly planning a news channel in order to combat the "left bias" of the media. The right-wing Canadian mogul Conrad Black, who owns more than half the daily newspapers in Canada and over 100 in this country (including the *Chicago Sun Times*) also whines about the liberal-left bias of the press.

The pitiful moguls are, of course, in the supremely privileged position of being able to create their own right-wing news and commentary operations and exclude those that don't meet their political standards. Murdoch personally funded the new conservative magazine *The Weekly Standard*, and he has placed Roger Ailes in charge of his new cable-news services. Ailes is the Republican specialist in media dirty tactics (famous for his role in the Willie Horton ploy in 1988), who came to the Murdoch news operation after a stint as Rush Limbaugh's producer.

Malone created his own talk-commentary program, *Damn Right!,* hosted by David Asman, the *Wall Street Journal* editorial page writer. He has also welcomed TCI cable Pat Robertson's Family Channel and the exclusively right-wing National Empowerment Channel (NET). (Excerpted from *Z Magazine*)

*Edward S. Herman is coauthor of* The Global Media: The New Missionaries of Corporate Capitalism.

## COMMENT

*Rupert Murdoch is far more right-wing than is generally thought, but will curb his ideology for commercial reasons. In the 1988 American presidential election his favorite for the Republican nomination was Pat Robertson, the right-wing religious fanatic who claims to speak in tongues and have direct access to God, takes credit for having persuaded the Lord to spare his headquarters from Hurricane Gloria, and believes in a Jewish money conspiracy. Murdoch regarded Oliver North, Reagan's wayward White House assistant, as a national hero: "He sold weapons to the Iranians, freed hostages, and used Middle East money to finance the contras," he once said to me admiringly. "The man deserves the congressional Medal of Honor."*
*— Andrew Neil,* Vanity Fair

*continued from page 31*

the most subversive shows on TV. Well-written dramas like *Homicide* and *ER* dish out a weekly feast of social issues. *Roseanne* and *Grace Under Fire* reflect the lives of real working families, and the *Ellen* controversy has no doubt sparked kitchen-table discussion about gay life and prejudice.

Independent television producers can—and should—contribute more to this mix. But we have to keep asking ourselves, Who are we trying to reach and what are we up against?

For the television-viewing public, there are rules. The content we want to put before a broader audience—thoughtful points of view that challenge politics-as-usual and the culture of exclusion—is pushing the limits of those rules. Since we're already breaking one rule by adding more substantive content, we should excel at the rest of the

game, which includes quality production values, compelling writing, strong character appeal, and strategically wrapping a content message around stories that capture the public mood.

Here are a few ideas of how independent producers might work together to communicate more effectively to American TV viewers:

**1.** Create an "echo." Print, radio, and television journalists, for example, could share a mission to elicit comments from the audiences we are already reaching about their needs and perceptions. If publicized widely enough, such a buzz would create a public lobby to support our positions with programming decision makers.

**2.** Heighten our visibility. One of the biggest obstacles for independent TV is simply letting the audience know where and when to find our programs. Why not create an alternative TV guide? Or enlist a

publicity firm to promote not just individual programs, but the whole idea of independent television?

**3.** Don't give up on PBS and public television. Securing a regular slot for mass audience-oriented programming on public television could be the first step toward popular viewership. Currently, Rory O'Connor from Globalvision and I, with support from the Independent Television Service, are putting together a two-hour bloc of humor/pop culture weekend programming, called Boom TV, for public TV aimed at a baby-boomer audience. Why should *Saturday Night Live,* a show that lost its punch years ago, remain unchallenged in the realm of funny, relevant, political and social satire?

*Patrice O'Neill is executive producer at The Working Group, producers of the public TV series* We Do the Work *and* Livelyhood.

## Free Speech TV

 Free Speech TV (FStv) is a part-time cable TV network that grew out of The 90's Channel. The 90's Channel launched FStv in July 1995 to reach a broader national audience through public-access cable channels. Today, FStv has access to over 7 million homes weekly (more than 10 percent of the cable market) with progressive programming. It acquires its programming from sources such as activist organizations, community-based media

groups, and independent film and video artists. The programming philosophy is to work closely with progressive groups and campaigns across the country. This is not only building a progressive network—it is using television to build a progressive movement.

Free Speech TV presents challenging programming on political, cultural, and social issues, including *Network Q*, a gay/lesbian/bisexual news and entertainment show; *America's Defense Monitor*, a watchdog feature produced by the Center for Defense Information; and *Termite*

*TV*, an experimental social-commentary magazine program.

The FStv website introduces users to FStv's cable programming using realtime video clips. The website features FStv's experimental "webzine and netcasting station" FSnet, a provocative blend of the latest Internet technology. Free Speech TV lends its services and technological expertise to help others use the Internet .

*Contact: Free Speech TV, P.O. Box 6060, Boulder, CO 80306; Tel: (303) 442-5693; http://www.freespeech.org/.*

# CHANGING THE CHANNEL

### BILL MOYERS

The best thing we have going for us is that the American people are behind us. They want public television to succeed . . . because they get it. In their gut they know what we're about. Millions of Americans look to us for the best that television can deliver, and even when we let them down they seem to keep the

faith and grant us a second chance.

Do we often miss the mark? You bet. Do we sometimes discombobulate and disappoint people who believe in us? Of course we do. But I have found that deep down the public harbors an intuitive and irrepressible understanding that for all the flaws of public television, our fundamental assumptions come down on their side, and on the side of democracy.

Public television was meant to do what the market will not do. We believed there should be one channel that was not only free of commercials but free from commercial values; a channel that does not represent an economic exploitation of life; whose purpose is not to please as many consumers as possible, in order to get as much advertising as possible, in order to sell as many products as possible; one channel—at least one—whose success is measured not by the numbers who watch but by the imprint left on those who do.

Every indication then was that millions of Americans shared those assumptions, and supported public broadcasting from the beginning.

As the cab drivers keep telling me, there is certain information that empowers us as moral agents to occupy the

*continued on page 34*

COMMENT

*"The explosion in the number of channels has just resulted in a multiplicity of mediocrities, that what you have is a greater selection of sameness....The whole concept of local television, local broadcasting, is threatened by the Telecom Bill, because if some big communications superpower can buy all these local television stations, there ain't gonna be local television stations anymore. They're going to be like USA Today....They're just going to be prepackaged, freeze-dried, the way every airport looks alike, every television station will look alike."*
— *Tom Shales,* Washington Post

*continued from page 33*

highest office of the land, the office of citizen. The commercial networks have abandoned this work. They are interested in what you buy, not in what you need to know. And you matter to them only if you are a consumer between the ages of 18 and 49. When one network reported its Nielsen results for the most recent season, it didn't even include figures for viewers who were not in that category. That's the only standard that counts, the network argued, because that's all that interests advertisers.

In crisis, or panic, or in desperation, it must be tempting sometimes for us to think of following suit. The subversive thought worms its way from under the rock and whispers seductively: Why hang on to a distinctive noncommercial nature? Times are changing! Just invite aggressive advertising, allow outside parties to purchase time on your stations, turn over whole blocks of the schedule for ratings-driven commercial programs. Here's the big apple: Bite and be like the big guys!

But that, surely, is the slippery slope to serfdom, where we wind up the stepchild of industry: ruled by the iron imperative of commercialism, in hock to the lowest common denominator, our decisions of what to produce and program determined not by educational or cultural needs but by the size of our back-end deals.

It would be the end of the alternative. Divided by bargains the strong could make with the strongest, we would be conquered by the very market forces that both dictate to popular culture and devour it. We would have forfeited the franchise granted us as public educators; a franchise where manners need not be coarse, standards diminished, or intelligence insulted in order to justify our existence. And we would lose favor with the very people who believe in us, who so passionately rallied to our cause last year, those many and diverse constituencies who are too small at any given time to be a mass audience but who over time compose the American public—the people we serve. (Excerpted from a keynote speech to the PBS annual meeting, San Francisco, 1996.)

### Paper Tiger Television

Since 1981, Paper Tiger Television has appeared across the country on public-access cable channels. Paper Tiger programs analyze and critique issues involving media, culture, and politics and feature scholars, community activists, critics, and journalists addressing the ideological assumptions and social impact of the mainstream media. Many programs examine a particular aspect of the communications industry, from print media to TV to movies, looking at its impact on public perception and opinion. Other videos present people and views that are largely absent from the mainstream media.

*Contact: Paper Tiger TV at 339 Lafayette St., New York, NY 10012;*
*Tel: (212) 420-9045;*
*http://flicker.com/orgs/papertiger.*

### Globalvision

When producers Danny Schechter and Rory O'Connor first developed the series *Rights & Wrongs,* a weekly half-hour news magazine devoted to human rights conflicts around the world, it was nearly impossible to find a broadcaster who would touch it. PBS told them that human rights was "an insufficient organizing principle for a TV series."

"Every outlet we went to refused the program. One executive was kind enough to explain why. 'I like the concept,' he told us. 'But we're only doing reality-based programming.' In other words, the concept—ongoing coverage of real-life human rights abuses and triumphs—was too real to be real," says O'Connor.

Four seasons later, *Rights & Wrongs* is one of the most informative and provocative programs on television. The series offers intelligent, balanced reporting on subjects that decry the need for social justice and human dignity. Although the higher ups at PBS still don't recognize the importance of a series that examines real-life issues through an unflinching lens, more than 140 local public television stations have seen fit to air the show, a growing number of them in prime time.

Hosted by award-winning anchor Charlayne Hunter-Gault of the *News Hour* with Jim Lehrer, *Rights & Wrongs*

*continued on page 35*

*continued from page 34*

features hard-hitting exposés from independent journalists armed with little more than a camcorder and courage. From the conflict in Kashmir, the aftermath of Rwanda's genocide and the barbarity of the Balkan war, these chilling documentaries reveal human rights abuses worldwide and the need for an international order built on justice and accountability.

Globalvision, which produces the show, was launched in 1987 "to prove that a socially responsible company could flourish in an industry increasingly known for producing trivia and sleaze." In addition to outstanding documentaries on such timely subjects as South Africa and Los Angeles race relations, Globalvision has focused on community groups working to protect the environment, foster interfaith dialogue and increase affordable housing.

By 1997, the future of the series looked bleaker. "We've come up against funder fatigue. The plug could be pulled at the height of our success," says co-producer Schechter whose new book *The More You Watch, the Less You Know* details the *Rights & Wrongs* story.

*Contact: Globalvision at 1600 Broadway, Suite 700, New York, NY 10019; Tel: (212) 246-0202; http://www.igc.apc.org/globalvision/*

## Independent Television Service

 The Independent Television Service (ITVS) supports independently produced public television programs which illuminate stories, issues and concerns for unserved or underserved audiences, in particular minorities and children. Created by Congress, ITVS has become the largest single source of funding for independent productions, and has funded more than 115 single programs, 17 series, and 55 interstitial "spots" for children, including: Richard Gordon and Carma Hinton's *The Gate of Heavenly Peace,* released via *Frontline* to coincide with the tenth anniversary of the Tienamen Square Massacre; George Stoney and Judith Helfand's *The Uprising of '34,* about the General Textile Strike of 1934; *The United States of Poetry*, celebrating the spoken word in America; *Positive: Life With HIV; The Question of Equality,* addressing the struggle for equal rights for gay men and lesbians; and *When Billy Broke His Head…and Other Tales of Wonder,* the critically acclaimed disability civil rights documentary. And there's more to come.

ITVS provides the bulk of its programming (about 60 percent to date) to stations via PBS's program service, and programs without the PBS logo are fed direct to stations via satellite. ITVS coordinates press support, works with the vast non-profit and academic community around issues-based organizing, and works in cities and rural areas to increase support for independent, non-commercial production and broadcast. ITVS provides these efforts to every funded program, including more controversial work such as *Coming Out Under Fire* by Arthur Dong, *Stolen Moments: Red Hot + Cool,* and Marlon Riggs' final work, *Black Is…Black Ain't.*

*Contact: ITVS at 190 Fifth Street East, Suite 200, Saint Paul, MN 55101, Tel: (612) 225-9035 ext. 226.*

## Ideas in Action . . .

Does independent television actually address the needs of underrepresented audiences? Larry Deressa, a founding board member of the Independent Television Service, says "No." Community leaders have consistently expressed the need for programs on education, jobs, and health issues, he explains, yet independent producers, in contrast, have been primarily interested in "cultural politics" or "personal documentary," not surprisingly in "the areas of their own immediate interest."

According to Deressa, the first step toward truly effective community media is an audience-based approach. He warns against "producing programs and then trying to attract audiences" rather than identifying underserved audiences and developing programming to meet their needs.

*continued on page 36*

*continued from page 35*

The mainstream media "have done so much to turn us from citizens into consumers," says Deressa. It's up to independent producers to reshape the debate along audience-driven lines and remind Americans of their public lives.

## Livelyhood

 We find common ground in everyday life, and nothing is more common than going to work. We pound the alarm clock, grab a cup of joe, hit the road, and try to make it through the day as best we can. But the real meat of our work day is rarely explored on TV (sorry, *Baywatch* doesn't count).

Moving into this uncharted ground is *Livelyhood,* a new public television series about our work lives—and its relationship to our families, communities, and the larger questions the country faces as the economy shifts at lightning speed. *Livelyhood* is being produced by The Working Group, producers of the award-winning series *We Do the Work* and presented by KQED-TV in San Francisco.

Hosted by humorist Will Durst, the new series takes viewers on a cross-country journey into the everyday lives of working Americans. The show reveals that their extraordinary and ordinary stories are much more satisfying than fiction. *Livelyhood* approaches serious subjects with a journalistic eye, and, most important, a weapon we all need on the job: plenty of humor.

*Contact: The Working Group at (510) 547-8484 or visit http://www. livelyhood.org*

# Commercialization

## Part II

**A**dvertising is more about projecting into our consciousness all the values of a consumer material culture. It is the religion that we worship in. How many kids do you know who grow up thinking they want to be priests or gardeners or carpenters? There may be a few but by and large the consciousness is pervasive that the criteria for success is the size of your house, the car you drive, and the clothes you wear — and advertising is that whisper in the ear that says that's true.

— Herbert Chao Gunther, Public Media Center

# INTRODUCTION

### JULIE WINOKUR

Commercialism is the Western world's equivalent of the *kamseen*, the legendary dust storm that sweeps across the Sahara desert with such force it buries people alive and burrows its grit into seemingly inaccessible places.

Commercialism is everywhere. It's in the ads that line our highways, the 30-second spots that interrupt our news, the children's television programming that threatens to infiltrate our schools. In an increasingly corporatized media, it barrels through the boardrooms and seeps into the newsrooms. It makes the underwriters the gatekeepers who determine which programs are "viable," which stories get killed, and whether books ever get published. It is driven by profits and has an urge to sell things, be they products or opinions, that is so strong it sweeps across the surface of our lives and infiltrates our ideas and perceptions.

The most obvious sign is advertising, for which the term "ubiquitous" is an understatement. Having exhausted its traditional venues—newspapers, magazines, television, and radio—advertising has metastasized into what was previously considered sacred public space. In the following pages you'll see the pervasiveness of advertising and its impact on our collective conscience. We'll also take a look at censorship that results from advertiser pressure so that media becomes the servant of corporate interests rather than of the people.

In what is perhaps the most disturbing section of this chapter, we'll examine commercialism's nefarious image factory—the public relations industry, whose job it is to put a pretty face on an often toxic reality. The flaks in the PR industry are in the business of swaying public opinion, even if that means twisting the truth or silencing information, and we'll look at some of the sacrifices the public interest has made in the process.

The option, short of shutting yourself off from the media, is to watch television more discriminately, to pay attention to who's selling what, to support noncommercial media. Rather than succumb to the stay-tuned syndrome, the challenge is to become media literate, to watch with a critical eye and reject media that doesn't meet your criteria. The people in the growing media-literacy movement featured in this chapter are working to educate people to become a more vital part of that process.

*Julie Winokur is a freelance writer and editor.*

# 1. Advertising

# MOVING BEYOND THE AMERICAN DREAM

### SUT JHALLY

It is four decades since Arthur Miller wrote *Death of a Salesman*. The Pulitzer Prize–winning play tells the story of an ordinary middle class family trapped within the aspirations of the American Dream, a story that becomes tragic as the gap between the family's actual life and the dream becomes increasingly evident. The play's frustrated protagonist, Will Loman, becoming desperate with the ordinariness of his own life, finally loses his grip on reality altogether. It is a sobering lesson that the United States has failed utterly to learn.

The American Dream is sustained by its massive presence in popular culture. The TV and film industries churn out fable after fable, reducing us to spellbound passivity. The success we are encouraged to strive for is always linked to the acquisition of goods. This whole materialistic charade is fueled by the most influential cultural industry in the United States: advertising.

*continued on page 40*

| Rank (%) | Company | Advertising | Share (%) | Cumulative |
|---|---|---|---|---|
| 1 | Time Warner Inc. | 899.4 | 19.0 | 19.0 |
| 2 | Hearst Magazines | 328.0 | 6.9 | 25.9 |
| 3 | Conde Nast Publications Inc. | 325.3 | 6.9 | 32.8 |
| 4 | Hachette Filipachi Magazines | 304.4 | 6.4 | 39.2 |
| 5 | Meredith Corporation | 255.4 | 5.4 | 44.6 |
| 6 | Parade Publications | 198.3 | 4.2 | 48.8 |
| 7 | Gruner & Jahr USA Publishing | 178.6 | 3.8 | 52.6 |
| 8 | Ziff Davis | 177.1 | 3.7 | 56.3 |
| 9 | News America Publishing | 173.9 | 3.7 | 60.0 |
| 10 | Newsweek, Inc. | 135.7 | 2.9 | 62.8 |
| 11 | New York Times Company | 133.5 | 2.8 | 65.6 |
| 12 | KIII Communications Corporation | 120.4 | 2.5 | 68.2 |
| 13 | Times Mirror Magazines, Inc. | 119.5 | 2.5 | 70.7 |
| 14 | Readers Digest Association, Inc. | 111.2 | 2.3 | 73.1 |
| 15 | McGraw–Hill Publications | 106.3 | 2.2 | 75.3 |
| 16 | Gannett | 92.9 | 1.9 | 77.2 |
| 17 | U.S. News/The Atlantic | 91.2 | 1.9 | 79.2 |
| 18 | Forbes, Inc. | 75.5 | 1.6 | 80.8 |
| 19 | Rodale Press | 84.4 | 1.8 | 82.5 |
| 20 | Wenner Media | 57.3 | 1.2 | 83.8 |
| 21 | American Express Publishing Corp. | 46.9 | 1.0 | 84.8 |
| 22 | Petersen Publishing Co. | 46.8 | 1.0 | 85.7 |
| 23 | CMP | 37.7 | 0.8 | 86.5 |
| 24 | Pace Communications, Inc. | 37.4 | 0.8 | 87.3 |
| 25 | National GeographicSociety | 29.6 | 0.6 | 87.9 |
| 26 | Goldhirsh Group | 28.5 | 0.6 | 88.5 |
| 27 | Weider Publications Inc. | 28.3 | 0.6 | 89.1 |
| 28 | Johnson Publishing Company | 26.8 | 0.6 | 89.7 |
| 29 | Lang Communications | 25.1 | 0.5 | 90.2 |
| 30 | Walt Disney Publications | 20.1 | 0.4 | 90.7 |
| 31 | Essence Communications Inc. | 20.1 | 0.4 | 91.1 |
| 32 | American Airlines Magazine Publications | 19.4 | 0.4 | 91.5 |
| 33 | Playboy Enterprises, Inc. | 17.4 | 0.4 | 91.9 |
| 34 | General Media Publishing Group | 13.0 | 0.3 | 92.1 |
| 35 | Heigher Communications | 3.4 | 0.1 | 92.2 |
|  | Other | 368.6 | 7.8 | 100.0 |
|  | Total for Industry | 4,736.9 | HHI=643 | |

# Top Magazine Publishing Companies by Advertising Dollars

(January – May 1996)

Source: Data on individual companies and "other" category from Magazine Publishers of America from Publishers Information Bureau, Inc., 1996. Total, percentages, and HHI were calculated from these numbers.

The "cumulative" column shows the overall amount of advertising dollars when you combine the companies, e.g., the first six companies collect 48.8 percent of the advertising dollars.

*continued from page 38*

Advertising is everywhere in the United States. Billboards loom over us whether we're in the city or the country, and posters and handbills decorate nearly every public place. Shopping areas from downtown districts to suburban malls to the ubiquitous small-town strip are littered with logos and commercial messages. Television, radio, newspapers, and magazines are saturated with advertising. It clutters our mailboxes and even our clothing. With commercial slogans emblazoned across baseball caps, T-shirts, and sneakers, we become walking advertisements.

Though such artifacts are not unique to the United States, this nation carries advertising to an unmatched excess. And what do these advertising messages say to us? Consume; then aspire to a level where we can consume more. Our contentment is anathema to the advertising industry: we have to be encouraged to be in a state of constant material desire. The economic logic of the industry requires that we never be happy. We can exist only on the verge of happiness, always at least one more consumer item away from contentment.

The key word in this acquisitive lexicon is "aspiration." Consumers do not usually see themselves in commercials; they see a vision of a glamorous and affluent world they aspire to be part of.

---

**Scary but True...**

 One minute of air time during the 1996 Super Bowl cost $2.4 million

 Federal Express Corporation paid $2.5 million to become the official sponsor of the Orange Bowl

 Reebok International spent an estimated $35 million to associate itself with the Olympic Games in Atlanta. (*New York Times*)

Between 1992 and 1994 *Forbes* magazine sold more pages of ads than any other magazine. What's *Forbes*' secret? According to an exposé in rival publication *Fortune* (2/5/96), it's the cozy relationship the magazine has with advertisers like GE and Rockwell. "*Forbes* systematically allows its advertising executives to see stories—and command changes—before they run," *Fortune*'s Jeanie Russell Kasindorf reported. "Certain companies have even been said to be 'untouchable'—exempt from tough editorial criticism—because of the amount of advertising they place in *Forbes*." (*EXTRA!*)

 "PBS has one of the most valued brand names in America. I don't think one can say that it's a brand name that's being effectively merchandised," declared Van Gordon Sauter, general manager of Sacramento's PBS affiliate KVIE, as quoted in the *New York Times*. The *Times* went on to describe the former CBS News chief's proposal to privatize public TV: "Mr. Sauter is uncertain about how such a private industry–public television partnership would work: whether, for instance, a media giant like Time Warner or Gannett would 'adopt' PBS or whether an entirely new corporation should be formed." (*EXTRA!*)

 According to the 1991 Census of Manufacturers published by the Department of Commerce, newspapers receive about 75 percent of their revenue from advertising dollars. Taking in nearly $40 billion in ad dollars in 1994, newspapers reserve 60–70 percent of their space for ads.

 Each day, 260 million Americans are exposed to at least

18 billion display ads in magazines and daily newspapers
2.6 million radio commercials
300,000 television commercials
500,000 billboards
40 million direct-mail pieces and leaflets

Advertising consumes approximately

60 percent of newspaper space
52 percent of magazine pages
18 percent of radio time
17 percent of network television prime time

(Michael Jacobson & Laurie Ann Mazur, *Marketing Madness*)

Underlying the preponderance of middle- and upper-middle-class characters on display is the relentless message that the world of happiness and contentment looks like their world.

This is the language of advertising. It is now also the discourse of the American Dream. This discourse of aspiration permeates our popular culture. Few other industrial nations allow their cultural industries to be as dependent upon advertising revenue as does the United States. Little happens in the popular culture of the United States without a commercial sponsor. In this lightly regulated free-market economy, cultural industries are not accountable to a notion of public service, only to the bottom line of profitability. Unlike most other Western governments, the United States spends little public money on art and culture. In 1990, the government spent only $171 million on the National Endowment for the Arts, less than it allocated to the Pentagon for military bands. This amounts to around 70 cents per capita spent on art and culture. In

West Germany the per capita figure, over $70, is 100 times greater. Even the British, after more than a decade of free-market policy, spent nearly 20 times as much per capita.

Moreover, broadcasters in the United States are required to do little in the way of public service. No regulations encourage quality, diversity, innovation, or educational value in programming. This means that the influence of advertising is twofold. Not only does it create a cultural climate that influences the form and style of programs that fill the spaces between commercials, it also commits television to the production of formulaic programming. Once television establishes cultural patterns, it is reluctant to deviate from them for fear of losing the ratings that bring in the station's revenue. (Excerpted from *Enlightened Racism* by Sut Jhally and Justin Lewis)

*Sut Jhally is a professor of communication at the University of Massachusetts at Amherst and founder of the Media Education Foundation.*

# SELLING OUR SOULS

### JEAN KILBOURNE

In the world of advertising, we are encouraged to have relationships with products. "The best relationships are lasting ones," a Toyota ad announces. Although a couple is featured, the ad implies that the lasting relationship will be with the car.

Advertising could be considered the propaganda of American society. It teaches us to be consumers, to value material possessions above all else, to feel that happiness can be bought, to believe in instant solutions to complex problems, and to turn to products for fulfillment of our deepest human needs.

More and more people are taking advertising seriously. They realize that the $130 billion advertising industry is a powerful educational force in the United States. The ads sell a great deal more

*continued on page 42*

*continued from page 41*

than products. They sell values—images and concepts of success and worth, love and sexuality, popularity and normalcy. They tell us who we are and who we should be. Although individual ads are often stupid and trivial, their cumulative impact is serious.

Advertising is the foundation and economic lifeblood of the mass media. The primary purpose of the mass media is to sell audiences to advertisers; the primary purpose of television programs is to deliver an audience for the commercials. Advertising is partially a reflection of the culture that created it. Because of its power, however, it does a great deal more than simply reflect cultural attitudes and values; it plays an important role in shaping them.

Far from a passive mirror of society, it is an effective medium of influence and persuasion, both a creator and perpetuator of the dominant attitudes, values, and ideology of the culture, the social norms, and the myths by which most people govern their behavior. Advertising performs much the same function in industrial society as myth performed in nonindustrial societies.

Targeting the young, advertisers are aware of their ability to create a kind of national peer pressure that erodes individual as well as community values and standards. They do not hesitate to take advantage of the insecurities and anxieties of young people, usually in the guise of offering solutions: a cigarette provides a symbol of independence;

designer jeans or sneakers convey status; the right perfume or beer resolves doubts about femininity or masculinity. Because so many anxieties center on sexuality and intimacy and because advertising so often offers products as the answers, gender roles may be the most deeply affected cultural concept.

Advertising creates a mythic, white, middle-class world in which people are rarely ugly, overweight, poor, elderly, struggling, or disabled, whether physically or mentally (unless one counts the housewives who talk to little men in toilet bowls). Women are shown almost exclusively as sex objects or as housewives pathologically obsessed with cleanliness. These days, however, they are likely to announce that they also

have a career: "I'm a brain surgeon, but right now my trickiest problem is how to get the grease off this stove." Men are generally rugged authority figures, dominant and invulnerable. Men who are married or engaged in "women's work" are often portrayed as idiots and buffoons.

In recent years, consumer activism has demonstrated that advertising campaigns no longer simply interrupt the news, they have become the news. Community groups successfully halted the marketing of Uptown, a new cigarette that targeted inner-city African-Americans. People were and still are outraged by a cartoon camel called "Old Joe," who successfully sells Camel cigarettes to children. The Surgeon

Match the advertisement with the product it advertises:

a. Beer
b. Jeans
c. Perfume
d. Diet clinics
e. Plastic surgery
f. Breast implants

KIRK—92

General and other public health activists called for restrictions on alcohol and cigarette advertising. The Swedish Bikini Team, featured in beer commercials, was also featured in a sexual harassment suit brought by female workers in the beer company.

As media becomes increasingly globalized, the Western model of beauty has become an international fantasy, spread by advertising, the media, and multinational corporate power. American television programs are shown worldwide. Strategies of global advertising lead to uniformity of desires as well as of images.

To combat the insidious impact of advertising, we have a number of options. They range from writing letters to advertisers and boycotting products to more powerful strategies such as teaching media literacy in all our schools, beginning in kindergarten. Parents should be educated to control their children's television viewing and to watch television with their children to counter its effects. We should also encourage the government to restrict certain kinds of advertising and we must work to eradicate sexism, to abolish damaging stereotypes of women and men, and to create avenues to real power for all people. Above all, as always, we must break the silence. (Excerpted from *Adolescent Medicine: State of the Art Reviews*)

*Jean Kilbourne is an internationally known media critic and award-winning creator of* Killing Us Softly *and* Still Killing Us Softly.

## COMMENT

*Women's bodies are not only dismembered in advertising but often gratuitously insulted. A recent ad for Dep hair-styling products in many women's and teen magazines had the following copy:*

*Your breasts may be too big, too saggy, too pert, too full, too far apart, too close together, too A-cup, too lopsided, too jiggly, too pale, too padded, too pointy, too pendulous, or just two mosquito bites. But with Dep styling products, at least, you can have your hair the way you want it. Make the most of what you've got.*

*At about the same time, a Calvin Klein ad made national news by featuring a nude man in a shower, holding a pair of jeans over his crotch. Some reporters claimed that men are now treated as sex objects exactly as women are. But the difference becomes obvious when we try to imagine the ad with the following copy:*

*Your penis may be too small, too droopy, too limp, too lopsided, too narrow, too fat, too jiggly, too hairy, too pale, too red, too pointy, too blunt, or just two inches. But at least you can have a great pair of jeans. Make the most of what you've got.*
*–Jean Kilbourne*

---

The average American is exposed to over 1,500 ads a day and will spend one-and-a-half years of his or her life watching television commercials.

## The Ad & the Ego

 Hats off to Harold Boihem's documentary *The Ad and the Ego,* which takes an unflinching look at advertising as the great social manipulator of the 20th century. In a relentless hour of fast edits and flashy images, Boihem's film depicts how the market economy has metastasized into the most intimate corners of our lives. In less than a century, advertising has transformed from a mere purveyor of information into a creator of markets and maker of dreams.

Leading media critics and scholars demonstrate how living in an advertising-infused environment creates a psychology of need, massaging our anxieties, doubts, and discontents into a boundless hunger for more things. One message you'll never hear in an ad, sociologist Bernard McGrane observes, is "You're OK."

*The Ad and the Ego* draws the link between our debased public discourse and a culture that defines freedom as consumer choice rather than civic discourse. It analyzes the "selling" of political beliefs to demonstrate how citizenship has increasingly been replaced by spectatorship, civil society by consumer culture.

Contact: The Ad and the Ego *is available as part of The Mediated Mind series for rent or sale from California Newsreel, 149 Ninth St., San Francisco, CA 94103; Tel: (415) 621-6196.*

# ADS IN THE SKY AND ON THE FLOOR

**JIM HIGHTOWER**

There's a Texas honky-tonk I know that has a motto carved above its bar: "Too much is not enough!"

Well, *enough already* with all these advertising messages that assault us everywhere we turn. Now, don't get me wrong—not only do I appreciate the value of advertising, but I rely on it to keep my message on the radio. Advertising definitely has its place—but every place?

Our children's classrooms now have television screens that periodically blare yet another commercial message at the little tykes; championship tennis players have become a phantasmagoria of commercials, with assorted company logos branded on their shirts, shorts, shoes, socks, wristbands, headbands, knee-bands, elbowbands, bandannas, rackets, carrying case, and crying towels; our gasoline pumps are being mounted with miniature TV sets that broadcast quickie "infomercials" while you tankup; one visionary company is even exploring a low-flying satellite that literally will beam product logos back to earth from the night sky so there'll be the moon, the Milky Way—and McDonald's. How romantic.

And get ready for this—advertising soon will be right underfoot. A marketing firm has begun selling ad space on supermarket floors. "The floor is a barren environment," this marketing manager declared disapprovingly—and I'm sure we can count on him to clutter it up. Sure enough, Safeway and Winn-Dixie are among the chains beginning to rent out their floor space for ads. For about $75 a month, Coca-Cola, Spam, Cheez Whiz, you-name-it can rent a floor tile with their name on it. I tell you, if they keep it up, you won't be able to find the food because the ads will be in the way.

Advertisers are beaming their sales pitches at you from all kinds of unexpected spots these days, including from police cars. Police in Crown Point, Indiana, for example, are raising revenues for lights and sirens by selling space on their cars, including ads for a car wash and a funeral home. The commercialized cop caper is just part of the retailing of local government, as public budget cutbacks have left front-line officials scrambling for funds. Speaking of which, New York City sure knows its market niche. For a fee, you can put your ad on a Big Apple garbage truck.

Is no surface sacrosanct? Think of the possibilities: church walls are a perfect opportunity for advertisers to catch consumers in a quiet and reflective moment; there are entire trees out there crying out to be plastered with brand-name labels; and what about your pets—aren't they just walking billboards waiting to happen? (Alternet)

*Jim Hightower hosts a daily radio show and is a former Texas agriculture commissioner.*

# THE HUNCHBACK ON HORMONES

**CHARLES FLEMING**

It was a figure that leapt off the page: last year the Walt Disney Co.'s consumer products division generated $17 billion in gross retail sales. *Seventeen. Billion. Dollars.* That's $12 billion more in *Aladdin* lunch boxes and *Hunchback* headbands than the total value of movie-ticket sales in North America. That's $7 billion more than the total value of movie ticket sales in the world. And this is just one movie studio. The total gross retail sales for licensed merchandise driven by the entire movie industry—from *Mission: Impossible* sweatshirts to *Ace Ventura* dental floss —is estimated to be somewhere around $40 billion a year.

That number affects more than Hollywood's bottom line; it also affects what you see at the movie theater. It's why Disney, Warner Bros., and the fledgling DreamWorks have made such huge financial commitments to the animated movie business: that big $40 billion revenue pie is the site of fierce competition, especially between Disney and its keenest competitor, Warner Bros.

Though neither side will acknowledge the rivalry, it's getting to be a close match. Disney, which has dominated animation and licensed its animated movie characters for use on pajamas and paperweights for decades, opened its first official Disney Store in the Glendale Galleria in March 1987. Five years later, Warner opened its first Warner Bros. Studio Store at the Beverly Center. Disney now has 517 Disney Stores worldwide, 380 of them in the United States, and plans to add another 100 by the end of fiscal 1997. Warner Bros. has 135 more retail outlets domestically, 21 more overseas; 13 additional stores are in the works. In May 1996, Disney opened its flagship United States outlet in a 40,000-square-foot New York retail space at Fifth Avenue and 55th. Warner opened its flagship store, all 75,000 square feet of it, a month later, at Fifth Avenue and 57th. And they say they're not competing?

Neither studio releases dollar figures on a division-by-division basis, but earlier this year head of Warner Bros. Worldwide Consumer Products, Dan Romanelli, estimated his division would soon exceed $1 billion in annual sales, reflecting a gross retail sales total of 10 times that figure. Disney's 1995 consumer products division numbers reflected income of $2.2 billion against total retail sales of $17 billion.

Both studios are acutely aware that a bad movie won't move any merchandise. (Seen any *A Troll In Central Park* toothbrushes lately?) They're also aware that merchandising a movie means putting the movie title first, the merchandise second, and making sure the toys and the title are an appropriate mix. Both studios are also aware that kids drive the sales of movie-themed merchandise—not their parents—and that kids don't connect to adult-themed movies. (No matter how big a hit it is, don't expect to see any shredded designer T-shirts like the one the kidnapped tot wears in *Ransom*.) This is part of the reason both studios are ramping up on animated movie production at a time when both are decreasing the total number of movies they make each year; animation moves merchandise. (*LA Weekly*)

*Charles Fleming is a freelance writer.*

## COMMENT

Even at big, corporate-owned media outlets, there are still a number of journalists inclined to uncover truths about society: who holds economic power, why wages are falling, why the military budget is still so bloated while central cities are decapitalized. But mergers can be intimidating to journalists, and not just because of the layoffs that often follow.

Think back to *1990*, before Disney owned ABC, when that network's Prime-Time Live *aired a hard-hitting report on the negative impacts of Disney theme parks on the environment and communities of central Florida. The report—* titled Tragic Kingdom? — focused on Disney's greed. Can you imagine such a report airing now on ABC?

The Disney company has political interests in trade, labor, tax, and telecommunications policy. Disney sells items of clothing in the United States for $11 that Haitian workers get paid 7 cents apiece for. With Disney as ABC's corporate parent, journalists may well avoid certain stories about labor exploitation and "free trade."

—*Jeff Cohen, Executive Director, Fairness & Accuracy In Reporting (FAIR)*

### Synergy = Poison when...

 *Newsweek* published a "From the Publisher" issue devoted to "celebrating" the 20th anniversary of Disney World. The issue, prepared by a "special publishing team of *Newsweek*," was paid for by Disney World and did not appear to be what it was—namely, an advertising supplement. When *Newsweek*'s publisher was asked why the magazine didn't tag the issue as an advertisement, the reply was, "The Disney people don't want to see that on the cover." Likewise, *USA Today* published a front-page teaser drawing attention to a four-page, inside spread on Clint Eastwood and his latest western. It turned out to be a Warner Bros. special advertising section touting the film's debut.

**Assets: $24 billion**

The Disney stores promote the consumer products, which promote the theme parks, which promote the TV shows. The TV shows promote the company. Roger Rabbit promotes Christmas at Disneyland.

**—MICHAEL EISNER,** Chairman, CEO, and President of the Walt Disney Company

**Sid R. Bass et al.**
(crude petroleum and natural gas production, 6.02% owners before merger)

**Home video**
Buena Vista

**Retail**
429 Disney stores
Childcraft Education
(mail order toys)

**Book publishing**
Hyperion Books
Chilton Publications

**Motion pictures**
Walt Disney Pictures
Touchstone Pictures
Hollywood Pictures
Miramax Film Corp.
Buena Vista Pictures
(distribution arm)

**TV and cable**
Disney Channel
Disney Television (58 hours/
week syndicated
programming)
Touchstone Television
(*Ellen, Home Improvement*)
A&E (37% with Hearst
and GE)
Lifetime Network (50%)
ESPN (80%)
ESPN 2 (80%)
Buena Vista Television
(*Home Again*)

**Magazines**
Chilton Publications (trade
publications)
Fairchild Publications
(*W., Women's Wear Daily*)
*L.A. Magazine*
Institutional Investor
Disney Publishing Inc.
(*FamilyFun* and others)

# Walt

**Music**
Hollywood records
Wonderland Music
Walt Disney Records

**Newspapers**
*Fort Worth Star-Telegram*
*Kansas City Star*
*St. Louis Daily Record*
*\*Narragessett Times*
*Oakland Press and Reminder*
(Pontiac, MI)
*County Press* (Lapeer, MI)
*Times-Leader* (Wilkes-Barre, PA)
*Belleville News-Democrat* (OR)
*Daily Things* (Ashland, OR)
*Sutton Industries* and
*Penny Power* (shoppers)

**Multimedia**
Disney Interactive
Disney.com
Americast (with some Baby Bell
companies; in development)
ABC Online (interactive network for
America Online)

**Mighty Ducks**
(N.H.L. ice hockey team)

**California Angels**
(American League
baseball team; 25%
ownership and control
ling interest, with
option to buy remaining
shares upon the death
of Gene Autry)

The global media market is forcing corporations to vertically integrate, so that they have the means not only to create shows but to broadcast them and market spin-offs. When Disney produces a film, for example, it can also guarantee the film shows on pay cable television and commercial network television, it can produce and sell soundtracks based on the film, it can create spin-off television series, it can produce related amusement park rides, CD-ROMs, books, comics, and merchandise to be sold in Disney retail stores. Moreover, Disney can promote the film and related material incessantly across all its media properties.

Even films that do poorly at the box office can become profitable in this climate. Disney's 1996 *Hunchback of Notre Dame* generated a disappointing $96 million at the global box office. According to *Adweek* magazine, it is expected to generate $500 million in profit (not just revenues), however, after the other revenue streams are taken into account. And films that are hits can become spectacularly successful.

Disney's 1994 The Lion King earned over $300 billion in global box office, and generated over $1 billion in profit for Disney.

Media conglomerates can and do use the full force of their various media holdings to promote their other holdings. Firms without this cross-selling and cross-promotional potential are simply incapable of competing in the global marketplace.

**— ROBERT MCCHESNEY**

**State Farm Insurance** (6% owners prior to merger)

**Berkshire Hathaway Inc.** (Insurance; Warren Buffet, C.E.O.; ranked #60 in Forbes 500; 12% owners prior to merger with Disney)*

# Disney Co.

**Theme parks/resorts**
Disneyland
Walt Disney World resort
Disneyland Paris (39%)
Tokyo Disneyland (royalties and fees only)
Disney Vacation Club:
  Vero Beach, FL
  Hilton Head Island, SC
  Orlando, FL
WCO Vacationland Resorts (recreational vehicle parks, country general stores)
Disney Institute (75-acre fitness resort in Orlando)
Celebration (community near Orlando)
Disney Cruiseline (planned)

**ABC TV stations** (covering 24.5% of U.S. housholds)
WABC-New York
WLS-Chicago
KFSN-Fresno
KTRK-Houston
WPVI-Philadelphia
KGO-San Francisco
WTVD-Raleigh-Durham
WJRT-Flint, MI
WTVG-Toledo
KABC-Los Angeles
(KCAL in L.A. for sale by agree ment with Justice Dept.)
Also owns 14% interest in Yougn Broadcasting, which owns:
WTVO-Roakford, RI
WTEN-Albany, NY
WLNS-Lansing, MI
KLFY-Lafayette, LA
WKRN-Nashville, TN
WATE-Knoxville, TN
WRIC-Richmond, VA
WBAY-Green Bay, WI

**ABC Network News**
*Prime Time Live*
*Good Morning America*
*Good Morning America* (Sunday)
*World News Tonight* (Saturday and Sunday editions)
*World News This Morning*
*World News Tonight With Peter Jennings*
*World News Now*
*Nightline*
*This Week With David Brinkley*
*20/20*

**ABC Video**

**ABC Radio** (owns 21 stations, largest radio network in U.S., serving 3,400 stations and covering 24% of U.S. households)

# FORCE-FED TELEVISION

**ADAM HOCHSCHILD**

Some friends from Moscow once introduced me to a lovely Russian custom. Before embarking on a trip, you "sit for the journey." Sitting quietly for a few minutes, you guarantee yourself a safe return by getting into the right, meditative frame of mind as you begin a major voyage.

Anyone looking for a few quiet moments in the place where most Americans begin longer voyages these days—an airport departure gate—is in for big trouble. Besides all the other distractions, there's often a new one: a flickering TV set. I first began encountering these TVs some months ago, and did some research to find out how widespread they are. It turns out that TVs are now installed at over a thousand gates in more than 25 major American airports. The number is growing rapidly.

These TVs usually hang from the ceiling, exasperatingly out of reach of an angry foot or a hand trying to turn the sound off. Woe to the traveler who has an extra hour or two and hopes to read a book. You can't escape. And surely many people want to. At gates cursed with these TVs, most passengers are trying to talk, work, or read. But with little luck, for that penetrating TV sound relentlessly needles its way into a conversation or onto the page.

## Adbusters

The Media Foundation, which publishers *Adbusters* magazine, is a media activist organization counteracting those who would pollute our mental environment. They are neither left nor right, but straight ahead. Their supporters are a global mix of media and environmental strategists, teachers and students of media literacy, communications professors, media professionals, ad agency executives, think tanks, and average citizens worried about what television is doing to their kids. The Media Foundation also runs Powershift Advocacy Agency.

The Powershift Agency pushes the boundaries of ad acceptability with its 30-second TV spots and print ads, which it will provide to anyone who wants to test commercial free speech. Among the recent spots was an ad for Buy Nothing Day (November 29, 1996) that was rejected by ABC, CBS, and NBC. In October Richard Gitter, vice president of advertising standards at NBC, told Powershift, "We don't want the business. We don't want to accept any advertising that's inimicable to our legitimate interests." Another spot, called "Obsession Fetish," features the naked back of a woman in what appears to be a stylized high-fashion commercial. With music in the background, the screen reads, "Obsession for Women," and a voice-over asks, "Why do nine out of ten women feel dissatisfied with some aspect of their own bodies?" The camera pans around the sexy, undulating back to reveal a woman throwing up into a toilet. The screen then reads "The Beauty Industry Is the Beast." Powershift tried to air this spot on CNN's Style with Elsa Klensch. Steve Mizer, the network's head of commercial clearance, rejected it on the grounds of "bad taste."

Kalle Lasn, publisher and editor of Adbusters, concedes that it makes business sense for media to censor advertising, but he wonders: Does it make sense for a democracy to deny media access to opposing points of view? Do restrictive advertising policies on the public airwaves truly serve the public interest and reflect community standards?
—MiHi Ahn

*Contact: Adbusters Media Foundation, 1243d West 7th Ave., Vancouver, British Columbia, Canada, V6H 1B7; Tel: (604) 736-9401; Fax: (604) 737-6021; E-mail: adbusters@adbusters.org. Visit the Adbuster website at http://www.adbusters.org/adbusters/*

Nobody can claim that this is a service that travelers have asked for. They haven't. The TVs are there because there's big money to be made from them. Last year, Nielsen Media Research reported that 8.4 million people a month saw airport TV ads. Many millions in advertising dollars get divided between three parties to a deal: the airport, the airline whose gate it is, and the CNN Airport Network, which provides the programming. CNN employs retired baseball home run king Hank Aaron to sign up new airlines and airports.

A TV set in a public place is different from one in your home. You can't turn it off. This force-fed TV is proliferating in part precisely because advertisers know that air travelers are likely to be working-age professionals—who usually watch less TV than children, housewives, retired people, and the poor. Furthermore, at home, everybody is more likely to turn off the sound during commercials. But airport TV is zap proof.

Not only in airports is television busy finding captive audiences, a phenomenon known in the advertising business as "place-based media." Despite strenuous opposition from parent and teacher groups, Channel One carries its commercials into thousands of school classrooms. Café USA is a TV network aimed at shopping-mall food courts. The Commuter Channel's silent screens hang above many cities' subway platforms. Happily, a recent Turner empire attempt aimed at supermarket shoppers, the Checkout Channel, failed. (NBC has been test-marketing the idea, however. "Our mission is to sell eyeballs to advertisers," the executive running the program has said.) Specially tailored TV programming is already creeping into doctors' waiting rooms. What sort of captive audience will they find next? Watch out for the Traffic Jam & Toll Plaza Network.

What is to be done the next time you fly? It won't work to courteously ask airport ticket agents to turn the TV off. They can't. Inadvisable for different reasons is using a sledgehammer or wire cutters to do the job yourself: This could land you in a place where you'd *really* be a captive audience, with nothing to do except watch TV all day long.

But there are other things you can do. You can support one of the organizations working to reduce the noxious effects of TV on American life, like UNPLUG or TV-Free America. And you can complain to the public authority that runs your local airport. What is a public place if not a spot where you can carry on an uninterrupted conversation?

In public places, TV is a form of pollution, like cigarette smoke. Smoke can at least be partly sucked away by a good ventilation system. The noise of an unwanted TV can't be. Regulation of unwanted noise is nothing new: many communities place restrictions on jet skis, leaf blowers, and snowmobiles. Thirty years ago people would have laughed at the idea of limiting smoking in public, but today, in the airport in my home city of San Francisco and in many others, smokers have to go to a special room. Why not a room for TV watchers? (*New York Times*)

*Adam Hochschild's books include* Finding the Trapdoor: Essays, Portraits, Travels.

### AdBusters' Media Manifesto

WE will take on the archetypal mind polluters—Marlboro, Budweiser, Benetton, Coke, McDonald's, Calvin Klein—and beat them at their own game.

WE will uncool their billion dollar images with uncommercials on TV, subvertisements in magazines and anti-ads right next to theirs in the urban landscape.

WE will take control of the role that the tobacco, alcohol, fashion, cosmetics, food and automobile corporations play in our lives. We will hold their marketing strategies up to public scrutiny and set new agendas in their industries.

WE will culture jam the pop culture marketeers—MTV, Time Warner, Sony—and bring their image factories to a sudden, shuddering halt.

ON the rubble of the old media culture, we will build a new one with a non-commercial heart and soul.

# ADVERTISING FOR THE OTHER SIDE

**HERBERT CHAO GUNTHER**

"Public-interest advertising" may sound like an oxymoron, but that's what we at the San Francisco–based Public Media Center (PMC) have been doing for the past twenty years.

PMC is the only public-interest, nonprofit ad agency in the country. In conceptualizing and executing media strategies for other nonprofits, PMC helps groups maximize their effectiveness by framing issues and telling their stories in order to change public opinion. PMC's approach—advocacy advertising—flows directly from its belief that nonprofits have a special obligation to communicate to people what they stand for and believe in.

Nonprofits are fundamentally about values and the basic, defining value of democracy: helping people gain some measure of control over their own lives. You don't just sit in a room by yourself talking about values. You have to tell others. You have to educate. You have to persuade. And you have to do so in an environment that's noisy, competitive, and often disinterested.

Advocacy advertising is about agenda setting. It's not about reacting. It's not just firing back. Advocacy advertising isn't about mass audiences. It's not about reaching everybody. It's about targeting the few who can make a difference. It's about starting a chain reaction. It's about getting to critical mass.

Nonprofits' IRS documents state explicitly that part of their public benefit or purpose is education, public education. Too many nonprofits forget this part of their fundamental charter—to tell others what they do and why. Nonprofits that are most successful in achieving their objectives and in recruiting supporters regularly invest in media and advertising in order to drive home their issues and project their values.

Advocacy advertising is about making democracy work. It's about giving people information. It's about empowering them. It's about correcting biases, sometimes by stating in extreme terms what we believe in. It's about digging in for the long haul. The battles we fight are about today. The war, however, is about tomorrow.

With this in mind, PMC has developed the following list of principles for effective advocacy campaigns:

1. *Communicate values*. Effective advocacy communications is predicated upon the strong, clear assertion of basic values, moral authority and leadership.

2. *American political disclosure is fundamentally oppositional*. People are more comfortable being against something than for something.

3. *Most issues are decided by winning over the undecided*. Typically, the percentage on one side of an issue is offset by a roughly equivalent percentage on the other side. It is the undecided or conflicted percentage left in the middle that determines the outcome.

4. *More than anything else, Americans want to be on the winning side*. The dominant factor influencing the undecided to choose one side or another is the perception that they're joining the winning side. So, for advocacy campaigns, acting like a winner—projecting confidence, asserting the morally higher ground, aggressively confronting the opposition —is a prerequisite to winning.

5. *Make enemies, not friends*. Identify the opposition and attack their motives. Point your finger at them and name names.

6. *American mass culture is fundamentally alienating and disempowering*. Most Americans don't feel they can make a difference or that they count, and they feel unqualified or unprepared to make important decisions about complex social questions. The key is to educate, empower, and motivate your target audiences.

7. *Successful advocacy and social marketing campaigns, which generally have limited budgets, mainly utilize communications strategies based on social diffusion through opinion leaders and not on mass media*. Effective social-policy movements develop through empow-

ering, challenging, and substantive messages targeted at a few key audiences that in turn influence larger constituencies.

8. *Responsible extremism sets the agenda.* To move the media, you must communicate as responsible extremists, not as reasonable moderates. You have to pick up the margin on your side of an issue and take it to an extreme to change the terms of the debate in your favor. The presence of an extreme right—acknowledged by mainstream media—puts the plain vanilla right in the middle, and the centrists on the left. The real left never gets heard from. We don't even register in the debate. In other words—thanks to media—extremism works.

9. *Social consensus isn't permanent and must continually be asserted and defended.* Social advocacy is an ongoing process that doesn't end with the passage of a law or resolution of a specific problem.

10. *In the same way that biological diversity is essential to planetary survival, strategic diversity is critical to successful social movements.* Multiple, independent advocacy campaigns on a single issue should be encouraged, while centralized, monocultural efforts should be avoided.

Public Media Center campaigns in conjunction with advocacy organizations have resulted in these victories and initiatives, among others, over the past two years:

1. Prevented the elimination of one of the country's most effective government antitobacco education campaigns mandated by California voters through the passage of Proposition 99.

2. Defeated forest "salvage" legislation that would have exempted hundreds of thousands of acres of national forest timber sales from any environmental oversight or public review.

3. Blocked efforts to reverse hard-won dolphin protections in legislation that would have changed the definition of "dolphin safe" tuna to allow the slaughter of thousands of dolphins annually.

4. Stopped Tokyo's giant Kumagi Gumi Company from destroying the San Francisco Bay Area's Bair Island (the single-largest potential addition to the bay's natural wetlands).

5. Derailed the passage of California Assembly Bill 180 (also known as the "Deadbeat Dad Relief Act"), which would have cut child support awards by 25 percent.

6. Launched a major multiyear "Teen Pregnancy Prevention Initiative" opinion leader campaign to reframe the issue of teen pregnancy as an adult responsibility.

7. Answered the one-sided debate on Proposition 209, the California initiative that would end all affirmative-action programs, by providing a series of public-education radio and television ads to help people understand critical policy issues raised by the proposition and its potential impact on public health.

For more information contact Public Media Center, 466 Green Street, San Francisco, CA 94133; Tel: (415) 434-1403; Fax: (415) 986-6779.

---

**Scary but True...**

In 1990 there were 24.6 million people in the United States ages 13–19. That number is expected to grow to 30 million by the year 2010. (Census Bureau)

During the first nine months of 1996, the collective ad revenues for the leading teen publications were up 18.9 percent, compared with an 8.5 percent increase for the industry on the whole. More important, their ad pages were up 8.3 percent while ad pages for the industry were down 1.1 percent. (Publishers Information Bureau)

Advertisers are excited not only by the growing numbers of potential teenage readers but by the increase in teen-agers' disposable incomes. "They have a lot of money," said Christina Ferrari, editor-in-chief of *YM*. "They have their own jobs and they're getting money from their parents and the only people they have to spend it on is themselves. We're starting to break prestige advertising accounts. They're realizing teens want the brands." (*New York Times*)

*Seventeen* magazine promises prospective advertisers, "Reach a girl in her *Seventeen* years and she may be yours for life." Mike Searles, president of Kids 'R' Us, doesn't believe in waiting that long. "If you own this child at an early age," he says, "you can own this child for years to come. Companies are saying, `Hey, I want to own the kid younger and younger.'" (*Marketing Madness*)

# THE END OF HIP

**THOMAS FRANK**

Why are the hippest minds of my generation so puzzled when, dragging themselves through the angry streets of Wicker Park or North Beach or Greenwich Village at dawn, they invariably find themselves joined by ad executives, network presidents, and bankers? Our problem is that we have a fixed idea of what power is, of how power works, and of how power is to be resisted. It's an idea called "hip" and it holds that the problem with capitalism is that it oppresses us through puritanism, homogeneity, and conformity, and that we resist by being

ourselves, by having fun, by pushing the envelope of uninhibition, by breaking all the rules in pursuit of the most apocalyptic orgasm of them all. It's an idea that hasn't changed at all in 40 years, even as capitalism has undergone revolution after revolution. And it's an idea that is now obsolete as a mode of dissent.

Hip is not revolutionary; hip is not radical; hip is no different from the official culture that we're trying to figure out how to fight. Pick up any recent book of management theory: today hip is the orthodoxy of information-age capitalism; it's being your own dog, it's Reebok letting U.B.U.; it's Finding Your Own Road in a Saab; it's Ginsberg shilling for the Gap and William S. Burroughs for Nike; it's business texts quoting Gurdjieff and Bob Dylan and bearing titles like *Thriv-*

*ing on Chaos* and *The Age of Unreason.*

The problem with cultural dissent in America isn't that it's been co-opted, absorbed, or ripped-off. Of course it's been all of these things. But the reason it has proved so hopelessly susceptible to such assaults is the same as the reason it has become so harmless in the first place, so toothless even before Mr. Geffen's boys discover it angsting away in some bar in Lawrence, Kansas; it is no longer any different from the official culture it's supposed to be subverting. The basic impulses of hip, as descended from Norman Mailer and the holy Beats, are about as threatening to the new breed of information businessmen as casual days are to worker efficiency.

These people don't correspond to any of the old symbols by which we

## Sisters Network

Representatives from three unique young magazines are joining forces. *New Moon: The Magazine for Girls and their Dreams, Teen Voices,* and *HUES (Hear Us Emerging Sisters)* are alternative magazines with a shared vision of providing a forum for expression for girls and women. All the magazines are "reader driven," meaning that they draw heavily from their readership to supply content and themes, but each serves a different age group.

"The Sisters Network" has a mission to "increase our collective power and influence to create positive social

change by and for girls and women in every life stage."

There is a national audience of 10 million girls and young women, and the members of Sister Network provide forums for their struggles, interests, strengths, and vision. "We're about asserting the fact that girls have the power to be what they want to be as they grow up," says *New Moon*'s publisher Nancy Gruver. The combined circulation of the three magazines is currently about 26,000, with *New Moon* having the bulk of the readers. Ultimately, these magazines want to compete with the advertising-driven high gloss of *Seventeen* and *Glamour*—a tall order for a few small-time, alternative, politically motivated and

socially challenging publications.

The collaboration wants to reach a much wider audience and attract girls and women of all income levels from age eight onward. By teaming up, they hope to learn from each other and help each other survive. —Melinda O'Grady

*Contact: Sisters Network website at http://www.hues.net/sisterpress/ or New Moon: P.O. Box 3587, Duluth, MN 55803; Tel: (218) 728-5507; E-mail: newmoon@ newmoon.duluth.mn.us; Teen Voices: P.O. Box 116, Boston, MA 02123; Tel: (617) 262-2434; E-mail: womenexp@ usa1.com; HUES (Hear Us Emerging Sisters): P.O. Box 7778, Ann Arbor, MI 48107; Tel: (800) HUES-4U2; E-mail: hues@hues.net*

understand the problems of the corporate world. They're hipper than you can ever hope to be because hip is their official ideology, and they're always going to be there at the poetry reading to encourage your "rebellion" with a hearty "right on, man!" before you even know they're in the auditorium. You can't outrun them, or even stay ahead of them for very long: it's their racetrack, and that's them waiting at the finish line to congratulate you on how outrageous your new style is, on how you shocked those stuffy prudes out in the heartland.

Hip is false populism on a par with Pat Buchanan; the same bogus MTV individualism as that of business writers Charles Handy or James Champy. Hip is the faith of the marketplace, simultaneously the blank blue stare of TV passivity and the howl of unreflective consumerism. The Man isn't who you think he is. He wears Henry Rollins tattoos, not gray flannel. He's Tom Peters, screeching subversive of the boardroom; he's Ben Nighthorse-Campbell, new convert to the Contract With America, in ponytail, on motorcycle, decked out and proclaiming his nonconformity from Banana Repub-

lic ads all across town. Not only is he going to gut labor law, workplace safety, and what remains of the welfare state, but he's going to convince the public that it's the rebel thing to do.

It's time to acknowledge that new hairstyles aren't going to change the relations of power in America. Nor is buying soda X instead of soda Y, no matter how subversive you believe your decision to be.

Clearly hip is exhausted as a mode of dissent. As the affluent society amid which it once made some sense drains away, we need to recover that much more powerful strain of dissent that built the affluent society in the first place, to rediscover the language of class, the non-market-friendly concept of industrial democracy. We can no longer think of the left as a subculture. But there's also an urgent task: there is hard journalistic work to be done, a million stories of cupidity and excess and hypocrisy to be told. It may not be as much fun, but there's a vast quantity of hard political work for us to do. The rise of the Culture Trust constitutes the most arrogant reworking of people's lives to suit private interests to come down the pike in a hundred years, and that shiny Third Wave capitalism is turning out to be a lot like that grinding old 19th-century capitalism. The cultural battle into which we must throw ourselves is not MTV reporters getting access to the presidential candidates, but information-age muckraking. (Excerpted from *The Nation*)

*Thomas Frank is editor-in-chief of* The Baffler.

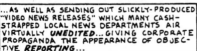

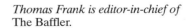

## Viacom Entertainment Group

### Television:
Viacom Television (syndication rights to *Cheers*, *I Love Lucy*, *The Honeymoners*, *Star Trek*, *Happy Days*, *The Twilight Zone*, *Taxi*, *Hawaii 5-0*)
11 TV Stations
Viacom Productions
Showtime
The Movie Channel
Flix
SET Pay Per View
The Sundance Film Festival Channel
BET & BET Pictures
Comedy Central
All News Channel
USA Network
MSG
MTV
VH-1
Nickelodeon
Lifetime Networks

### Radio:
15 Radio Stations
One World Entertainment (distributes programming from Viacom, MTV Networks and third-party sources)

### Theatres:
Famous Players (a 465-screen theatre chain in Canada)
Cinemacircuit (349-screen theatre chain in western U.S.)
United Cinemas International (424 movie screens in nine countries)

### Book Publishing:
Simon and Schuster Audio Book, Software, and Interactive
Pocket Books
Scribner
Silver Burdett Ginn
Prentice-Hall
Allyn and Bacon
The Free Press
Macmillan Publishing USA

# Viacom

## Blockbuster Entertainment Group

### Music:
Blockbuster Music
Sound Warehouse
Music Pass
Super Club Music

### Video:
Blockbuster Video (4,100 stores in 50 states and 18 countries around the world)

This vertically integrated company can take a creative idea and turn it into a film at its studio (Paramount), show it on one of its cable channels (Showtime and the Movie Channel), publish it as a book through its imprint (Simon & Schuster), rent out the video at its chain of stores (Blockbuster), then roll out the spin-off characters at one of its regional theme parks (Paramount). Its chairman, Sumner Redstone, age 74, began in 1987 to transform his National Amusements movie-theater chain into a media conglomerate by purchasing most of Viacom.

Redstone bought Paramount for $10.4 billion in 1994, the company that is responsible for *Frasier, Forrest Gump, Star Trek* and *Hard Copy,* among other TV and film titles. He later bought Blockbuster Entertainment for $7.8 billion, which includes Spelling Entertainment Group, adding *Melrose Place* and *Beverly Hills 90210* to the list of popular shows.

Viacom also owns MTV, VH-1, Nickelodeon, and the Comedy Channel.

**Spelling Entertainment**

**Film:**
Spelling Films International
(Ten films annually produced
by major studios)

**Television:**
Spelling Television (140 hours
of television including *Beverly
Hills 90210*, *Melrose Place*)

**Spelling Satellite Networks**
(Tele Uno Mexico)

**Spelling Worldvision**
(Distributes more than 12,000
hours of film and television)

**Republic Entertainment**

**Laurel Entertainment**

**Home Video**

**Paramount Communications, Inc.**

**Theme parks:**
5 Paramount parks in the U.S. and Canada
Discovery Zone
Fun Centers

**Paramount Pictures**
Paramount Home Video
United International Pictures
UPN Network
Paramount television (*Star Trek,
Deep Space Nine*, *Fraiser*, *Wings*,
*Entertainment Tonight*, *Hard Copy*,
*The New Price Is Right*)

**Cable:**
Viacom Cable (1.2 million
subscribers)

## Incredible Shrinking Media: Film

In cinema, the stakes have been raised for commercial success, resulting in huge investments in blockbusters, and less resources for more modest films. *Variety* concluded after a 1996 study of 164 films that films with budgets greater than $60 million are more likely to generate profit than cheaper movies. One Hollywood producer notes that media mergers accelerate the trend toward "greater emphasis on the bottom line, more homogenization of content and less risk taking. As has been noted elsewhere, the action genre has the greater "upside" since violent movies require less subtlety than comedy or drama. As one executive explained it: "Butt kicking plays everywhere."

The big movie studios are dominating market share. Total revenues for 1996 showed Disney with 20.9 percent of the market, Warner Bros. with 15.7 percent, Fox with 12.6 percent, Universal with 8.4 percent, Sony with 6.2 percent; thus five studios controlled 63.8 of the market.

— Robert McChesney

# DICTATING CONTENT

### RONALD COLLINS

In modern America, censorship is far more likely to be imposed by advertisers and advertising-related pressures, and far more likely to be tolerated by our commercially supported media.

Today, the notion of freedom of expression is seriously threatened in ways not envisioned by the architects of the First Amendment. Imagine attempts to kill a television story because it documented the dangerously substandard condition of parts used to construct jet planes. Or picture a small political group's nonlibelous message being suppressed because it dared to criticize a company believed to profit from the deaths of Third World people. Imagine, further, certain topics such as abortion, religion, or gun control being declared off-limits for discussion of any kind, liberal or conservative.

Further, imagine stories being written or produced as if they were news when in fact they are commercial messages masquerading as news. The content of these "stories" is first conceived and then contoured to suit advertisers. In the extreme, the result can be an advertiser-influenced press perpetuating half truths or even untruths.

Picture this and more and you soon enter the ugly and real world of private economic censorship. Private economic censorship occurs when an advertiser (or an influential corporation) formally or functionally dictates to the mass media what the public shall or shall not hear. Private censorship occurs whenever an editor, reporter, or producer either hushes or slants a report in order to placate some real or perceived demand of an advertiser or sponsor. Often the censorship is self-imposed, even though an advertiser never expressly objected to a story. Call it the Sponsorship Syndrome. To the extent that advertisers continue to foot the media's bills, they remain in a unique position to influence, and in some instances direct, the content of America's news and entertainment.

As the lines between journalism and commercialism become increasingly blurred, the result is a change in the very nature of the public-information enterprise. The old public-minded ideal of the press was one in which the primary mission was providing trustworthy information; the secondary mission was to obtain revenue by providing commercial messages in the form of paid ads. Press and profit in that order. Today's private-minded model, by contrast, reverses that arrangement. Commerce and content in that order. Where private profits collide with the public trust, business interests (of whatever magnitude) often triumph.

*Ronald Collins is cofounder of the Center for the Study of Commercialism.*

## Scary but True...

In a confidential survey of 42 real-estate editors by the *American Journalism Review*, nearly half said publishers and senior editors had prohibited critical coverage of the industry for fear of offending advertisers. More than 80 percent said advertisers had threatened to pull ads because of negative coverage. Over a third knew of advertisers that had done so.

In February 1992, Michael Jacobson, executive director of the Center for Science in the Public Interest, appeared on KKTV-TV in Colorado Springs to discuss health and fast food. The producer pleaded with him not to criticize McDonald's and asked that he not mention brand names at all. It turned out that about four years earlier the station's medical reporter commented unfavorably on McDonald's. The local McDonald's operators were incensed and yanked their advertising for three months.

## Recommendations for a Freer Press

**1.** *Deny tax deductions for advertising.* Currently, advertising is 100 percent deductible as a business expense. Considering that advertising is a $130 billion industry, these write-offs cost the American public a considerable amount of financing.

**2.** *Tax advertising and use the proceeds to help fund public broadcasting.* Establish a direct relationship in which advertising revenues would directly finance non-commercial television.

**3.** *Establish voluntary guidelines* governing the practice of private censorship. These uniform guidelines should be established to discourage advertiser censorship, whether imposed directly by the advertiser or indirectly by an editor or producer, etc.

**4.** *Extend whistle-blower laws* to protect reporters, editors, or any other members of the media who publicly disclose advertiser or commercial conflicts of interest that affect editorial content. These laws would prevent a media company from threatening or taking retaliatory action against an employee who, in good faith, makes such disclosures.

**5.** *Outlaw advertiser censorship.* Institute legislation that outlaws an advertiser's attempt to use its economic relationships with a media enterprise to influence the enterprise not to print or broadcast content that it would otherwise choose to present.

**6.** *Clearly identify advertiser influence.* The law should require that any content that an enterprise pays to influence should clearly and continuously identify the firm as an advertiser or sponsor. Similarly, video news releases provided by corporate public-relations departments should be identified as such. Additionally, the same kind of public disclosure would be required whenever an advertiser or agent acting on its behalf makes content arrangements with an editor or producer, etc. —Ronald Collins

## Annual Planetary Buy Nothing Day

On November 29 (the day after Thanksgiving) thousands of people in the rich countries of the world will celebrate voluntary simplicity by buying absolutely nothing for 24 hours. Buy Nothing Day is about discovering the joys of buying less and living more simply, with less environmental damage, less stress, more happiness and personal fulfillment.

Buy Nothing Day is an attempt to draw attention to what many groups and individuals believe is the primary environmental problem in the world: overconsumption by people in the affluent, industrialized west.

Buy Nothing Day is the brainchild of Vancouver, BC, artist/activist Ted Dave. He started it as a "gesture of protest for those of us who feel as if our lives and dreams have been marketed back to us." The concept has spread worldwide—first to the United States, then Ireland and England, and recently the Netherlands and beyond. Although previously held on September 24th, it has been moved to the first day of Christmas shopping to more directly confront the obligatory consumerism of the season.

For more information, call (800) 663-1243.

# DECODING THE COMMERCIAL WORLD

**LESLIE SAVAN**

Advertising infects just about every organ of society, and wherever it gains a foothold it tends to slowly take over, like a virus. How do we ward off the effect of billions of words and images from our sponsors? No perfect antidote exists, but I can suggest some tactics to keep in mind:

1. *When watching, watch out.* Literally. Watch as an outsider, from as far a distance as you can muster (farther even than irony)—especially when watching ads that flatter you for being an outsider.

2. *Big lie, little lie.* All advertising tells lies, but there are little lies and there are big lies. Little lie: This beer tastes great. Big lie: This beer makes you great. Don't get me wrong; many products do live up to their modest material claims: This car runs. But all ads must tell big lies: This car will attract babes and make others slobber in envy. Don't be shocked that ads lie—that's their job.

3. *Read the box.* Look not just at whether an ad's claims are false or exaggerated, but try to figure out what portion of an ad is about the culture as opposed to the product. Read the contents as you would a cereal box's: Instead of how much sugar to wheat, consider how much style to information.

4. *Assume no relationship between a brand and its image.* Marlboro was originally sold as a woman's cigarette, and its image was elegant, if not downright prissy. It wasn't until 1955 that the Marlboro Man was invented to ride herd on all that. The arbitrary relationship between a product and its ads becomes even clearer when you realize how much advertising is created to overcome "brand parity"—a plague more troubling to marketers than bodily odors. Brand parity means that there's little or no difference between competing brands and that the best a brand can do is hire a more appealing image.

5. *We don't buy products, we buy the world that presents them.* Over the long run, whether you actually buy a particular product is less important than that you buy the world that makes the product seem desirable. Not so long ago a BMW or Mercedes was required if you seriously bought the worldview that their ads conveyed. Still, buying an attitude doesn't automatically translate into product purchase. If your income precluded a BMW, you might have bought instead a Ralph Lauren polo shirt or even a Dove bar (which is how yuppie snack foods positioned themselves—as achievable class). Sure, GE wants you to buy its bulbs, but even more it wants you to buy the paternalistic, every-thing's-under-control world that GE seems to rule. Buying that will result, GE is betting, not only in more appliance sales but also in more credibility when spokesmen insist that defrauding the Pentagon is not really what GE's all about. That is to say. . . .

6. *The promotional is the political.* Each world that commercials use to sell things comes packed with biases: Entire classes, races, and genders may be excluded for the coddling of the sponsored one. Lee Jeans' world (circa 1989) is a place where young people are hip, sexual, and wear jeans, while old people are square, non-sexual, and wear uniforms. The class and age politics here is more powerful than the Young Republicans'. There is politics in all advertising (and, more obviously, advertising in all politics). It makes sense that these two professions call what they do "campaigns."

7. *Advertising shepherds herds of individuals.* When Monty Python's mistaken messiah in *The Life of Brian* exhorts the crowd of devotees to "Don't follow me! Don't follow anyone! Think for yourselves!...You are all individuals!" they reply in unison, "We are all individuals!" That is advertising in a nutshell.

Advertising's most basic paradox is to say: Join us and become unique. Advertisers learned long ago that individuality sells, like sex or patriotism. The urge toward individualism is a constant in America. Commercial nonconformity always operates in the service of…conformity. Our system of laws and our one-man-one-vote politics may be based on individualism, but successful marketing depends on the exact opposite: By identifying (through research) the ways we are alike, it hopes to convince the largest number of people that they need the exact same product. Furthermore, in modern pop culture, we construct our individuality by the unique combination of mass-produced goods and services we buy. I sip Evian, you slug Bud Light; I drive a Geo, you gun a Ford pickup; I kick sidewalk in cowboy boots, you bop in Reeboks.

8. *It's the real ad.* The one question I'm most often asked is, Does advertising shape who we are and what we want, or does it merely reflect back to us our own emotions and desires? As with most nature-or-nurture questions, the answer is both. The real ad

in any campaign is controlled neither by ad makers nor ad watchers; it exists somewhere between the TV set and the viewer, like a huge hairball, collecting bits of material and meaning from both. The real ad isn't even activated until viewers hand it their frustrations from work, the mood of their love life, their idiosyncratic misinterpretations, and, most of all, their everyday politics. On which class rung do they see themselves teetering? Do they ever so subtly flinch when a different race comes on TV? In this way, we all coproduce the ads we see. *Follow the flattery.* I use the word flattery—a lot. When trying to understand what an ad's really up to, following the flattery is as useful as following the money. You'll find the ad's target market by asking who in any 30-second drama is being praised for qualities they probably don't possess. When a black teenager plays basketball with a white baby boomer for Canada Dry, it's not black youth

that's being pandered to. It's white boomers—the flattery being that they're cool enough to be accepted by blacks. Ads don't even have to put people on stage to toady up to them. Ads can flatter by style alone, as do all the spots that turn on hyperquick cuts or obscure meanings, telling us —uh, some of us—that we're special enough to get it.

9. *We participate in our own seduction.* Once properly flattered, all that's left is to close the sale—and only we can do that. This is seduction: We're stirred to a state so that not only do we close the image but, given the right image at the right time, we open our wallet. All television is erotically engaged in this way, but commercials are TV's G-spot. The smart ads always hold back a little to get us to lean forward a little. Some ads have become caricatures of this tease, withholding the product's name until the last second to keep you wondering who could possibly be sponsoring such intrigue. The seduction may continue right to the cash register, where one last image is completed: you and product together at last. It'd be nice to say that now that you've consumed, you've climaxed, and everyone can relax.

But sponsorship is a lifetime proposition that must be renewed every day. (*Excerpted from* The Sponsored Life.)

*Leslie Savan is the advertising columnist for the* Village Voice *and three times a finalist for the Pulitzer Prize in criticism.*

---

**Scary but True…**

When Neil Armstrong first set foot on the moon and announced our "great leap," many people may have wondered where we were leaping. The answer was unveiled recently when two Russian cosmonauts trailed a four-foot high replica of a Pepsi can behind the space station Mir. They went outside and placed a banner on the station that read "Even in space…Pepsi

is changing the script." The stunt was for a TV commercial for which the Russian space agency was reportedly paid millions of dollars. Space as a backdrop for Pepsi ads…but where's Coke? On the *Endeavor* space craft in a $1.5 million dispenser. When asked if our astronauts might appear in a Coke commercial, NASA rep Jeff Bangle said the agency "is looking at new and different kinds of things to involve commercial enterprises." (*American Newspeak*)

11-7-96-A

# 2. The Box

# THE WORLD ACCORDING TO TELEVISION

### JOHN PERRY BARLOW

For most of The Market, reality is almost entirely based on The World According to Television. This has been the case since the Kennedy-Nixon debates and will continue to be the case for some time. The World According to Television is not a reality that arises from direct experience with events or phenomena. It is a processed world, both eviscerated of context and artificially fortified toward no greater purpose than entrancing the audience.

In the time since the Kennedy-Nixon debates, the organism of television has learned a lot about which elements of the political process keep people locked in even through the ads. It learned a lot during Watergate and has been busily offering up "-gates" of one sort or another ever since. It has also learned that fear, violence, and sex all fertilize attention marvelously, so it continually churns up virtual demons and scandals that not only jolt the audience into paying attention, but completely transform the political debate.

Voters are now more concerned with imaginary threats than real ones, and so they elect representatives who will address these "problems" without regard to their existence.

Looking to raise shares and beat back the future, the media raise an imaginary problem, say, a cybertsunami of online kiddie porn. Out in Televisionland, parents who have already been driven into a state of omniphobia by TV depictions of kidnappers, child molesters, and Calvin Klein commercials freak out and call their congressperson.

Of course, the congressperson doesn't actually know whether or not there's a flood of Kiddie porn online. He (or she) has never been online and isn't about to go there. But he does know that his constituents have seized on An Issue that they are truly passionate about.

Under such circumstances, it takes a brave man to do nothing. So the congressperson gets together with his colleagues and passes a law that effectively addresses a problem almost no one has ever actually experienced, while issuing forth a whole new set of real ones.

This is democracy in the Television Age, working with hideous efficiency. It is government by hallucinating mob. A push-me, pull-you that is self-contained and almost completely detached from anything I would call "real." (Excerpted from *Wired*)

*John Perry Barlow is a nationally known commentator on technology.*

## TV-Free America

 TV-Free America is the brainchild of Henry Labalme. Young, quiet, amazingly energetic, Labalme and his friend Matt Pawa shared lofty ideals of saving the world from mindless consumption, violence, illiteracy, incivility, and intolerance. Both saw TV as a major cause of these problems. For years they just talked, until Pawa did the legal work to set up an organization called TV-Free America, and turned to Labalme to make it happen.

Labalme expected the idea of life without television to be met with resistance. Instead he found himself riding a wave of enthusiasm. TV-Free America held its first National TV Turnoff Week in April 1995. Four thousand schools signed up. The American Federation of Teachers and the American Medical Association supported it. A volunteer sent a kit to Governor Angus King of Maine, who held a press conference to praise the 25 participating Maine schools. Four more governors signed on. "We thought we were being too radical. Now we wonder if we're being radical enough," said Labalme.

In 1996, TV Turnoff Week was endorsed by seven governors, the American Federation of Teachers, the National

# LEAVE IT TO BEAVER

### WILL DURST

Sucking up to an electorate with the brazen arrogance of a teacher's pet armed with bushels of freshly picked apples in the faculty lounge, Bill Clinton announced an agreement with the TV industry to require broadcasters to program three hours of educational shows a week for children. In an election year. Who knew?

Officials familiar with the agreement say this time the networks are going to certify the programs are designed to be educational, because when a 1990 law linked TV stations' license renewals to serving the educational needs of children, the FCC received documents informing

them that *Leave It To Beaver* and *The Jetsons* were informational programs. *The Jetsons* was obviously an abstract analysis of futurism, and *Leave It To Beaver* had to have been a nostalgic time-travel trip down memory lane designed to visit one of our many alternative American fictional histories.

It'll probably be this time next year when a network executive files a report claiming that *Teenage Mutant Ninja Turtles* is a nature show teaching survival skills and *Scooby Doo* is a burning indictment of the perils of substandard veterinarians. Unfortunately, this rule will not apply to cable TV, meaning kids won't get to watch *World Wrestling Federation* and receive physical-education credit.

*Political humorist Will Durst hosts the public television series* Livelyhood.

## COMMENT

*I'm convinced that knowing about television and growing up with it provides my daughter with a form of cultural literacy that she will need, that will tie her to her friends and her generation and help her understand her place in the world. So instead of killing my TV, I've tried to show my daughter basic bullshit-detecting techniques. Don't think your choices are either no TV or a zombified kid. Studies show that the simple act of intervening — of talking to your child about what's on television and why it's on there — is one of the most important factors in helping children understand and distance themselves from some of the box's more repugnant imagery.*

*— Susan Douglas, Professor of Media Studies, University of Michigan*

Association of Elementary School Principals, the American Psychiatric Association, the Family Research Council, and others. The American Medical Association sent out flyers to 20,000 schools. A businessman in Mississippi distributed posters at his own expense to all the schools in his state.

Like Smoke-Out Day, TV Turnoff Week gives us a chance to step away from our addiction. We might discover that, as author Wendell Berry wrote to Labalme, "it isn't as though we can entertain and instruct ourselves in no other way. We have the literature of several thousand years—more than anyone can read in a lifetime. We have each other to talk to and listen to. Music can still be made locally. We can play and walk and dance without deference or payment to any organization. The world contains many beauties that we can look at directly, without the intervention of any equipment. Let us live our lives while we have them."
—Donella H. Meadows

Contact: TV-Free America at 1611 Connecticut Avenue, NW, Suite 3A, Washington, DC 20009; (202) 887-0436; Fax (202) 518-5560; E-mail: tvfa@essential.org; website: http://www.essential.org/orgs/tvfa

## Television Saturation

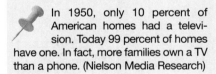 In 1950, only 10 percent of American homes had a television. Today 99 percent of homes have one. In fact, more families own a TV than a phone. (Nielson Media Research)

 Number of TV sets in the average United States household: 2.24. (TV-Free America)

The average American spends more than four hours a day watching television. Four hours a day, 28 hours a week, 1,456 hours a year. That's 60 days—two months! If you keep it up for a 72-year lifetime, you will spend 12 years in front of the tube. Assuming eight hours of sleep a night, that's one fourth of your waking life. (TV-Free America)

 Percentage of Americans who regularly watch TV while eating dinner: 66. (TV-Free America)

The number of books checked out of public libraries in the United States every day is 3 million. In contrast, the number of videos rented every day is 6 million, and the amount Americans spend each year in late fees for failing to return videos on time totals $3 billion. (TV-Free America)

Almost three quarters of the public cites TV as at least one of the primary sources of news, compared to about 40 percent who mention newspapers and 25 percent who mention other sources. Almost half the public cites television as their sole source of news. (*Journal of Broadcasting and Electronic Media*)

# PARENTS: IT'S OK TO LIMIT TV VIEWING

**PETER DEBENEDITTIS**

Let's make it official. You have permission to limit how much and what kinds of TV your children watch. Of course, your children will complain, but they complain when you make them eat healthy food too. You're the parent. The research is pretty conclusive. Unrestricted television viewing is harmful.

Here's the problem, most parents spend about 1,000 minutes a week watching TV, and only 38 minutes a week in quality conversation with their children. On the other hand, parents and kids are watching between three to four hours of television a day.

Kids are crying out for attention, recognition, and love. Instead we give them a steady diet of television messages promoting sex, violence, drinking, fatty-sugary foods, and, of course, diet products. Start with something simple. Try turning off the TV during dinner.

If you have preschool children, I strongly urge you to limit their television viewing to an hour a day or less. Most

*continued on page 64*

*continued from page 63*

major medical associations in this country agree on this point, including doctors, pediatricians, and psychiatrists. Children need unstructured play time for their brains to develop properly. Children who watch a great deal of TV as preschoolers tend to do poorly in a wide variety of cognitive skills, with many developing attention deficit disorder.

Media literacy helps: In addition to turning the TV off during meal times, you might consider watching some shows with your children. Take a look at what your kids are seeing and then talk with them about it.

And if you're serious about encouraging your children to grow up with moral values they learn from you instead of values pushed by advertisers whose only concern is profit, you might

consider removing TVs from your children's bedrooms. Putting a TV in your child's bedroom is the same as saying watch whatever you want. You may as well just install a vending machine for beer, cigarettes, junk food, and diet products.

The effects of excessive television viewing are serious. The question remaining is, Parents, what are you going to do about it? (*Los Alamos Monitor*)

### Children Watching TV

Two thirds of kids live in households with three or more sets; over half have a TV in the their bedroom and usually watch TV without their parents. (Children Now)

The number of hours spent in front of a television or video screen is the single biggest chunk of time in the waking life of an American child. (American Medical Association)

The greatest amount of television viewing takes place among children and young adolescents and peaks around age 12. By age 18, the average child will have watched 22,000 hours of TV—more time in front of the tube than in the classroom. (Children Now)

### Prime-Time Violence

Most kids watch adult TV, including nighttime soaps heavy on sex and violence. In the 1994–1995 season, nine out of the top 10 shows watched by kids ages two to eleven ran in primetime. (Children Now)

The average American child will witness 8,000 murders on TV by the time he or she is 12. He or she will see 20,000 commercials a year and have viewed over 20,000 acts of violence by the time of high school graduation. (Center for Media and Public Affairs)

60 percent of the information that children receive comes from TV. (American Medical Association)

### TV Influence

A 1994 *Newsweek* poll found that 67 percent of those asked blamed TV and other popular entertainment for the country's moral crisis. (Children Now)

Percentage of Americans who believe TV violence encourages real-life violence: 79. (TV-Free America)

SUPERIOR V-CHIPS

# THE LARGEST CORPORATIONS TAKING OVER THE CLASSROOM

### MARIANNE MANILOV

Young people today are a $150 billion market. They see an average of 100 TV commercials a day, and some 16,000 billboards, print ads, and corporate logos, as Leslie Savan notes in *The Sponsored Life*. Schoolgoers beware: The day of the submarket is upon us, and schools are one of the final frontiers—seen as places to put messages, logos, public relations material and direct advertising —all in the name of brand loyalty but covered up by the catch-all of "schools in need."

While the fact remains that low teacher-student ratios and parental or mentor involvement improve graduation and literacy rates, the push to hook up the next generation as early as possible is crashing through school doors. In addition, the Clinton-Gore effort to get every school on the information superhighway has become yet another venue for collecting marketing information from young people and their families. As the Center for Media Education noted in the "Web of Deception," World Wide Websites allow advertisers unprecedented access to collect direct marketing information from young people on their ideas, opinions, and families by asking the students questions about their dreams, goals, buying habits, and, of course, their parents' home address.

Here's a look at the corporate feeding chain of one of the largest multiconglomerates involved in commercializing United States schools:

### Kohlberg Kravis Roberts & Co.

Leveraged-buyout kings—most famous for its $25 billion leveraged buyout of RJR Nabisco—brought the art of stripping a car and selling its parts for cash to the corporate world.

Investors include teacher pension funds and educational institutions—like the State of Oregon retirement fund, the State of Washington investment board, and the Massachusetts Institute of Technology.

Owned by partners Henry Kravis and George Roberts. Jerome Kohlberg left the firm in 1987. Kravis is the chair of the board of WNET, New York City's public TV station.

### UNPLUG

Formed to fight the rising tide of commercialism in U.S. public schools, the Center for Commercial-Free Public Education/UNPLUG was started "by youth, for youth" in 1993. Recognizing that commercialism is most insidious when it preys on those in need while masquerading as a gift, the initial focus of UNPLUG's ire was Channel One, a daily "infotainment" program that makes viewing commercials for junk food and beauty products compulsory viewing for 8 million sixth through twelfth graders in the country's most underfunded schools. Since its founding, UNPLUG has expanded to support not only students but also parents, teachers, and entire communities in their battles against Channel One as well as other sinister examples of classroom commercialism.

Working in coalition with a broad range of activists and organizations, UNPLUG has put classroom commercialism on the map in the national debate on education reform. Through its tenacious media activism and dedication to grassroots organizing, UNPLUG is helping to overcome the dangerous complacency that would abandon public schools in dire need of resources to the highest corporate bidders. In 1996, UNPLUG helped oust Channel One from its showcase high school in San Jose, California and in 1997, it is garnering national media attention to an ongoing community-led campaign against classroom commercialism in Seattle.

*Contact: UNPLUG at 360 Grand Avenue #385, Oakland, CA 94610; Tel: (510) 268-1100; E-mail: unplug@igc.apc.org*

*continued on page 66*

continued from page 65

K-III Communications Corp. is started in 1989 by KKR, using over $460 million in cash.

## K-III Communications Corp.

KKR controls 82.2 percent of K-III's stock.

Best known for its ownership of *New York*, *Seventeen*, *Weekly Reader*, and Funk & Wagnalls.

School-based properties include the Classroom Channel, Films for the Humanities and Sciences, Macmillan Early Science Program, and the Katharine Gibbs Schools.

Several of K-III/KKR's properties are directly involved with classroom commercialism—making it one of the largest companies involved with the efforts to sell America's students' time directly to the highest corporate bidder.

## Channel One

Bought by K-III Communications from Whittle Communications for $300 million in August 1994.

Controversial in-school news and advertisement program sent to what it calls a "captive audience" of 8 million students a day for close to $200,000 per 30-second ad (compare to the Super Bowl rate at $1 million a minute).

Advertisers on Channel One include: McDonald's, M&M/Mars, Pepsi, and Reebok.

## Channel One = Reebok = "PE-TV"

12 minutes of physical-education programming sponsored by Reebok are broadcast on the Channel One network.

Promotes the contradictory idea of learning sports while sitting and watching TV.

## Weekly Reader

Distributed to 1.2 million fourth graders, 840,000 fifth graders and 478,000 sixth graders each week.

## Lifetime Learning Systems

Purchased by K-III Communications in 1994.

Produces sponsored education materials that it claims help companies reach "63 million young people, their parents and their 2 million teachers cost effectively."

*Stepping Into Adolescence: Produced for Anheuser-Busch for Grades 6–8 by Lifetime Learning Systems*

Warns students of the dangers of drinking too much, but forgets to mention the idea of not drinking at all. The program represents an attempt to legitimize and sanitize Anheuser-Busch's name, while the Budweiser frogs—the ones that say "Bud-Weis-er" like a Sesame Street spelling game—are now more recognizable to children ages 9–11 than Tony the Tiger, Smokey Bear, and Mighty Morphin Power Rangers, according to a recent study by the Center for Alcohol Advertising.

*Count Your Chips: Produced for the National Potato Chip Board for Grades 2–4 by Lifetime Learning Systems*

Encourages students to "strengthen skills in computation, problem solving, conducting research and creative writing"—all through learning with potato chips.

### Ideas in Action...

If you're against commercialism in schools, let your voice be heard.

Contact Henry Kravis, KKR, 9 West 57th St., New York, NY 10019; Tel: (212)750-8300. Tell him you think classroom commercialism is a bad investment, and that KKR can afford to donate schools the TVs now on loan. Or write Paul Fireman, CEO Reebok, 100 Technology Center Drive, Stoughton, MA 02072; Tel: (612) 341-5000. Tell him that there is no way that investing in Channel One and "captive audiences" of young people is part of leadership in human rights and education. (*EXTRA!*)

*Marianne Manilov is director of the Center for Commercial-Free Public Education.*

# PBS'S PAST, PRESENT, AND FUTURE

**ROBERT MCCHESNEY**

Not everyone grew up with *Sesame Street*. In fact, commercial broadcasters were wary of public broadcasting and fought it tooth and nail well into the 1960s. After many halting starts, Congress passed the Public Broadcasting Act of 1967, which led to the creation of the Corporation for Public Broadcasting (CPB), and soon thereafter PBS and NPR. The commercial broadcasters finally agreed to back down, primarily because they believed the new public system could be responsible for the unprofitable cultural and public-affairs programming that critics were constantly lambasting them for neglecting. There was a catch, however. The initial plan to have the CPB funded by a sales tax on the purchase of new radio sets and television sets, akin to the British Broadcasting Company method, was dropped, thus denying public broadcasting the stable source of income necessary for planning and editorial autonomy.

Although United States public broadcasting has produced some important fare, the system has been undermined by its funding structure and is farcical in comparison to the powerful public-service systems of Europe. Indeed, in international discussions of public broadcasting, the term "PBS-style system" is invoked to refer to a public system that is marginal and ineffective. It is the fate that the BBC, Canadian Broadcasting Corporation, and others wish to avoid.

The funding system is the primary culprit. The United States government only provides around 15 percent of the revenues; public stations depend on corporate donations, foundation grants, and listener/viewer contributions for the balance. In effect, this has made PBS and NPR stations commercial enterprises, and it has given the large corporations that dominate its subsidy tremendous influence over content in a manner that violates the fundamental principles of public broadcasting. It has also encouraged the tendency to appeal to an affluent audience rather than a working-class audience, because upscale viewers/listeners have far more disposable income.

Conservatives live in fear of a journalism not constrained by commercial support. It is true that much of public-broadcasting journalism and public-affairs programming is indistinguishable from commercial journalism. Nonetheless, on occasion stories slip through and programs get produced that would never clear a commercial media hurdle. This is especially true on public radio and with some of the more progressive community stations that would suffer the most without any federal grant money.

The right-wing assault on journalism and public broadcasting is not an isolated or exceptional phenomenon. It is part and parcel of a wholesale attack on all those institutions that possess some autonomy from the market. Thus public libraries and public education are being primed for privatization and advertising-supported schools and schooling-for-profit—notions regarded as obscene only a decade ago—are moving to the center of education policy debates.

*Robert McChesney is the author of* Corporate Media and the Threat to Democracy.

# KILLING IT SOFTLY

**NORMAN SOLOMON**

There's more than one way to kill public broadcasting. It can be murdered outright...or gradually strangled by corporate embraces with the aid of government. The latter process is well underway.

"Over a period of many years, the external pressure from Congress has induced a sort of self-censorship on the part of PBS," says Ruby Lerner, executive director of the 5,000-member Association of Independent Video and Filmmakers. "The network has gotten very cautious about what they're going to air. They don't want to be harassed by politicians who are, in turn, harassed by a lot of the organizations on the right."

Today, you won't see much of the public on "public television." None of the

*continued on page 68*

*continued from page 67*

regular PBS programs, for instance, are devoted to exploring the lives of working people. (The show *We Do the Work*, distributed independently, was not on the national PBS schedule.) Nor does a single ongoing PBS show explore the outlooks of environmentalists or consumers.

Meanwhile, huge companies keep pouring serious money into public TV programs they appreciate, such as *Wall $treet Week, Firing Line*, the *McLaughlin Group, Washington Week in Review* and the *Nightly Business Report*—literally made possible by corporate backing.

Each edition of the *NewsHour With Jim Lehrer* includes a pair of colorful pitches for agribusiness giant Archer Daniels Midland, "supermarket to the world." Likewise, on a daily basis, National Public Radio airs flattering descriptions of ADM. Those "enhanced underwriter credits" symbolize the steady privatization of public broadcasting.

ADM pays $5.8 million a year to the *NewsHour*. It also gives plenty of money to NPR for *All Things Considered*—but the radio network won't say how much. Suffice to say that when ADM began donating to *All Things Considered* last year, it made possible the expansion of the radio program from 90 minutes to two hours. A secretive policy exists "as a courtesy to our underwriter," says NPR spokesperson Pat Lute. Notice: NPR's courtesy to ADM outweighs informing the public about "public radio."

A highly political firm with billions of dollars riding on public perceptions

and legislation, ADM has gained enormously from a federal ethanol subsidy averaging $500 million per year during the past decade. But don't hold your breath for the *NewsHour* or *All Things Considered* to broadcast a series of investigative reports about ADM—the world's biggest producer of ethanol.

For many programming executives, deference to the private sector has become so routine that it seems normal, even wise. In the process, big checks determine more and more of what's on the air.

As federal appropriations slowly dwindle, stepping into the breach more than ever will be corporate America. It's a perfect scenario for winning bipartisan applause in Washington. The only losers

 Federal funds for the Corporation for Public Broadcasting amount to less than $1 a year for every United States citizen, with a projected annual drop of a few cents until 1999.

Less than 10 percent of the total public-television audience is black.

will be Americans who want public broadcasting in fact as well as in name. (Alternet)

*Norman Solomon is a syndicated columnist and co-author of* Through the Media Looking Glass: Decoding Bias and Blather in the News.

# WHEN IS A COMMERCIAL NOT A COMMERCIAL?

**JANINE JACKSON**

A luxury car tools along a mountain road. A Citicorp bankcard gleams behind the slogan, "Anyhow. Anywhere. Anytime. Right Now." Chase Manhattan advises viewers: "We believe that helping our customers realize their dreams is the best investment we can make."

Typical commercials? No—because they're on "noncommercial TV."

According to PBS, these are not commercials, but "enhanced underwriter acknowledgments." According the Communications Act of 1934, they may well be illegal.

The law specifically forbids noncommercial stations to accept compensation for broadcasting messages that "promote any service, facility or product offered by any person who is engaged in such offering for profit."

But since the era of deregulation beginning in the late 1970s, this law has been virtually ignored. In March 1984, the Federal Communications Commission (FCC) officially "relaxed" the noncommercial policy to allow public broadcasters to expand or "enhance" the scope of donor and underwriter "acknowledgments" to include such things as "value-neutral descriptions of a product line or service" and corporate logos or slogans that "identify and do not promote."

In a 1986 public notice, the FCC explained that this action was part of an "on-going effort to strike a reasonable balance between the financial needs of public broadcast stations and their obligation to provide an essentially noncommercial service." "Enhanced underwriting," the FCC said, would offer "significant potential benefits to public broadcasting in terms of attracting additional business support. (*EXTRA!*)

*Janine Jackson is co-host and producer of FAIR's radio show,* Counter Spin.

# THE MEDIA LITERACY ANTIDOTE

**JAY DOVER AND VIVECA GREENE**

At a time when the Beatles' "Help" is used to sell phone service, culturally correct actors sing about how Blockbuster is making the world "one," prepackaged politicians hawk their wares on Larry King, and an Internet "community" is a bunch of people at home alone in front of a computer, the champions of media literacy education insist that children—and adults—should all be taught how to engage the media critically.

Their tool is media literacy education: learning to ask questions about media, from how commercials are put together to why only a handful of corporations own almost all the world's newspapers and TV stations. Its main goal is to help people, especially kids, construct a deeper understanding of media, its place in society, and its influence on individuals. The end result of media literacy education, we hope, is that people make informed choices when "consuming" media. In media literacy education, inquiry is centered around five "core principles":

1. All media are manufactured products, stuffed with myths, illusions, messages, and values. For example, the quick cuts in music videos on MTV both generate and reinforce the ironic hipness of their audience of disaffected Gen-Xers.

2. All media are different. Obvious, maybe, but there's more to it since the same news story will differ in appearance, content, and meaning between newspapers, on television, or on the radio.

3. Media is Big Business. Media mission statements are simply: Show Me the Money. In this corporate environment, whether or not a piece of media (TV show, film, album, news story) can *make a profit* determines whether or not it will see the light of day or the glow of night.

4. Media have values. This simplest TV commercial is saturated with all sorts of values, messages and meanings. Political ads such as the "nuclear nightmare"ones used against Barry Goldwater and George Bush's "Willie Horton" spot are vivid examples.

5. Audiences are different. One need only flip through the cable TV channels or visit a magazine rack to see how media caters—and thus increases its market share—to include every type of audience.

These concepts help determine the shape of media literacy curriculum and practice. Because media take many forms and are constantly shifting in content and delivery, the concepts serve as a way to get everybody asking the same kind of questions and thus a way to organize media literacy education.

Because media show up in many areas of our lives, media literacy education is utilized in equally as many environments and by an array of groups: public and private schools, government agencies (i.e., the Center for Substance Abuse Prevention), community-based programs (i.e., the Poetry Video Project), nonprofit organizations (i.e., the Media Education Foundation), and enclaves of the media industry (i.e., the National Cable Television Association's Critical Viewing Project).

At present, however, only 6 percent of graduating high school seniors receive any sort of media literacy education in the United States. We are woefully behind countries such as Canada, Great

*continued on page 70*

*continued from page 69*

Britain, Australia, the Philippines, and most of Europe in educating our citizenry on how to consume media with conscious awareness. Unlike many of these other countries, American media is consumer based, and its primary purpose is to serve the needs of a market economy. Thus, media literacy education, in emphasizing critical thinking and informed choice, runs counter to the core message of American media: Don't think, just buy.

In smaller countries, it is considerably easier to implement media literacy through a national curriculum. In the United States, educational standards and practices are set by 16,000 school districts in 50 autonomous states. Currently there are "pockets" of media literacy education in a few states—New Mexico, North Carolina, and Massachusetts. The inconsistent reality of media literacy education in America is one of the pressing issues in the media literacy field.

There are certainly obstacles to a media-literate citizenry. But, even more certainly, we live in a media-saturated culture. As Neil Postman maintains, media literacy is one of few antidotes for such a culture where data are substituted for knowledge, where violence is the dominant form of entertainment, where we allow technology to dictate our lives without contemplation or scrutiny, and where we amuse ourselves to death.

In academic parlance, media literacy education is critical thinking about social, cultural, and our individual and collective relationships. It has the potential to be a rather radical educational

# CHRISTIAN ANGST

Gee, Honey...Without our daily dosage of the evening TeeVee news, how would we *ever* know which information is truly relevant in our ever changing world?

Terry Everton

process, too, because it addresses the impact of media on political policies, economic forces, social agendas, and cultural viewpoints.

In everyday terms, media literacy education helps people look at media in "The Big Picture" rather than just as an

appliance of diversion after a long workday. It helps people see the connection between McDonald's commercials and public landfills; televised images of African-Americans and public perception of welfare; the lack of news coverage of labor issues and the choices American voters face.

It is this kind thinking and questioning that fuels the fire in the media literacy field. It also helps validate media literacy as a process for creating serious and effective public debate on cultural, social, and political issues that affect all of us. Activism is a controversial camp within the movement, but as Wally Bowen, director of Citizens for Media Literacy, warns: "Media literacy is fundamentally about power relations. If practiced in a way that ignores or sidesteps issues of power, then media literacy is nothing more than media appreciation."

*Jay Dover and Viveca Greene created and organized the 1996 National Media Literacy Conference in Los Angeles.*

## Media Literacy Organizations

*CAMEO* (Canadian Association of Media Education Organizations) in Toronto, Ontario, advocates, promotes, and develops media literacy in Canada through its member organizations.

*Center for Media Literacy* in Los Angeles, California, publishes both text and media resources for use in classroom and media study activities. The center publishes the quarterly newsletter *Connect* and an annual resource catalogue.

*Citizens for Media Literacy* in Asheville, North Carolina, serves as a clearing house of information and curriculum materials, as well as offering workshops and symposia on media literacy for teachers and parents.

*Just Think Foundation* in Sausalito, California, develops media literacy programs for students, teachers, and parents in schools and community centers. The foundation creates positive messages to accompany TV shows, films, CD-ROMs, and on-line sites and works with the entertainment industry and educational organizations.

*Media Education Foundation* in Northampton, Massachusetts, produces educational materials (primarily videos) that highlight the important role the media play in the lives of all Americans. MEF is proposing an expanded media literacy program that would include a summer institute, curriculum guidelines, and educational resources developed for national use.

*Media Literacy On-line Project* in Eugene, Oregon, maintains an information-rich website for media literacy–related events, publications, sites, etc.

*National Telemedia Council* in Madison, Wisconsin, is a nonprofit educational organization that serves as a clearing house and center for media literacy. NTC publishes the quarterly *Telemedium*, which contains articles by leading media literacy specialists, book reviews, and classroom activities.

*New Mexico Media Literacy Project* in Albuquerque, New Mexico, launched the nation's most ambitious statewide initiative on behalf of media literacy in March 1993. Developed by the Downs Media Education Center, the New Mexico Media Literacy Project has introduced a rigorous media literacy curriculum into many of the region's schools.

*Turn to our Resource Rolodex for contact information.*

# 3. The Image Factory

*The public-relations industry is a 20th-century phenomenon. No one knows exactly how much money is spent each year in the United States on public relations, but $10 billion is considered a conservative estimate. "Publicity" was once the work of carnival hawkers and penny-ante hustlers smoking cheap cigars and wearing cheap suits. Today's PR professionals are recruited from the ranks of former journalists, retired politicians, and eager-beaver college graduates anxious to rise in the corporate world. They hobnob internationally with corporate CEOs, senators, and presidents. They use sophisticated psychology, opinion polling, and complex computer databases so refined that they can pinpoint the prevailing "psychographics" of individual city neighborhoods. Press agents used to rely on news releases and publicity stunts to attract attention for their clients. In today's electronic age, the PR industry uses 800-numbers and telemarketing, advanced databases, computer bulletin boards, simultaneous multilocation fax transmission, and "video news releases"—entire news stories, written, filmed, and produced by PR firms and transmitted by satellite feed to hundreds of TV stations around the world. Video news releases typically used as "story segments" on TV news shows without any attribution or disclaimer indicating that they are in fact subtle paid advertisements.*

*—John Stauber and Sheldon Rampton, authors of* Toxic Sludge Is Good for You

**Scary but True...**

 The number of PR flacks in the United States is greater than the number of working journalists.

 PR Newswire, which claims to be "the world's acknowledged leader in the distribution of corporate, association and institutional information to the media and the financial community" for 40 years, has 19 offices in the United States and distributes some 100,000 news releases a year to 2,000 newsrooms for more than 15,000 clients."

 "Most of what you see on TV is, in effect, a canned PR product. Most of what you read in the paper and see on television is not news." —Senior vice-president for Gray & Company public relations

"Persuasion, by its definition, is subtle. The best PR ends up looking like news. You never know when a PR agency is being effective; you'll just find your views slowly shifting"—PR executive

"This is the secret of propaganda: Those who are to be persuaded by it should be completely immersed in the ideas of the propaganda, without ever noticing that they are being immersed in it."—Joseph Goebbels (March 1933)

"The conscious and intelligent manipulation of the organized habits and opinions of the masses is an important element in democratic society. Those who manipulate this unseen mechanism of society constitute an invisible government which is the true ruling power of our country."—Edward Bernays, one of the founding fathers of American PR, in his book *Propaganda*

Kathie Lee Gifford was caught off guard when labor-rights activist Charlie Kernaghan and the National Labor Committee revealed the unperky truth: The Wal-Mart clothing line that bears her name (and picture) was partly made in sweatshops by Central American kids. But with help from damage-control king Howard Rubenstein (PR consultant to Leona Helmsley and Donald Trump), Kathie Lee became a "committed labor activist," according to the *New York Times*. Suddenly it was Gifford, not Kernaghan, who had "called for a crackdown on sweatshops," and all without giving up the profits form her lucrative "Kathie Lee" line of clothes.

Conveniently equipped with a live, national, daily TV show—syndicated by Disney, which also reaps profits from child labor—Gifford launched her defense in person. "I started my clothing line to benefit children.... Up to 50 percent of the profits go to the little children." With no TV program of their own, labor-rights activists couldn't immediately contradict the uncontrite Kathie Lee. In fact, only $1 million of the reported $9–$10 million profits from the Kathie Lee line goes to children's charities; the rest Gifford keeps. "One for the kids, nine for Kathie Lee," Kernaghan told FAIR's radio show *CounterSpin*. (*EXTRA!*)

# SOAKING IN SLUDGE

## JOHN STAUBER AND SHELDON RAMPTON

A romantic mythology surrounds the journalistic profession. We like to think that reporters are all like the guys on *N.Y. News*, relentlessly digging until the truth is exposed and villains receive their just punishment.

For the people who really shape the news—the public-relations industry—this myth serves an obviously useful function. It is also a useful myth for the news media itself, which perpetuates the image of the crusading press with frequent self-congratulatory editorials and newspaper mastheads proclaiming that "the only security of all is a free press."

In reality, according to scholars who study the media, at least 40 percent of all "news" today flows virtually unedited from public-relations offices. Media critics note that the media habitually fails to report on itself. It also fails to report on the PR industry. To do so would reveal the extent of its dependency on PR for access, sources, quotes, stories, and ideas.

Today's PR firms organize phony "Astroturf" grassroots groups that lobby for the tobacco, automobile, and insurance industries and create biased "video news releases" that often air unedited on the evening news, fooling viewers into thinking they are watching TV journalism. PR practitioners help the food and chemical industries deep-six books about dangerous pesticides, use "greenwashing" to divide and conquer environmentalists, and are presently campaigning to clean up the image of toxic sewage sludge, renaming it "biosolids" and calling it a "vitamin pill for the earth" so sewage treatment plants can sell it as fertilizer to unsuspecting American farmers.

One firm, Sawyer/Miller, even masterminded a PR campaign on behalf of the government of Colombia, one of the world's most egregious human-rights abusers and a compliant haven for the world's worst drug cartels. By the time Sawyer/Miller got through, President Bill Clinton was referring to Colombia as a democratic leader and "one of our strongest allies. . .in the effort to free the world of the scourge of narcotics trafficking."

These revelations may shock you, and they *ought* to shock even seasoned flacks, but practices that most people find outrageous are simply another day at the office for PR megafirms like Burson-Marsteller and Hill & Knowlton. Accusing the PR industry of manipulating the truth is like criticizing sharks for eating meat or snakes for poisoning their victims. They do what they do because it's in their nature.

Actually, the people we *ought* to be criticizing are the journalists who let the PR industry get away with manipulating the truth.

With the computer information banks and other information resources now available, investigative journalism is easier to practice than ever before. Reporters could and should use these resources to dig behind the scenes, exposing the PR industry's manipulations and the scandals that emanate from corporate boardrooms and government bureaucracies.

Instead, we get superficial journalism, news by press release, and endless regurgitation of easy-to-cover no-brainers.

At the very least, the news media ought to offer truth in labeling. "News stories" that are merely edited press releases ought to include disclaimers identifying the PR firm, government agency, or corporation that wrote them. Video news releases should include subtitles stating "footage supplied by Hill & Knowlton PR."

C'mon newspeople, clean up your act —do the job you're paid for. If you try, you might discover that even the public-relations industry is rooting for you to succeed.

PR pro Kirk Hallahan hopes to preserve a place at the table for the traditional news media, and he worries that its usefulness may be lost if "media organizations cheapen the value of their product.... When a news medium covered a story in the past, the information sponsor gained more than mere exposure. The client, product or cause gained salience, stature and legitimacy."

That legitimacy will be lost, he warns, if the public ceases to see a difference between news and paid propaganda. "While PR people might circumvent the press occasionally, we aren't going to want to do so all the time," Hallahan writes. "We can't kill the goose that laid the golden egg. A loss of public reliance upon and confidence in the mass media could be devastating."

*John Stauber and Sheldon Rampton write and edit the quarterly* PR Watch *and are the authors of* Toxic Sludge Is Good For You: Lies, Damn Lies and the Public Relations Industry.

# REWRITING THE TRUTH

## ROBERT MCCHESNEY

With fewer journalists, limited budgets, low salaries, and lower morale, the balance of power has shifted dramatically to the public-relations industry, which seeks to fill the news media with coverage sympathetic to its clients. In the United States today, one expert estimates that there are 20,000 more PR agents than there are journalists. Their job is to offer the news media sophisticated video press releases and press packets to fill the news hole, or contribute to the story that does fill the news hole.

The effects of this PR blitz on journalism can be seen on the two most important issues in United States politics in the 1990s: foreign trade and health care. These two issues are unusual because they provided clear public-policy debates on the types of all-important long-term issues (globalization of the economy and collapse of living standards and economic security) that professional journalism usually avoids. In the case of GATT and NAFTA, the large transnational corporations were almost unanimous and aggressive in their support of "free trade." While there was not the same unanimity in the business community regarding health care, the insurance industry had an enormous stake in maintaining control of the health sector. In both cases, these powerful interests were able to neutralize public opinion, even though, initially, based on personal experience, it was against GATT and NAFTA and for a single-payer health system.

The demise of journalism was readily apparent in this process. In each of these issues, big business mounted sophisticated, multimillion-dollar PR campaigns to obfuscate the issues, confuse the public, and, if not weaken the opposition to the business position, at least make it easier for powerful interests to ignore popular opinion. In effect, corporate America has been able to create its own "truth," and our news media seem unwilling or incapable of fulfilling the mission our society so desperately needs it to fill. And this is the likely pattern for the new global commercial journalism of the media giants.

*Robert McChesney is the author of* Corporate Media and the Threat to Democracy.

# ASTROTURFING

## KEN SILVERSTEIN

The PR industry also orchestrates many of the so-called grassroots citizen campaigns that lobby Washington, state, and local governments. Unlike genuine grassroots movements, however, these industry-generated "Astroturf" movements are controlled by the corporate interests that pay their bills. In defense of these activities, the PR industry claims that it is simply participating in the democratic process and contributing to public debate. In reality, the industry carefully conceals most of it activities from public view. This invisibility is part of a deliberate strategy for manipulating public opinion and government policy. Following is a short list of several currently active Astroturf groups:

*The Advancement of Sound Science Coalition* (ASSC)—An industry-funded front group linked to a beltway PR group. ASSC opposes federal regulations and dismisses threats posed by pesticides and other toxic chemicals.

*National Smokers Alliance*—Created by the PR firm Burson-Marsteller with money from Philip Morris, this "grassroots" group champions smokers' rights.

*Coalition to Save Medicare*—Goal: To destroy Medicare. Allied with big insurers like Cigna and Prudential.

# THIS MODERN WORLD by TOM TOMORROW

Seniors Coalition—a conservative group funded with support by right-wing direct-mail specialist Richard Viguerie.

*Citizens for a Sound Economy*—Fortune 500–backed think tank with primary support provided by the Koch family, the owners of the nation's largest private oil and gas company

*American Tort Reform Association*—Attacks "frivolous" lawsuits by posing as a friend of the little man and woman. The real goal is to protect its corporate supporters such as the tobacco, chemical, and drug industries from being sued over the manufacture and sale of faulty or inherently dangerous products.

*Ken Silverstein is co-author with Alexander Cockburn of* CounterPunch, *a biweekly newsletter of hard-hitting investigative reporting.*

### COMMENT

*"Today, with many more options available, PR professionals are much less dependent upon mass media for publicity. In the decade ahead, the largest American corporations could underwrite entire, sponsored channels. Organizations such as Procter & Gamble might circumvent public media altogether and subsidize programming that combines promotional and otherwise conducive messages — news, talk shows, infomercials, or sponsored entertainment or sports.… Channel sponsors will be able to reach coveted super-heavy users…with a highly tailored message over which they exert complete control." — Kirk Hallahan*

# CARMA SNOOPING

**BARBARA EHRENREICH**

Remember when former Energy Secretary Hazel O'Leary turned out to have been paying a private firm $43,500 to "evaluate" reporters according to how favorably they cover her and her department? "Enemies list" has been the charge of choice, but it is unlikely that O'Leary got the idea from studying the files of Richard Nixon or from anyone else in the vanishing public sector. The one interesting datum to emerge from "O'Leary Gate" is that corporations are increasingly paying to have journalists studied, snooped, and ranked.

My first reaction to this bit of news was, I admit, a light-hearted one. Too often in this business one has the sense of scratching out a message in fresh-drawn blood, corking it in a bottle, and tossing it out into the vast gray sea. So thank you, Ms. O'Leary, for inadvertently revealing that, somewhere, someone is actually reading what we write and taking note. It would be nicer, of course, to think that the corporate chieftains were undertaking this labor themselves. But at least now we know that our work is finding attentive readers, even if they have to be paid to do it.

Nor is this kind of surveillance likely to intimidate many journalists, at least any more than they are already intimidated by the moral imperatives of corporate profit taking. According to the *Wall Street Journal*, which broke the O'Leary

story, corporations are terrified of "aggressive, potentially prosecutorial news reporting." But wherever would this come from? Show me a mainstream journalist today and I will show you a broken creature living in mortal fear of being downsized or dismissed for offending some advertiser, some executive, or some company that happens to belong to this poor journalist's ruling media conglomerate.

Nevertheless, the business of snooping on the media is growing almost as fast as the Net-browsing industry. Carma International, the snoop firm O'Leary employed, has seen its revenues leap by 20 percent annually, and its list of clients expand to include Microsoft, Philip Morris, McDonald's, the National Rifle Association, the Republican Party, and the Scottish nuclear power industry. "Carma" stands for Computer-Aided Research and Media Analysis, and, given the company's prescience in discerning a ripe new market, it's a shame that "computer" couldn't have been spelled with a K, as in Mortal Kombat or Ku Klux Klan.

The media snoopers attribute the growing demand for their services to an innocent Pythagorean zeal for quantitative measurement. Corporations maintain PR departments for the purpose of massaging the press, so why not measure the success of those efforts? As Carma's managing director for Europe told the *Financial Times* in 1994, in a spirit

Archimedes would have applauded, "If you can't measure it, don't do it." Thanks to the new wisdom, Hewlett-Packard's PR director for Britain, Shirley Horn, is now monitoring such matters as the number of thank-you letters written by journalists who have been wined and dined at company expense. Science at work!

The real purpose of all this monitoring and measuring is to stamp out any lingering sparks of initiative and independence that may persist within the journalism profession—that is, to complete its transformation into a branch of public-relations. Some of the snoop firms sell corporations information on reporters' personal predilections—whether they are "spacey," for example, or divorced or vegetarians—and these tidbits can be used by corporate operatives to "avoid being blindsided by a reporter with whom you've had no previous experience," according to material from the firm Werle & Brim Ltd. The more staid Carma conducts qualitative studies of journalists' work and ranks them on a suck-up scale of 1–100. The recalcitrant can then be brought into line or, in severe instances, cut out of the loop.

Take the case of former low-scorer Tom Kenworthy of the *Washington Post*. When a Carma study found him deficient in admiration for the beef industry, the industry's PR people did a little remedial work and introduced him to "some live cattlemen." You can bet that this introduction did not take place in a Dunkin' Donuts, because the industry now reports being "a little bit happier with his reporting." Kenworthy says lamely he "doesn't know" if this had any

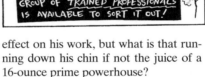

effect on his work, but what is that running down his chin if not the juice of a 16-ounce prime powerhouse?

For anyone who can still muster a flutter of pride at the concept of the "journalism profession," further disillusionment is at hand. Who does the arduous work of reading and rating at places like Carma? "Generally," the *Wall Street Journal* reports, "former academics or people with journalism backgrounds." This explains what has happened to our colleagues as newspapers eliminate unnecessary and tedious forms of news, such as that of the national and international variety. Not all of the thousands cast out by *Newsday*, the *Los Angeles Times*, the *Miami Herald* and others are writing novels in garrets. The more wretched and spiteful of them are spying on those few of us

who can still claim semihonorable modes of employment.

The ever-tangled relationship between journalism and PR achieves a new level of symmetry. Reporters report on the real world, while reporters *manqués* report on the reporters. PR has always been, at heart, a kind of proto-journalism, with its primary product, the press release, serving as a primitive template for news stories distinguished chiefly by the addition of a byline. Now, thanks to Carma and its ilk, companies can ensure that news stories deviate as little as possible from the corporate press releases that are designed to inspire them. (*The Nation*)

*Barbara Ehrenreich, a regular contributor to* The Nation, Z, *and* Time *magazines, is the author of several books.*

# A ROSTER OF PROGRESSIVE PUBLICISTS

**Fenton Communications**
David Fenton and Beth Bohart
Washington, DC
Clients include Greenpeace, the Center for Tobacco-Free Kids, and Environmental Media Services.

**ProMedia**
Rochelle Lefkowitz
New York, New York
Clients include the American Library Association, Neighborhood Preservation Coalition, and Planned Parenthood Federation of America.

**Riptide Communications**
David Lerner
New York, New York
Clients include Center for Constitutional Rights, William M. Kunstler Fund for Racial Justice, and Honor the Earth Campaign.

**McKinney & McDowell Associates**
Gwen McKinney and Leila McDowell
Washington, DC

**Public Policy Communications**
Bob Schaeffer
Belmont, Massachusetts
Clients include Project on Participatory Democracy, Public Employees for Environmental Responsibility, and Chemical Weapons Working Group.

**VoxPop**
Christine Triano and Brian Smith
San Francisco, California
Clients include Western States Center, Environmental Health Coalition, and California Food Policy Advocates.

**Kent Communications**
Stephen D. Kent
Garrison, New York
Clients include the American Assembly of Columbia University, Center for Responsive Politics, and Lawyers Committee on Nuclear Policy.

**Communication Works**
Michael Shellenberger and Tony Newman
San Francisco, California
Clients include the Headwaters Forest Coordinating Committee, Northern Coalition for Immigrant Rights, and Global Exchange.

**The Mainstream Media Project**
Mark Sommer
Arcata, California
Clients include Public Citizen, Friends of the Earth, and World Policy Institute.

**Millennium Communications Group**
Ann Beaudry
Washington, DC
Clients include Project on Participatory Democracy, Public Employees for Environmental Responsibility, and Chemical Weapons Working Group.

**We Interrupt This Message**
Kim Deterline
San Francisco, California
Clients includes Center for Commercial-Free Education/UNPLUG, San Francisco AIDS Foundation, Ella Baker Center for Human Rights.

**Valerie Denney Communications**
Valerie Denney
Chicago, Illinois
Clients include Association of Community Organizations for Reform Now (ACORN), Community Media Workshop, Youth Vision

**Miriam Zoll Communications**
Miriam Zoll
Brookline, Massachusetts
Clients include Ms. Foundation for Women, Gay Men's Health Crisis Center

*Turn to our Resource Rolodex for contact information.*

# 4. Incredible Shrinking Media: Books

*Plus comments by* Todd Gitlin

## COMMENT

*Conglomerate publishers have less and less need of Valhalla. They are in the business of providing content that moves. All the better if the movie division of the conglomerate can be tied into a presold novel that has been published by the hard-copy division. Better still if subsequent novelizations and auxiliary product can be spun off. You've read the paperback, now wear the T-shirt, buy the toy, play the game. This is not to say that serious books go lacking publishers. For now, they do find markets, often remunerative ones. But when a manuscript comes up for discussion at editorial meetings, every last one must be a plausible profit maker. God help the poor thing if the author is obscure and the manuscript is difficult; if the style is cerebral or unfashionable, the characters unpleasant, the plot not a recombination of the last six bodice-rippers. After all, their time to reach readers is decidedly limited. Even commercial books are going to get a few weeks on superstore shelves before they get revolved through the door straight back to publishers' warehouses.*

*— Todd Gitlin, New York University*

## LEADING RETAIL BOOKSELLERS

**(1st quarter sales, 1996)**

| SELLER | ($ MILLION) | % | CUMULATIVE (%) |
|---|---|---|---|
| Barnes & Noble | 508.8 | 25.3 | 25.3 |
| Borders Group | 404.0 | 20.1 | 45.4 |
| Crown Books | 62.5 | 3.1 | 48.6 |
| Books-A-Million | 56.6 | 2.8 | 51.4 |
| All other | 977.1 | 48.6 | 100.0 |
| Total | 2,009.0 | 100.0 | HHI: 1,063 |

Source: American Booksellers Association, from the United States Census Bureau and company reports.

# THE CORPORATIZATION OF PUBLISHING

**ANDRÉ SCHIFFRIN**

The mighty heads of America's conglomerate publishers, as well as a group of the small independent editors, converged on Paris in March 1996 at the invitation of the French government. The United States was the theme of the Paris Book Fair, and it was clear that the invitations had been arranged as if for a Feydeau bedroom farce. As the major players left from one salon door, the small independent publishers were ushered into another; the possibility of confrontation, discussion or debate was carefully avoided. The polarized U.S. publishing scene was represented accurately, but its extremes remained as separate as ever.

For the French, this polarization was no doubt a difficult concept to grasp. While the conglomerates there control some 60 percent of the publishing industry as a whole, the intellectual scene is still dominated by the traditional, family owned and serious publishers. Even the conglomerates find they have to vie for sales and respectability by keeping to a program that includes books many an American university press would envy.

For the rest of the continent, publishing is still close to what we had in the United States twenty years ago. The large media companies have not yet taken over all the major houses; the

profits expected from books are not yet those expected from film or television; and the bookstores are still filled with a wide variety of books, political and literary, that have long disappeared from most of ours. How has U.S. publishing come to resemble the mass media in so short a time?

We have seen in recent years the application of market theory to the dissemination of culture. Spurred by the Thatcher / Reagan changes in politics, the owners of publishing houses rationalize their policies by invoking the market. It is not up to elites to impose their values on the readers, they claim; it is up to the public to choose what it wants—and if what it wants is bad, so be it. Houses with histories as distinguished as Knopf have not hesitated to take on perverse and violent books that have been turned away by other conglomerates. The question is which books will make the most money, not which ones will fulfill the publisher's traditional cultural mission.

The development of the market ideology has been accompanied by legislation that has increasingly changed the nature of book publishing. In both the United States and Britain, funding for libraries has been drastically cut. There was a time in both countries when library purchases were large enough to cover much of the costs of serious fiction and nonfiction.

The editorial process has also been skewed by the fact that at large companies, decisions about what to publish are made not by editors but by so-called publishing committees, in which the financial and marketing people play a pivotal role. If a book does not look as if it will sell a certain number—and that number increases with every year—these people argue that the company simply cannot "afford" to take it on, especially when it is a new novel or a work of serious nonfiction. What the Spanish newspaper *El Pais* perceptively called "market censorship" is increasingly in force in a decision-making process that is based on whether there is a pre-existing audience for any book. The obvious success and the well-known author are the books now sought; new authors and new, critical viewpoints are increasingly finding it difficult to be published in the major houses.

Obviously, new ideologies did not develop out of thin air. They are part of the *Zeitgeist*, but they are also part of a new structure, in this case the rise of the large international conglomerates. Increasing concentration has brought with it a drive for dramatic increases in profits. Since the twenties, through prosperity and depression, the average profit for all publishing houses has been around 4 percent after taxes. This includes both the houses that were intensely commercial and sought (even then) to publish only those books they felt to be eminently profitable, as well as the important houses that we all recall as forming the culture of our time, houses that sought to balance profitability with responsibility. The owners of these latter houses, the Alfred A. Knopfs and others, did not retire in poverty. But they were happy to have the value of their house grow gradually from year to year; they did not bleed it each year of the capital necessary for the maintenance of its list.

It is instructive to look at the figures for those European houses that have not yet been corporatized. In France, the most prestigious of the traditional houses, Gallimard, makes an annual profit of little over 3 percent, despite what is probably the strongest backlist in Europe and a flourishing and imaginative children's book section. Le Seuil, probably the second most impressive of the French houses, came up last year with a profit of just over 1 percent. At this moment, both are still owned by the founding families and their allies.

In the United States and Britain, where more and more independent houses are being taken over by conglomerates, the new owners have insisted that the profitability of the book publishing arm should be similar to the high returns they demand from other subsidiaries like newspapers, cable television and film. New profit targets have therefore been established in the range of 12 to 15 percent.

To meet these new expectations, publishers have drastically changed the nature of what they publish. The "smaller books"—serious fiction, art history, criticism—have all but disappeared from the lists of major houses. The emphasis has been shifted to pay huge advances for what are hoped to be huge best sellers. But since every other major house has been following the same policy, advances increasingly go beyond what is reasonable to expect a book will earn. These huge advances are written off, vast losses are incurred and the publisher must cut back even more, eliminating the "midlist" and taking away from the smaller books what is left for marketing and advertising in order to try once again with a Jeffrey Archer or a Danielle Steele. Indeed, layoffs at HarperCollins in London last year have been reported in the British press as being a direct result of the enormous (and unearned) £32 million advance (close to $50 million) paid to Archer.

Needless to say, not all the houses are able to make their profit targets. Indeed, there are reports that some of the large corporations are far less profitable than they were five years ago, when they were pursuing their traditional and diversified policy. But if one house succeeds, all the others are told they must try harder. If someone does make 15 percent in a year, the others are expected to do the same, and the unfortunate front runner is then expected to make 16 percent. One of the most interesting lessons, yet one of the hardest to learn, is that there is no such thing as enough when such unrealistic profit targets are set. Newhouse, for instance, bought the Random House empire for some $60 million. Ten years later, his holdings had increased in value to over $1 billion. But this did not suffice. Greater annual profits were expected of each of the publishing units, so each of the houses changed its list accordingly, until the group as a whole had altered its character completely.

Another pressure on publishing is rising overheads. Publishing used to pay relatively low salaries. Editors earned roughly what a professor would, assistant editors roughly what a lecturer would and so on. Now publishers have raised their salaries to phenomenal heights, reaching into the millions. A recent *PW* survey shows the head of McGraw-Hill to be making more than $1.5 million a year, more than the head of Exxon or Philip Morris. One of the side-effects of corporatization is the increasing intent of book publishers to mimic the lifestyles of their colleagues in Hollywood. Publishers' offices become more and more showy, resembling banks rather than the offices of their predecessors; salaries and expense accounts have risen accordingly. The sales conferences at Random House were costing a million dollars each—twice a year—by the time I left. These overheads must be paid for even before the annual profits are declared. The reason so many publishers claim they cannot afford to publish a book that will sell fewer than 15,000 or 20,000

*continued on page 83*

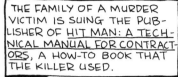
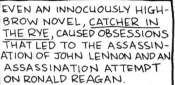

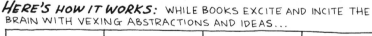

*continued from page 81*

copies is not that the book cannot break even at those numbers. The reason is that each book must throw off a certain contribution to overhead, often $100,000 or more, to justify its place on the list.

These internal demands are part of the transformation of the ideology of publishing. When people can no longer be proud of the books they publish, and justify their own careers by the books they have brought to the world, the cruder rewards of money and status are needed to fill the moral gap.

The third basic change is a political one. It can be illustrated by a recent event. Basic Books, the prestigious social science publisher now owned by HarperCollins, published a biography of Deng Xiaoping, by his daughter. It is badly written, full of excuses and lacking information—the kind of book that no Western publisher would look at twice under normal circumstances. But not only was the book published by Basic, it was launched with a massive publicity campaign, reported to have cost at least $100,000, in which the author was brought from China and presented to the press and public. Why was so much effort devoted to this book? For one thing, Rupert Murdoch, who owns HarperCollins, was eager to obtain from the Chinese government permission for his Sky cable network to broadcast in China. He had already agreed to censor the network so that the BBC News would be blocked, but

those assurances, apparently, were not sufficient to get the contract for him. A little additional persuasion was needed —*voilà*, the publication of this embarrassing volume.

To Murdoch, the use of publishing to obtain greater ends is simply part of business as usual. A great deal of press attention was paid to the initial proposal by HarperCollins to pay Newt Gingrich an advance of $4.5 million. The book's sales now look as if they will earn, at the very most, a third of that. Even with the promise of a paperback sale and a second book, it is clear that the amount first offered the Representative exceeded any reasonable expectation of what sales might be. Under the circumstances, Murdoch's eagerness to consult Gingrich on the fate of his immensely valuable TV franchises, even before the contract had been signed, becomes even more telling.

In the United States, the political nature of books has changed drastically since the conglomerates acquired so many houses. Harper, Random House, and Simon & Schuster were once bastions of New Deal liberalism. Yet the current output of U.S. publishing is markedly to the right. The editors involved are still basically the same people; one must assume that they are responding to new pressures. Indeed, one of the major reasons my colleagues and I left Pantheon after all those years was the clear directive from the new Random House management that we should move away from the kind of political publishing for which Pantheon

had been known, that we should consider books from the right instead. Random House, of course, denied afterward that it had made any such statements. But one has only to look at the Random House lists five years later to see the degree to which it has abandoned critical political and social commentary, and instead publishes authors from the right.

Now of course the larger houses will say that these decisions are market-driven. But it is hard to argue that there are no readers open to alternative views. Indeed, the market success of The New Press's own recent books dealing with politics confirms both the substantial nature of the audience and the need for publishers to play a countercyclical role. Books on political issues, particularly in election years, were for many years traditional fare of U.S. publishing houses. Yet in 1992, during the presidential election, there were virtually no books published for the general reader dealing with the major issues facing American citizens —NAFTA, national health insurance, the future of the welfare system—other than those taking a right-wing viewpoint, often subsidized by conservative foundations and then published by major conglomerates.

The problems of publishing have been exacerbated by the rise of major bookstore chains, which to a large degree share the profit-centered ideology of the media conglomerates. The

*continued on page 84*

*continued from page 83*

major chains focus their energies and very considerable resources on the best sellers. Bookselling has been divided by a civil war in which independent bookstores claim they are constantly threatened by the chains, which have an aggressive policy of opening new stores close to successful independents. As a result, more and more independents go out of business; in the center of New York City it is difficult to find more than a handful—that number has been diminished by three in recent months.

In a series of lawsuits brought by the American Booksellers Association, the independents have charged that the large publishers favor the chains through unfair practices. These publishers pay large amounts of so-called "co-op" advertising money to be sure best sellers are advantageously placed in stores. Smaller publishers, taking a gamble on a less accessible book, are hard put to pay the extra co-op money, and the chances of their books being stocked in any quantity diminish accordingly.

\* \* \*

What reversals of these trends are possible? The only major changes that could come would be by strict application of antitrust laws in the United States and Great Britain—the very laws that have been waived to allow media conglomerates like Murdoch's to gain ever-increasing power. Political leaders are wary of opposing those who control the media, and have been quick to give way to the demands.

It would be unrealistic at this point to expect either Clinton or the Republicans to challenge the major media conglomerates head-on. But this does not mean that no Congressional action is possible. Not many years ago Senator Paul Simon and others organized hearings on concentration in the media, supported by author groups such as PEN, then far more politically daring. Should no member of Congress be willing to run the considerable risks of taking on the media giants, citizen hearings, teach-ins and other tools are available. The most dangerous aspect of the current increase in conglomerate power is that is has gone largely unchallenged, that antitrust legislation is not even discussed, that other forms and structures of media ownership are hardly contemplated.

Another opportunity is the proliferation of small, independent houses. These are growing in the United States. Though their names—Dalkey Archive, Graywolf Press, Verso Books, Thunder's Mouth, Milkweed, etc.— are still largely unknown to the public, from them come a wide variety of serious and important books. In a vast cultural desert, the combined effort of all the independent presses does succeed in making a few flowers bloom. But only a few. The share of the market of these presses is minuscule, at most 1 percent of total book sales. Moreover, they do not have the strength or resources of the major firms, and do not have anywhere near as ready an access to bookstores.

The problem overall is a political and economic one. Until governments feel strong enough to challenge the power of the enormous conglomerates, the solutions that can be offered will have to be partial. Still, these new alternatives offer us the beginnings of choice. There is a new generation of young publishers willing to take on the "commercially incorrect" and, particularly in fiction and poetry, these new houses have come close to replacing their older and larger competitors.

The drive for profit that determines capitalism at the end of this century fits like an iron mask on our cultural output. Unlike Europe, we have lost most of the remnants of nineteenth-century capitalism, the family-owned firms whose owners could decide whether or not to maximize profit. If we were talking about similar changes in other industries, the results might not be as dangerous. If a few international manufacturers of clothing offer us an ever-more-limited choice of jeans, the culture is not deeply threatened. But if we have purveyors of culture who feel that one idea can fit all, then not only our future but our very ability to debate what it should be will be at risk. (Excerpted from *The Nation*)

*André Schiffrin is Director of The New Press.*

# HEARST

*Privately held; George Hearst Jr., chairman*

### HEARST BOOKS
*1995 combined revenues: $160 million (est.)*

**AVON BOOKS**
**WILLIAM MORROW & CO.**
Hearst Books
Hearst Books International
Hearst Marine Books
Quill Trade

### NEWSPAPERS
Albany (NY) Times Union, Beaumont (TX)
Enterprise, Edwardsville (IL) Intelligencer,
Houston Chronicle, Huron (MI) Daily Tribune,
Laredo (TX) Morning Times, Midland (MI)
Daily News, Midland (TX) Reporter-Telegram,
Plainview (TX) Daily Herald, San Antonio
Express-News, San Francisco Examiner,
Seattle Post-Intelligencer; 7 weeklies

### MAGAZINES
Esquire, Good Housekeeping, Colonial Homes,
Cosmopolitan, Country Living, Country Living
Gardener, ESPN, House Beautiful,
Marie Claire (with Marie Claire Album),
Motor Boating & Sailing, Popular Mechanics,
Redbook, SmartMoney (with Dow Jones),
Sports Afield, Town & Country, Victoria and
Harper's Bazaar. Also, 9 magazines in the U.K.
and 81 international editions

### CABLE
Part owner of Lifetime (50% with Disney);
A&E and History Channel (37.5% with Disney and
NBC); ESPN; ESPN2; and ESPNEWS (20% with
Disney); one foreign channel (partially owned)

### STATIONS
7 TV stations; 6 radio stations

### TV PRODUCTION
24-hour news channel in New England;
entertainment programming (Flash Gordon)

### MULTIMEDIA
Kidsoft (kids' software, 29.4%); Netscape (1.5%);
Books That Work (how-to software, 17.5%);
I/Pro (Internet provider; minority interest)

### COMICS
King Features Syndicate (Blondie, Beetle Bailey)
and others

### OTHER
Timber, ranching and real estate in California

1995 revenues:
## $2.3 billion

---

# NEWS CORPORATION

*C.E.O. Rupert Murdoch
controls about 30% of stock*

### HARPERCOLLINS
*1995 revenues: $550 million (est.)*

**HARPERCOLLINS**
Harper Reference
Harper Perennial
Harper Business
Basic Books
Harper Prism
Regan Books
Harper San Francisco
Westview Press

### NEWSPAPERS
New York Post;
The (London) Times,
The Sun and others,
together accounting for 30%
of newspaper sales in the
U.K.; more than 200 wholly
and partially owned papers
in Australia and New Zealand;
papers in Fiji and in Papua
New Guinea (partially
owned); inserts for 622
U.S. papers

### MAGAZINES
Pacific Islands Monthly,
Premiere (50%), TV Guide,
The Weekly Standard;
40% of 18 weekly and
monthly magazines in
Australia, New Zealand
and Europe

### TELEVISION
Fox Network; Twentieth
Century Fox Television
(The X-Files; Chicago Hope)

### CABLE & SATELLITE TELEVISION
In the U.S.: fXM:Movies from
Fox; in partnership with TCI-
owned Liberty Media (50%)

**VOL 1**

---

# NEWS CORPORATION

for: Fox Sports Net, Fox
Sports International and
fX; Fox Kids World-
wide(50%), Fox News
Channel;
in partnership with MCI
(50%) to develop ASkyB,
satellite TV in the U.S.;
STAR TV, satellite TV that
reaches all of Japan,
China, India, Southeast
Asia and into Africa;
BSkyB (40%), satellite TV
in the U.K., which holds
49% interest (with Kirch
Gruppe) in Germany's DF1;
developing JSkyB in Japan
(50% with Softbank);
FOXTEL (50%) cable
operator and two sports
networks (50%)
in Australia; Canal FOX,
cable TV in Latin America

### TELEVISION STATIONS
22, including 1 in each of
the top 4 markets
(N.Y., L.A., Chicago, Phila.)

### MOTION PICTURES
Twentieth Century Fox,
Fox 2000, Fox
Searchlight Pictures,
Fox Family Films,
Fox Studios Australia

### MULTIMEDIA
CD publishing;
about 20 Web sites
(including iGuide)

### OTHER
Sheep farming;
paper production
(46.2% of Australia's only
newsprint plant); an
Australian airline (50%)

**VOL 2**

1995 revenues:
## $9 billion

---

# PEARSON PLC

### THE PENGUIN GROUP
*Combined 1995 revenues: $617 million (est.)*

| | |
|---|---|
| **VIKING PENGUIN** | **PUTNAM BERKLEY** |
| Studio | G.P. Putnam's Sons |
| DUTTON/SIGNET/PLUME | Grosset/Putnam |
| Dutton | Boulevard |
| Donald I. Fine | Price Stern Sloan |
| Signet | Jeremy P. Tarcher |
| Onyx | Berkley Books |
| Topaz | Jove |
| Plume | Ace |
| Meridian | Perigee |
| Mentor | HP Books |
| | RIVERHEAD BOOKS |

### NEWSPAPERS
The Financial Times; newspapers and
magazines in Spain and France;
financial newspaper in South Africa

### MAGAZINES
The Economist (50%)

### TELEVISION PRODUCTION
Thames Television (The Bill);
Grundy Worldwide (Neighbors); Financial
Times Television (all in U.K.); ACI in L.A.;
BSkyB (4%); Hong Kong's TVB (10%);
U.K.'s Channel 5 (24% with others)

### SATELLITE TELEVISION
BBC Prime; BBC World (6% with BBC)

### MOTION PICTURES
Phoenix Pictures (20%)

### MULTIMEDIA
Mindscape

### FINANCIAL
Lazard Frères & Co. (9% profit interest);
Lazard Brothers (in U.K.) 50%

### THEME PARKS/AMUSEMENTS
Port Aventura theme park in Spain (40%);
Madam Tussaud's wax museum,
the London Planetarium, Rock Circus,
Alton Towers, Warwick Castle, Chessington
World of Adventures (all in U.K.);
Madam Tussaud's Scenerama (in Amsterdam);
Madam Tussaud's 42nd St. (coming to N.Y.C.)

1995 (est.) revenues:
## $2.8 billion

# VIACOM

## SIMON & SCHUSTER
*1995 revenues: $832.7 million (est.)*

| | |
|---|---|
| **SIMON & SCHUSTER** | **POCKET BOOKS** |
| Lisa Drew Books | Star Trek |
| Scribner | Minstrel Books |
| Touchstone | Archway |
| Fireside | Folger Shakespeare |
| Aguilar | Library |
| Libros en Español | Washington Square |
| **THE FREE PRESS** | Press |
| Lexington Books | MTV Books |
| Martin Kessler Books | Pocket Star Books |

*Also, largest educational publisher in U.S.*
*(1995 sales over $1 billion)*

■ ■ ■

**MOTION PICTURES:** Paramount Pictures

■

**MOVIE THEATERS**
Famous Players in Canada; UCI (50% with
MCA) and Films Paramount in Europe;
Cinamerica (50% with Time Warner)
in western U.S.

■

**CABLE**
MTV; M2: Music Television; VH1;
Nickelodeon; Nick at Nite's TV Land; Showtime;
FLIX; Sci-Fi Channel (50% with Seagrams);
Comedy Central (50% with Time Warner);
The Movie Channel; Sundance Channel
(45% with PolyGram & Robert Redford);
USA Network (50% with Seagrams);
Paramount Channel (in U.K. with BSkyB)

■

**TELEVISION**
UPN Network (50% with Chris Craft) includes
152 affiliates, reaching 92% of U.S. TV homes;
Spelling Entertainment (Melrose Place, Beverly
Hills, 90210), 75%; Paramount Television
syndication (Cheers, I Love Lucy) and
production (Frasier, Entertainment Tonight)

■

**TV STATIONS:** 11

■

**RADIO STATIONS:** 10

■

**HOME VIDEO**
Blockbuster stores; Paramount Home Video

■

**OTHER ENTERTAINMENT**
Theme parks (Kings Dominion,
Kings Island, Great America, Carowinds,
Canada's Wonderland)

**1995 revenues:**
# $11.3 billion

---

# ADVANCE PUBLICATIONS

**RANDOM HOUSE**
*1995 revenues:*
*$1.26 billion (est.)*

**RANDOM HOUSE**
The Modern Library
Times Books
Times Business
Princeton Review
**ALFRED A. KNOPF**
Everyman's Library
Pantheon
Villard
Schocken
Vintage
**FODOR'S**
**CROWN**
Crown Trade Paperbacks
Harmony Books
Clarkson N. Potter
Bell Tower
**BALLANTINE**
Del Rey
Fawcett

**NEWSPAPERS**
Birmingham (AL) News
and Post-Herald,
Mobile (AL) Press,
Huntsville (AL) Times,
Mobile (AL) Press Register,
New Orleans Times
Picayune, Springfield (MA)
Union News & Sunday
Republican, Ann Arbor (MI)
News, Flint (MI) Journal,
Grand Rapids (MI) Press,
Kalamazoo (MI) Gazette,
Bay City (MI) Times,
Muskegon (MI) Chronicle,
Saginaw (MI) News,
Jackson (MI) Citizen
Patriot, (Pascagoula)
Mississippi Press, St. Louis
Post-Dispatch,
Jersey Journal (Jersey

**VOL 1**

**1995(est.) revenues:**
# $5.3 billion

---

# ADVANCE PUBLICATIONS

City), (Newark) Star-Ledger,
Staten Island (NY) Advance,
The Times of Trenton (NJ),
Syracuse Herald-Journal
and Post-Standard,
Cleveland Plain Dealer,
The Oregonian (Portland),
Harrisburg Patriot-News;
business weeklies
in 35 cities

**MAGAZINES**
Condé Nast publications:
Allure, Architectural Digest,
Bon Appetit, Bride's, Condé
Nast House and Garden,
Condé Nast Traveler, Details,
Glamour, Gourmet, GQ,
Mademoiselle, Self,
Vanity Fair, Vogue; also,
NASCAR Winston Cup
Illustrated, NASCAR
Winston Cup Scene,
The New Yorker,
On Track, Parade

**CABLE**
Discovery Channel,
Animal Planet and
The Learning Channel
(24.6% with TCI, Cox
Communications and
John Hendricks)

**CABLE FRANCHISES**
4.5 million households
(33% with Time Warner)

**OTHER**
The Nature Company,
Scientific Revolution
and Discovery Channel
stores (24.6%);
Cartoon Bank

**VOL 2**

---

# BERTELSMANN AG

## BANTAM DOUBLEDAY DELL
*1995 revenues: $670 million (est.)*

| | |
|---|---|
| **BANTAM BOOKS** | **DELL** |
| **DOUBLEDAY** | **Delacorte Press** |
| Anchor Books | The Dial Press |
| Currency Books | Delta |
| Nan A. Talese Books | Island Books |
| Image Books | Laurel |
| | **BROADWAY BOOKS** |

*One of Germany's largest trade publishers. Also, 2.5
million book club members worldwide in the Literary
Guild and other book clubs in the U.S.; most of Western
Europe, Canada, Australia, New Zealand and, beginning
this year, in China (70% with state-run company)*

**MAGAZINES**
Family Circle, McCall's, Parents, Child,
Fitness, American Homestyle and Garden,
Ser Padres Network, YM; 34 magazines
in Germany, including Stern and Der Spiegel
(part owner); magazines in France,
Spain, England, Italy and Poland.
About 40 professional magazines

**NEWSPAPERS**
Six dailies in Germany; part-ownership of
papers in Hungary and Slovakia

**TELEVISION**
CLT-UFA (50%): largest European
broadcaster, with television and radio
stations and television
programming branches

**MUSIC**
Arista, RCA, others (14% of music sold
worldwide); music publishing

**MULTIMEDIA**
Includes partnership with America Online in
Europe; publishes reference CDs

**OTHER**
Printing; CDs for data storage

**1995 revenues:**
# $14 billion

---

# TIME WARNER

## TIME WARNER PUBLISHING
*1995 revenues: $325 million (est.)*

| | |
|---|---|
| **WARNER BOOKS** | **LITTLE, BROWN** |
| Warner Treasures | Bullfinch |
| Warner Vision | Back Bay |
| Aspect | |

**MAIL-ORDER BOOKS**

| | |
|---|---|
| Time-Life Books | Book-of-the-Month Club |
| Oxmoor House | Sunset Books |

◆ ◆ ◆

**MOTION PICTURES**
Warner Bros. (75%), Castle Rock Entertainment,
New Line Cinema, library of MGM, RKO and
pre-1950 Warner Bros. films

**CABLE & SATELLITE TV**
CNN, Headline News, CNNfn, CNN Airport Network,
CNN Interactive, CNN/SI, CNN Newsource, TBS
Superstation, Cinemax, Comedy Central (50%),
Court TV (33.3%), Sega Channel (33%), Turner Classic
Movies, TNT, Cartoon Network, HBO (75%);
Primestar (31% with others) satellite TV in U.S.

**CABLE FRANCHISES**
12.1 million subscribers
*(about 20% of U.S. TV homes)*

**TV PROGRAMMING**
Warner Bros. Television (Friends and ER);
WB Television Network with (Chicago) Tribune
Broadcasting (84% of U.S. TV homes); Warner Bros.
Television Animation (75%), Warner Bros. International
Television (75%), Telepictures Production,
Hanna-Barbera Cartoons (The Flintstones, The Jetsons),
World Championship Wrestling, Turner Original
Productions, Turner Sports, Turner Learning
(noncommercial daily newscasts for schools)

**MUSIC**
Atlantic, Elektra, Warner labels (22% of U.S. music sales)

**RADIO:** CNNRadio

**MAGAZINES**
Asiaweek, Baby Talk, Coastal Living, Cooking Light,
Dancyu, DC Comics, Entertainment Weekly,
Fortune, Health, Hippocrates, In Style, Life, Money,
Parenting, People, People en Español, President,
Progressive Farmer, Southern Living,
Southern Accents, Sports Illustrated,
Sports Illustrated for Kids, Sunset, This Old House,
Time, Time for Kids, Weight Watchers, Who

**THEME PARKS:** Six Flags (49%)

**SPORTS:** Atlanta Braves, Atlanta Hawks, Goodwill Games

**OTHER**
Home video and satellite, CD-ROM production,
some retail stores

**1995 revenues:**
# $8.1 billion

## EDUCATIONAL PUBLISHERS

*Privately held by Dieter von Holtzbrinck, president*

# HOLTZBRINCK

**FARRAR, STRAUS & GIROUX**
**Hill & Wang**
**Noonday Press**
**North Point Press**

**ST. MARTIN'S PRESS**
**Robert Wyatt Books**
**Thomas Dunne Books**

**HENRY HOLT & CO.**
**Metropolitan Books**

*1995 combined revenues:*
*$267 million (est.)*

Major trade publisher in
Germany and the U.K.

**NEWSPAPERS**
Dailies and weeklies
in Germany, including
Die Zeit and
Tagesspiegel

**MAGAZINES**
Scientific American

**MULTIMEDIA**
Part-owner of N.Y. firm
Voyager

**TELEVISION**
Part-owner of #2 rated
channel in Germany

*(Firms that no longer
concentrate on trade
publishing)*

**HARCOURT
GENERAL**
Publishes some
trade books
under both
Harcourt Brace
and the Harvest
imprint.
Publishes
extensively in
education
(8.6% of U.S.
market in 1995)
and professional
areas

**McGRAW-HILL**
Publishes some
trade, and
extensively in
education
(11% of U.S.
market in 1995)
and professional
areas

1995 (est.) revenues:
## $2 billion

# SOME INDEPENDENTS

### AN INCOMPLETE AND ARBITRARY LIST OF HOUSES THAT, EITHER BECAUSE OF SIZE OR CONTRIBUTION TO THE FIELD, WARRANT MENTION

*Franklin Mutual Advisers owns 5.3% of stock*
**HOUGHTON MIFFLIN**
*1995 revenues: $87.2 million*
**Clarion Books**
*Also publishes in education (5.2% of U.S. market)*

*Employee-owned*
**W.W. NORTON**
*1995 revenues: not disclosed*
**Norton Professional**
**COUNTRYMAN PRESS**
**LIVERIGHT PUBLISHING**

**GROVE/ATLANTIC INC.**
*1995 revenues: $13.5 million*
**Grove Press**
**Atlantic Monthly Press**

*Nonprofit; publishing arm of the Unitarian-Universalist Association*
**BEACON PRESS**
*1995 revenues: $4.5 million*

*Peter Workman, president & publisher*
**WORKMAN PUBLISHING**
*1995 revenues: not disclosed*
*Trade imprints:*
Algonquin of Chapel Hill
Artisan Publishing

*Privately held; largest shareholder is the nonprofit New Left Trust*
**NEW LEFT BOOKS**
*1995 revenues: $3.5 million*
**Verso**

*Nonprofit; associated with the Fund for Independent Publishing*
**THE NEW PRESS**
*1995 revenues: $3.5 million*

*Nonprofit*
**THE LIBRARY OF AMERICA**
*1995 revenues: $2 million (est.)*

# OTHER HOUSES OF NOTE

### A FEW HIGH-VOLUME NICHES

**UNIVERSAL PRESS SYNDICATE**
*Third-largest newspaper syndicate of columns (William F. Buckley, Mary McGrory) and comics (Doonesbury, Calvin and Hobbes)*

**ANDREWS AND McMEEL**
*1995 revenues: $92.4 million (est.)*
*10th-largest trade publisher*

**DISNEY**
*The second-largest media company (1995 revenues about $12 billion), the company's book division had estimated 1995 adult trade revenues of $75 million*
**HYPERION**
**Miramax Books**
As yet unnamed ESPN imprint

**THOMAS NELSON PUBLISHERS**
*1995 revenues: $145.7 million (est.)*
*9th-largest trade publisher, specializing in religious books*

**READER'S DIGEST**
*1995 revenues: $2.1 billion*
*Second-largest overall publisher in U.S. specializing in direct mail and condensed books*

*This chart does not include university presses or genre, large print or electronic imprints. Trade publishers' revenue figures come from the July 1996 "Book Publishing Report" or from the publishers themselves. They include adult and children's U.S. trade books only.*

# 5. Selling Vice

## HOLDING THE CEOS ACCOUNTABLE

### MAKANI THEMBA

Two seemingly unrelated events brought home, for me, the importance of media literacy: the 1996 passing of controversial rap artist Tupac Shakur and the Republican National Convention. The convention was full of talk about individual and family responsibility. Shakur's passing was a tragic example of how naive that talk is.

The truth is, young people grow up in a world today that is dramatically new and different—and dangerous. Much of what they learn is brought to them by corporate sponsors who care little for their interests beyond what they consume. They are constantly bombarded with exploitive and negative messages that undermine their self-image—messages designed using the brightest minds and the best technology money can buy.

Ellen Goodman once wrote that the call for parental responsibility seems to increase with corporate irresponsibility. Nowhere is corporate irresponsibility quite as blatant as in youth marketing. It is transforming the lives of our children—

and mostly for the worse. The death of Shakur is a poignant example.

The hip-hop culture that Shakur helped shape was once a relatively sober, drug-free culture. It was mainly marketing —not family disintegration—that made it synonymous with malt liquor and violence. And parents couldn't even monitor what was going on because the targeting was so narrow, so precise, that few adults were exposed to it.

It all started in the 1980s, when malt liquor companies aggressively pursued rap artists as spokespersons, sponsored concerts and events, and developed special products for this new market of young African-American and Latino males. Extra-large, 40-ounce, and even 72-ounce bottles of high potency brews exploded onto local inner-city neighborhoods. These products were pushed by an aggressive media strategy that sought to link them with high-profile, controversial rap artists. Key to its success was its piggybacking on the record industry's use of criminal stereotypes to sell hip-hop records.

No tragedy appeared too awful to exploit. One ad, featuring the rap group Get Boys, included a light-hearted reference to the shooting of group member Bushwick Bill. Bushwick, while under the influence of alcohol, held his thengirlfriend's infant out a window in order to force her to shoot him in an alleged suicide attempt. He lost an eye in the shooting. The group's promotion company took pictures right after the incident and published his injured face on the group's album cover. A malt liquor company followed with ads featuring Bushwick in an eye patch rapping references to the incident.

After decades of drinking and drugging less than their white cohorts, alcohol use among African-American youth rose dramatically in the 1990s. The sad results: while the Tupac Shakurs and the many not-so-famous young people who are influenced by these promotions suffer and die, a few continue to get rich.

So where do we lay most of the blame? OK, kids shouldn't drink. Yes, parents should watch them better. But yes, corporations know who listens to rap artists like Snoop Doggy Dog and

From 1988 to 1993, Halloween helped propel Stroh Brewery's October beer revenue from 6.5 to almost 8 percent of annual business. From 1992 to 1993, Pete's Brewing (which makes Wicked Ale) increased October sales by 125 percent.

they should not enlist them to market alcohol to kids. It just doesn't make sense to put all our efforts into restraining 15-year-olds from buying products that we give college-educated CEOs free reign to market. Call me crazy, but I expect a 40-something CEO to know better than a 15-year-old. I just do.

*continued on page 90*

## Scary but True...

Malt liquor companies have profited by targeting poor African-Americans and Latinos. One marketing executive of G. Heileman Brewing Company estimated that African-Americans consumed 75 percent of Heileman's leading malt liquor, Colt 45.

One 40-ounce bottle of St. Ides is equivalent to drinking a little more than five shots of whiskey.

A marketing brochure for Olde English 800 noted that the product is "brewed for relatively high alcohol content (important to the ethnic market!)."

The alcoholic beverage industry spends $1.3 billion a year on advertising.

Seagrams aired an ad for their whiskey in Texas in June 1996, breaking a voluntary television hard-liquor ban maintained since 1948. President Bill Clinton asked Seagrams to withdraw the ads "for the simple reason it was the right thing to do." Clinton's request was ignored. Arthur Shapiro, Seagrams vice-president of marketing, said that the company's decision, "in no way reflects any departure from our principles as a responsible marketer." (*Adbusters*)

Seagram's announced plans to air its liquor ads on TV after 9 pm, but at that hour in both New York and Los Angeles, the largest media markets in the country, 16 percent of the audience, or more than two million people, are under 17. (Center on Alcohol Advertising)

Alcohol abuse continues to be the No. 1 health problem in America, costing the nation more than $90 billion a year in expenses ranging from medical care to lost productivity, law enforcement, and premature death. (Alcohol Health and Research World)

*continued from page 89*

As teachers, parents, and practitioners who care, media literacy must be more than helping children and families take a discerning look at media. We need to work together to forge new partnerships—new covenants—that address corporate irresponsibility and government neglect.

We must not only talk with kids and admonish them to stay on track, we must also hold those businesses accountable who prey on our young people. I have seen mail-order ads for guns in magazines targeted to black teens. I have seen liquor store owners sell guns and malt liquor to youngsters, and when I ask them about it they tell me they are just trying to make a living. We cannot worship money so intensely that it doesn't matter who does what to our children in the name of making a living.

All over the country, people are refusing to accept the status quo. They write letters every time they see offensive ads. They talk to their neighbors, faith institutions, and coworkers to spread the word. And they even win. Ads have been removed and companies have been fined, all thanks to their efforts.

Together, we can move beyond education and let these companies know you cannot do that to my child, not to my brother's child, and to my community. We can draw the line.

*Makani Themba is codirector of the Praxis Project, a nonprofit organizaton dedicated to developing community-based approaches to policy development.*

### Scary but True...

A survey in a New Jersey Latino community found 145 billboards and store ads for liquor and beer, compared with seven in a nearby white neighborhood. (*EXTRA!*)

For the past several years, the alcohol industry has produced so-called Responsible Drinking ads. These star-studded commercials show race-car drivers who decide they know "when to say when" and athletes who drink until their speech is slurred. They never suggest abstinence as a socially acceptable choice, never encourage limited consumption, never mention separating drinking from driving altogether, and never draw a correlation between the hazards of mixing alcohol with drugs. According to researchers from Harvard, Michigan State, and University of California at Berkeley, "In the main, these 'moderation' ads reinforce the idea that beer consumption is a reward for hard work, an escape, a social lubricant, a device for furthering romance or sexual conquest, a facilitator of male comradeship, an emblem of group membership and acceptance, and a means of gaining social identity." (*Milbank Quarterly*)

In 1990, more than 400,000 deaths were attributable to tobacco and more than 100,000 to alcohol, while 20,000 were attributable to illicit drug use. But in a random sample of network news time devoted to coverage on alcohol, tobacco, or other drugs from that year, 77 percent of the time was spent on illicit drugs, 14 percent on alcohol, and 10 percent on tobacco. (Berkeley Media Studies Group)

Alcohol is seldom included in local TV news stories, even though it is associated with one half to two thirds of all homicides, 20 to 30 percent of all suicides, and more than half of all incidents of domestic violence. (Berkeley Media Studies Group)

Beer manufacturers spend up to $50 million a year on motor sports sponsorships that target the very population at greatest risk of drinking and driving—young, working-class men. (The Marin Institute)

In posters and ads, beer company logos share the billing with the Thurgood Marshall Scholarship Fund, the National Hispanic Scholarship Fund, and the Denver Indian Center's literacy project. Liquor company insignias are stamped on New York's Harlem Week promotions.

At the same time, government and private research reports that the cirrhosis mortality rate for African-Americans is nearly twice that of whites, Mexican-American men have a 40 percent higher risk of death due to cirrhosis than do white males, and adult Native Americans die from alcohol at four times the rate as Americans as a whole.

"The bottom line is that they steal our heroes, holidays and values in order to sell booze.

"Alcohol companies say that supporting us shows they're socially responsible. But they're pursuing minorities at a time when consumption is dropping in general. They will use any tactic they can to access these growing communities. Sponsorship and philanthropy are another way besides targeting in advertising to achieve this. It buys good will…If we're really talking corporate responsibility, we should have a pot of money, a consortium with a social justice agenda for African-Americans, Latinos and Native Americans, and companies making money off these people should give anonymously."

—Marilyn Aguirre-Molina, assistant professor of consumer health education at the Robert Wood Johnson Medical School and chair of the Latino Council on Alcohol and Tobacco

## CHRISTIAN ANGST

© 1994 Terry Everton

## Hands Off Halloween

The exploitation of Halloween by the beer industry has angered public-health advocates since it began in the early 1980s. By 1990, after years of beer promotions using jack-o-lanterns, paper masks, glow-in-the-dark bottles, trick-or-treat bags, and Halloween characters, children's health advocates began making their concerns public.

To bolster the claim that beer advertising targets only adults, brewers added the phrase "adult parties" to their promotions. Meanwhile, increasing numbers of brewers have adopted Halloween images in their advertising. "Monster profits" is the term the industry uses to describe the results of point-of-sale displays, promotional tie-ins, and broadcast advertising that link Halloween to beer drinking.

Prior to Halloween 1994, the Center on Alcohol Advertising urged the Beer Institute to amend its Advertising and Marketing Code to discourage the use of any Halloween icons or symbols in ads and promotions for beer, emphasizing that

*continued on page 92*

*continued from page 91*

Halloween belongs primarily to children. the Beer Institute president Raymond McGrath rejected the appeal.

As a result, the Hands Off Halloween campaign was launched. Starting in 1994, the Center on Alcohol Advertising helped groups across the country organize locally to pressure the beer industry into adopting more responsible advertising. Hands Off Halloween coalitions in 100 different communities participated. Many of these community groups established successful Responsible Merchants Cam-

paigns. Coalition members wrote letters to the editor, spoke on radio and TV talk shows, and took out newspaper ads to highlight their opposition to Halloween-theme beer ads. In 1995, thirty-seven Hands Off Halloween coalitions held media events in 19 different states, all orchestrated to coincide with a national press conference in Washington, DC.

Although media coverage of Hands Off Halloween was strong at both the national and local level, the beer industry still refused to give up Halloween promotions. The Center on Alcohol Advertising declared a partial victory in 1996 when

Anheuser-Busch dropped the *Cryptkeeper* theme in favor of a tie-in with the *Rocky Horror Picture Show* (arguably less appealing to children). Southland Corporation also agreed not to display Halloween beer ads in their corporate-owned stores.

—Laurie Leiber, Director, Center on Alcohol Advertising

For more information contact the Center on Alcohol Advertising, 2140 Shattuck Ave., Ste 1206, Berkeley, CA 94704; Tel: (510) 649-8942; Fax: (510) 649-8970

# WE'VE COME A LONG WAY, BABY?

**STACEY EIDSON**

Once upon a time, the cigarette was simply a symbol of women's growing power in a male-dominated society. That was before the United States Surgeon General estimated that among women under the age of 65, smoking is responsible for 40 percent of all heart disease deaths, 55 percent of lethal strokes, and 80 percent of lung cancer deaths in the United States.

If you think photos of the Marlboro Man riding out on the prairie or a loving couple scaling the Rockies while they enjoy a good smoke seem an improbable tactic for attracting teenage girls to the joys of smoking, you're probably right.

Tobacco companies have learned that those images are not the ones that grab young girls' attention. Consequently, cigarette advertisers have targeted the number-one issue guaranteed to impact sensitive young girls—weight gain.

The American Medical Association found that even in 1928, cigarette companies were using slogans such as "Reach for a Lucky Instead of a Sweet" to attract the women's market. They hired models to carry around Lucky Strikes and wear the package's signature color. This may seem like ancient history, but such tactics are still in evidence. The tobacco industry to this day tries to link smoking with the fashion world. *The Journal of the American Medical Association* noted that Kate

Moss, formerly queen of the waif world, was featured in *Esquire* magazine with a packet of Marlboro Lights.

Obvious examples of attempts to connect the fashion world and tobacco sales can be found inside any issue of young women's magazines such as *Glamour, Cosmopolitan*, or *Mademoiselle*. There will be an ad for cigarettes right next to an article on how to trim your waist to reach your ideal weight.

Such campaigns also reinforce in men the tendency to see women who smoke as sexy and sensual. *Maclean's* did a report in March 1996 on a video agency called Premier Productions. This company (which is in the business of catering to people's fetishes) began producing videos of women smoking after the agency's owner discovered such a huge male interest on the Internet. Premier Productions, which usually markets videos filled with half-dressed women, found its biggest seller of the year was a fully clothed woman wearing bright red lipstick, taking deep drags of a cigarette as she read a book.

Have you ever wondered why cigarettes were named Virginia Slims or Capri Superslims? It's not just a catchy name that refers to the size of the cigarette itself. Cigarette companies know that women are aware of the fact that nicotine is an appetite suppressant. What tobacco companies do not tell their customers is that once someone is addicted to nicotine, that person's metabolism will be altered. So, when someone quits smoking there's a good possibility of weight gain while the body tries to readjust to life off the drug.

One thing women of today must learn from the independent women of our past is not to play victim to anyone. Not to the tobacco companies, advertising agencies, the entertainment media, or even their own addictions. Because one thing's certain: If women continue to smoke at the same increasing rates as they are today, they will continue to die at increasing rates as well.

*Stacey Eidson is a writer for* Ace *magazine.*

---

### Scary but True...

Cigarette companies spend $6 billion annually on advertising and marketing campaigns to addict a new generation of customers. That's $16 million every day, according to the Federal Trade Commission. Meanwhile, cigarettes kill more than 400,000 Americans every year. That's more deaths than from AIDS, alcohol, car accidents, murders, suicides, drugs and fires —*combined*.

Hill & Knowlton helped set up a PR and lobbying organization, the Tobacco Institute, which grew by 1990 into what the *Public Relations Journal* described as one of the "most formidable public-relations/lobbying machines in history," spending an estimated $20 million a year and employing 120 PR professionals to fight the combined forces of the Surgeon General of the United States, the National Cancer Institute, the American Cancer Society, the American Heart Association, and the American Lung Association.

A study of adolescent smokers in the United States demonstrates that young people may be more influenced by advertising than older consumers. A 1993 survey revealed that Marlboro, still the leading cigarette among adolescents, had decreased in popularity by almost 9 percent, while Camel gained more than 5 percent. The change in adolescent brand preference could not be explained by changes in the overall market shares for Marlboro and Camel, but did reflect a significant variation in brand-specific advertising expenditures. (Center on Alcohol Advertising, citing a study published in *Morbidity and Mortality Weekly Report*, August 1994)

"We thought that Marlboro should be on the Internet. Most of the Internet audience is young and young people smoke these days, especially the 21-plus crowd they want to go after, because once they get somebody —you should pardon the pun—hooked on a brand, they probably stay with it the rest of their lives…. We told them, 'Get out there! Since there are no rules, no controls, since it's international and probably no one can regulate it, what can they do to you? Tell you to get off? Why not go for it, guys?'" (Joel Cohen, executive vice president of the New York promotion/marketing firm of Heller & Cohen)

An exhaustive study published in the January 30, 1992, issue of the *New England Journal of Medicine* found "strong statistical evidence that cigarette advertising in magazines is associated with diminished coverage of the hazards of smoking. This is particularly true for magazines directed to women." As a result of the scarcity of independent journalism, "Americans substantially underestimate the dangers of smoking as compared with other risks to health."

The cigarette industry spent $4.83 billion on advertising and promotional expenditures in 1994. That number was down nearly 20 percent from

*continued on page 94*

### Campaign for Tobacco-Free Kids

 William Novelli's name should be well known to those in the PR business: He cofounded and was president of Porter/Novelli, one of the country's 10 largest PR agencies. He retired in 1990, though it was short-lived. He was executive vice president of CARE, the world's largest private relief and development organization, before becoming director the Campaign for Tobacco-Free Kids, a national initiative to stop the sale and marketing of tobacco to children. The center acts as an umbrella organization for dozens of national health, medical, civic, and religious organizations (many of which contributed to the center's $30 million start-up).

*What are the center's goals?*

Our interest is changing the policy environment so that we can restrict the marketing of tobacco to kids and the access of tobacco to kids. If we can do those things, then those grass-roots programs, those parents, teachers, and scout leaders who are working with their children will have a much greater chance for success.

We are going to serve as a counterforce to the tobacco industry and its allies in terms of speaking out, in terms of being heard, in terms of setting the record straight, so they really don't have a monopoly on the media and the airwaves.

*continued from page 93*

the previous year even though spending on magazine advertising, outdoor advertising, and point-of-sale expenditures all rose. So where's the discrepancy? A drastic cut in discount coupons, "buy one, get one free" promotions, and giveaways such as key chains and lighters at point of sale. (Federal Trade Commission)

Smoking rates for students in grades 9–12 increased from 27.5 percent in 1991 to 34.8 percent in 1995. Rates for African-American male students almost doubled during that time, going from 14.1 percent to 27.8 percent. (Centers for Disease Control)

Adolescents are more than twice as likely as adults to smoke the most-advertised brands of cigarettes—Marlboro, Camel, and Newport.

Between 1991 an 1994, the prevalence of smoking among eighth graders rose 30 percent—a time that coincides with the controversial "Joe Camel" advertising campaign.

Of the 3,000 children who begin smoking each day, 1,000 will eventually die of a tobacco-related death. (American Lung Association)

One study showed that nearly one third of three-year-olds matched Joe Camel with cigarettes and that by age six, children were as familiar with him as with the Mickey Mouse logo on the Disney Channel! The cartoon Camel catapulted Camel cigarettes from a brand smoked by less than 1 percent of U.S. smokers under age 18 to a one-third share of the youth market—and nearly one-half billion dollars in annual sales—within three years. *(INFACT)*

Tired of negative advertising? So is Ackerly Outdoor Advertising, your friendly billboard people. Their sudden conversion occurred when Ackerly was confronted with the prospect of putting up antismoking billboards featuring a retired lawyer and ex-smoker named R.J. Reynolds proclaiming, "Smoking kills. Don't buy cigarettes." Said Ackerly President Randy Swain as they refused the ad, "The negativity was what we didn't like about it." Then he laid out his company's positive philosophy: "We support ads promoting a healthy lifestyle, but we won't allow ads that attack companies that are selling lawful products" (and providing 17 percent of Ackerly's earnings). Marlboro should be overjoyed to hear it is "promoting a healthy lifestyle." And one hopes the antismoking groups can find more "positive" ways to describe a drug that kills 300,000 people annually in this country. *(American Newspeak)*

*How do you expect to compete against the tobacco companies, who have much larger marketing budgets?*

Ah. that's where the great invention of PR comes in.

*How about an example?*

On January 2, the last day of the FDA comment period, the tobacco industry had a big press conference. So we set up our pop stand about 15 feet down the hall from them at the Marriott here in DC, and we had our own press conference. We had dueling press conferences. We refuted everything they had to say. That's an example of how we intend to take our seat on center stage with them. We have very strong media interests in the issue. The media are always, as we know in this country, interested in both sides of an issue. We intend to take advantage of that. Too many times, what happens is that tobacco companies will refute some scientific thing. You'll have 99.9 percent of all scientists saying "X," and some scientist employed by the tobacco industry is saying "Y," and he gets equal billing in the press. We're going to do something about that.

*What might some of those tactics be?*

Well, I'm talking about good, old-fashioned media relations work—providing really good background material to the media and good sources and resources to the media to make their work as balanced as it can be. If the media do objective and balanced reporting, we win.

*Are you using kids as spokespeople?*

They could be kids who are popular in today's entertainment world. There are many different role models kids can relate to. There's something really terrific called the Smoke Free Class of 2000, a group of more than 2 million eighth-graders nationwide who are committed to graduating high school tobacco free

*continued on page 96*

 Before the tobacco giant RJR Nabisco purchased the Weekly Reader, which reaches 8 million schoolchildren, 62 percent of their tobacco articles had an antismoking slant. After the purchase this dropped to 24 percent. Stanton Glantz, professor of medicine at the University of California, compared Weekly Reader articles to those in Scholastic News, a similar publication with no tobacco ownership. Glantz found that nine Weekly Reader articles gave the tobacco industry the last word while none of Scholastic News articles did. And the Weekly Reader was less likely to mention the effects of smoking that would turn off kids, such as yellow teeth, bad breath, and smelly clothes. (David Morris, AlterNet)

*continued from page 95*

in the year 2000. Some of them are media trained. They're very savvy kids. They've got home pages. Those kids are their own role models.

*How do you expect the tobacco companies will react to your campaign?*

They're already at work trying to impugn our veracity. One tobacco-state congressman has written to the Secretary of the Treasury asking for an IRS investigation into our tax status. Another congressman's staff is also snooping around. The tobacco industry has also taken this to the media. I got a call today from a broadcast reporter wanting to know where we get our money, and so on. It was clear where the source of this questioning came from. And this is all part of the game. The tobacco industry plays hardball. If we're going to be a counterforce, we have to be able to stand the heat. At the same time, we're going to be attacking them.

*How do you view Philip Morris' recent disclosure that it is preparing a $10–$20 million magazine ad campaign to discourage youths from smoking?*

As I understand it, they're directing that magazine campaign toward adults, to tell adults that they don't want kids to smoke. It's really an attempt to refurbish their public-relations image, which, of course, is almost laughable. They have a very substantial problem—the hypocrisy of their position is very obvious. On the one hand, they say they don't want kids to smoke. On the other hand, if kids don't smoke, they won't have any business because 90 percent of their replacement smokers—to replace the people who died or quit—come from kids.

*Why would anyone want to take on the tobacco industry?*

[Laughs] I guess Don Quixote lives.

Contact: National Center for Tobacco-Free Kids at (800)284-KIDS or (202)296-5469; 1707 L Street, NW, Suite 800, Washington, DC 20036; Fax: (202)296-5427.

## The FDA Rules at a Glance

On August 23, 1996 President Clinton approved a comprehensive initiative to reduce teenage tobacco consumption by 50 percent. Here's a summary of the major provisions:

Requires age verification for all over-the-counter sales

Limits vending-machine sales and self-service displays only to places where minors are not allowed

Prohibits the sale of single cigarettes and packages of fewer than 20

Prohibits free sampling of cigarettes

Bans outdoor advertising within 1,000 feet of schools and playgrounds

Permits black-and-white text-only advertising in publications with significant youth readership

Prohibits the sale or giveaway of tobacco products like caps, jackets, or gym bags that carry brand names or logos

Prohibits the brand-name sponsorship of sporting or entertainment events

A separate rule requires the six tobacco companies with significant sales to children to educate young people about the real health dangers associated with the use of tobacco products. This national multimedia campaign will be monitored by the FDA.

# Content                    Part III

The trend in local TV news over the last *10* years has been more and more emphasis on violence — rape, murder, mayhem. The trend of actual life has, by most social science reports, been less of those things. I would argue that the trend in local news has still exaggerated the degree to which most people feel hostage to crime every day. And there's not any kind of coherence, context, explanation, etc., that would at least make people feel they had some control over their destinies, some way to improve the things that are troubling to them.

*— James Fallows, author of* Breaking the News: How the Media Undermine American Democracy

Only 5 percent of reporters in the United States are black, making journalism one of this country's most segregated professions. That's a shameful statistic in and of itself — but just as important is how it affects the news. The dearth of black journalists is one of the key reasons why the media consistently overreports the violence and weaknesses of the black community and underreports black everyday life and its strengths. The body of overwhelmingly white reporters don't seem willing or able to locate hardworking African-Americans, but are able to home in on urban deprivation, which they at least know where to go to find. The media's constant attention to certain stories — like crime — in the black community borders on obsession; the trend of ignoring others — like black community watch and self-help groups — borders on true pathology. And too often, news organizations are smug about their strengths, blind to their weaknesses and surly when these weaknesses are pointed out.

*— Farai Chideya, author of* Don't Believe the Hype: Fighting Cultural Misinformation about African-Americans

# INTRODUCTION

### JULIE WINOKUR

At the offices of the Institute for Alternative Journalism, a humorous sign for the San Francisco Examiner declares: For a mere 25 cents you too can blame the media for everything. If you look at the results from various polls, these words seem to reflect the genuine sentiment of many Americans.

According to the Times Mirror Center for People and the Press, the general public strongly faults the news media for its negativism and goes so far as to say the press gets in the way of society solving its problems.

Despite the fact that members of the press perceive themselves as watchdogs, the facts tell a different story. Biased reporting is the rule rather than the exception. In the news, African-Americans are portrayed most often as perpetrators of crime while whites appear more frequently as victims. This doesn't "watchdog" anything, let alone accurately portray reality. And when more than half of the stories that top local news involve violent crime, despite that fact that such crime has fallen in many cities, the press has not only skewed our picture of the world, it has contributed to the fear and anxiety of the citizenry. Don't even mention coverage of women! Although women constitute more than half the population, we only appear in 15 percent of front-page newspaper stories, the affect of which is to virtually silence a major voice from the national agenda.

Typically scapegoated by the press are youth (who have become synonymous with drugs, promiscuity, and violence), single mothers (the scourge of our welfare state), the elderly (who rank second to single mothers on the welfare black list), and minorities (who are lucky if they appear in media in any capacity other than negative stereotypes).

The bias of the press plays out in insidious ways. Whether it's merely a matter of overlooking entire segments of the population or literally misrepresenting the facts, the press impacts public perception and thereby prejudices important policy debates. When the press gets lazy and falls back on violence or "fluff," the chatty filler that turns newscasters into wannabe stand-up comics, it's a sorry substitute for diversified news. The absence of coverage on vital issues has resulted in a distorted view of the world.

At its best, the independent press is aware of the bias and distortion in mainstream media and tries to give voice to the very people who are usually voiceless. Several organizations have taken a targeted approach, such as the American News Service, a wire service that only features solution-oriented stories, *Hip Mama*, a zine launched by a former welfare mother with stories by and for single moms, and *National Native News*, an internationally broadcast radio show about Native Americans.

*Julie Winokur is a freelance writer and editor.*

# 1. Glorification of Violence

COMMENT

*We are assaulted on every front today by what the scholar Cleanth Brooks of Yale University called "the bastard muses."*

*The "bastard muses" are propaganda, which pleads, sometimes unscrupulously, for a special cause at the expense of the total truth; sentimentality, which works up emotional responses unwarranted by and in excess of the occasion;* *and pornography, which focuses on one powerful drive at the expense of the total human personality.*

*The mass media pipe these forces directly into our hearts and minds, through images that shape our collective imagination. We are everywhere bombarded by the pernicious and debilitating effects of nonsense, trivia and violence,* *by what* Newsweek *calls "a stream of mass-produced and mass-consumed carnage masquerading as amusement and threatening to erode the psychological and moral boundary between real life and make-believe."*

*I am a journalist, not a social scientist, and I have to leave it to the researchers to study what this phenomenon does to a* person's sensibility. What does it mean to see 81 corpses in a single movie? Or to laugh while watching Arnold Schwartzenegger blow his wife away after telling her, "Consider this a divorce?" Or what it means that by the age of 18, the average American reportedly will have seen 200,000 acts of violence on the television screen, including 40,000 murders? Psychologists at the University of Illinois who studied a set of children for 20 years found that kids who watch significant amounts of television violence at the age of eight were consistently more likely to commit violent crimes or engage in child or spouse abuse at 30. No wonder half a million people are ready to buy a record with the lyrics: "She begged me not to kill her. I gave her a rose, then slit her throat, watched her shake until her eyes closed, had sex with the corpse before I left her, and drew my name on the wall like Helter Skelter" (The Geto Boys).

I don't know what to make of all this. But I know it doesn't make the future a friendlier place for my small grandsons, Henry and Thomas. And I know it must be countered. That's why you and I have the best jobs in broadcasting. For all our frailties, despite the strange ways we make decisions and the bizarre means by which we have to raise money, despite our Byzantine paths to creativity, we are free — you and I — to regard human beings as more than mere appetites and America as more than an economic machine.

Leo Strauss once wrote that "liberal education is liberation from vulgarity." He reminded us that the Greek word for vulgarity is apeirokalia, the lack of experience in things beautiful. In contrast, a liberal education supplies us with that experience and nurtures the moral imagination. A liberal education is what we're about; in our best moments public television is a strategy of affirmation. Performing arts, good conversation, history, travel, nature, critical documentaries, public affairs, children's programs — at their best they open us to other lives and other realms of knowing.

You know what we're about? The ancient Israelites had a word for it. They called it hochma, the science of the heart. Intelligence, feeling and perception combine to inform your own story, to draw others into a shared narrative, and to make of our experience here together a victory of the deepest moral feeling of sympathy, understanding and affection.

When you and I succeed at this kind of programming, the public square is a little less polluted, a little less vulgar, and our common habitat a little more hospitable. When we fail, well, we get up and try again. Out there, the public waits — for something real. They will give you an hour of their life — they never get it back — and you give them something of value in return. A moral transaction. That expectation, that hope; the unarticulated but patient trust that as producers and programmers we will try our best — that is what's at stake. Henry Thoreau got it right: "To affect the quality of the day, is the highest of the arts." That is our mission.

— Bill Moyers. Excerpted from a keynote speech to the PBS annual meeting (San Francisco, 1996).

# THE FEAR YEARS

## JON CARROLL

You've heard it: "Three people are dead in one Bay Area community, and police fear the killing is not over."

"Is there a convicted sex criminal in your neighborhood? We'll have an exclusive report at 11."

"How safe are you really? Tonight, we'll have the facts that will allow you to rescue at least some of your internal organs."

And so on. The marketing of fear is relentless. We are told every day from every talking box that there are predators on every street corner; poisons in every box; danger in the inner city, on the highways, in our bedrooms, in our very chemistry.

Most people get their news from television, and it is television where the fear is most palpable. The teasers are the worst, because they are purposely vague —"one Bay Area community"—and

continued on page 100

*continued from page 99*

thus they generalize the fear. Someone dies in San Jose and people in Sonoma lock their doors.

And the news teasers are mixed with other teasers for "entertainment" shows about malign aliens, serial killers, women with psychotic husbands, airplane crashes, plagues, explosions, fires. Your entire future is encapsulated in 60 seconds, and there is no good news.

You are surrounded; throw down your arms; ha ha blam blam. Over to you, Pete.

This is not actually your reality. In your reality, people are nice, days go by with some order and cheerfulness, children smile and dogs run and flawed people make sincere efforts to overcome obstacles. That's the world you experience.

But our environment is saturated with media. It is hard to perceive the knock-on-wood world because we are lost in the fog of powerful, impressionistic electronic sensation. It is hard to perceive the knock-on-wood world because we are scared all the time. When we are scared, we do not seek information; we seek solace.

Solace is in advertising. In the electronic world, children smile only when they are using products.

It is not necessarily the fault of TV news people. They are working in a long tradition. The media have always lived on sensational news stories, scandal, double homicides, killer chemicals, police standing by helplessly as terror stalks the city.

But in previous eras, the media was understood as a sideshow. It was just a roller coaster; no one confuses a roller coaster with real life. No one is afraid that a roller coaster is stalking their neighborhood.

But times changed; the power of the information agencies grew; the people in the media did not. They are still using rationales invented in the 19th century.

"We're just giving the people what they want," says the news director. "The ratings prove it. Give'em blood and

terror; see the viewers flock."

Question: If a man were standing on your street with a bullhorn yelling, "Maniac loose in streets. I'll tell you more if you keep listening," would you keep listening? Yes. Would you say the man with the bullhorn is giving you what you want? Not exactly.

If the First Amendment were put to a vote today, it would not pass. It's like: We gave it a chance, but it did not work out. The deal was, the media would understand that with constitutional protection came a kind of citizenship, a kind of mandate.

That mandate has been forgotten. The media are now the tool of tyrants and despots. Tyrants and despots encourage fear, because fearful people will accept extreme political solutions, will demand extreme political solutions.

But our mandate has changed too. We have to stop being credulous. We have to stop believing the scare stories. We have to trust the evidence of our senses. Bad things happen, but mostly bad things do not happen.

Today you will not be killed by a maniac. Today your biggest challenge will be to understand that you are capable of love. Your biggest challenge will be to ignore the bogus fear. More tomorrow. (*San Francisco Chronicle*)

*Jon Carroll is a columnist for the* San Francisco Chronicle.

## Berkeley Media Studies Group

 By current standards, the media's coverage of violence looks more like drive-by journalism than responsible reporting. When a news crew goes out to cover a violent crime, a.k.a. a "hot story" they usually miss the real story: the cause of the crime. Violent crime is rarely depicted in context, with in-depth reporting on the social factors that might have led to bloodshed. Poverty, environment, family conflict, and lack of education are rarely discussed in the same breath as murder, assault, gunshot wound, or abuse.

For years, the Berkeley Media Studies Group (BMSG) has been working with other advocates to reframe violence as a public-health issue. By treating crime as a health issue rather than a criminal-justice problem, there's a greater chance of rectifying the source of the trouble and instituting preventive measures. A focus on public health rather than criminal justice could help reroute funds away from prisons and toward social services.

Berkeley Media Studies Group monitors and analyzes the media with the objective of supporting media advocacy training, professional education, and strategic consultation. The group recognizes the significant influence of mass media on people's beliefs and actions regarding public health and social issues. It aims to have news stories told from a public-health perspective emphasizing prevention and policy development.

Given that in the state of California, for example, more than half of all violent offenders are under the influence of alcohol or other drugs when they commit crimes and most homicides happen between people who know each other, BMSG argues that reporters have to probe beneath the superficial details of an assault. Did the people know each other? Was alcohol involved? Were victims and perpetrators employed? Did they have histories of child abuse or battering? What preventive action is being taken by law enforcement, public-health agencies, and community organizations? These are the types of questions that could shed some light on violent crime, say the members of BMSG. This is the type of reporting that could make the media part of the solution rather than adding to the problem.—Julie Winokur

*Contact: BMSG at 2140 Shattuck Ave., Suite 804, Berkeley, CA 94704; Tel: (510) 204-9700; Fax: (510) 204-9710.*

A survey by Berkeley Media Studies Group of more than 22 hours of local television news revealed that violence dominates coverage but only one story out of more than 8,000 had an explicit public-health frame. "If our nation's most popular source of news continues to report on violence primarily through crime stories isolated from their social context, the chance for widespread support for public health solutions to violence will be diminished," the study concluded.

## Scary but True...

Children's TV shows contain about 26 violent acts each hour. During an average prime-time hour there are five violent acts. MTV has at least one occurrence of violence in more than 50 percent of its videos. (American Medical Association)

In 1974, 58 percent of prime-time television dramatic programs had overt physical violence. By 1994 that number had risen to 75 percent. (Cultural Indicators)

A 1994 study of local news by the University of Miami found that time devoted to crime averaged 32 percent while violent crime in the city remained constant, involving less than one tenth of 1 percent of the population.

According to the National Television Violence Study, the context in which violence is portrayed is as important to its impact as the amount of violence. Of the shows with violent content three quarters demonstrated unpunished violence; when violence occurred, victims were not shown experiencing pain 58 percent of the time. (Mediascope)

According to a *U.S. News and World* report, 92 percent of Americans believe television contributes to violence.

The typical viewer of prime-time television drama sees, every week, an average of 21 criminals arrayed against an army of 41 public and private law enforcers. Crime and violence engage more characters than all other occupations combined. About one out of three speaking parts, and more than half of all major characters, are involved in violence either as victims, victimizers, or both. (Cultural Indicators)

The United States exports 30 percent more violent actions series than are aired at home. (Cultural Indicators)

On local Los Angeles TV news, crime was the focus of the lead story 51 percent of the time, and 27 percent of the violent crime coverage concerned murders. But during the period, murder accounted for only 2 percent of felonies in Los Angeles, so the frequency of murder was exaggerated by a ratio of 14 to 1. In fact, reported crime fell 9.3 percent overall in the first six months of 1995, although you never would have known it by watching television. (UCLA)

# FOR "ACTION" MOVIES, IT SEEMS THE BODY COUNT RISES WITH EACH SEQUEL

| MOVIE | Original Body Count | Sequel Body Count | Second Sequel Body Count |
|---|---|---|---|
| Robocop | 32 | 81 | |
| Death Wish | 9 | 52 | |
| Rambo | NA | 62 | 106 |
| Die Hard | 18 | 264 | |
| Godfather | 12 | 18 | 53 |

Source: *New York Times* and Cultural Indicators, a television monitoring project.

# PAVLOV'S TV DOGS: A SNAPSHOT OF LOCAL TV NEWS IN AMERICA

### PAUL KLITE

The Pavlov Index is a measure of audience manipulation and conditioning in local television newscasts in the United States.

Ivan Pavlov, the astute observer of animal behavior, demonstrated the necessity for repetition (reinforcement) in the conditioning process. Just as rats in a cage become tolerant to the effects of repetitive painful stimuli (such as electric shocks), Americans have become numb to the unbalanced and unhealthy diet of TV news. This conditioning required increasing doses of mayhem and fluff over time to hold audience attention.

You will recall that Pavlov was able to associate a variety of stimuli to elicit reactions in dogs:

Present a dog with food.
*He salivates.*

Ring a bell with the food.
*He salivates.*

Eventually, just ring the bell.
*He salivates.*

For our analogy with local newscasts, substitute news for food, emotion for salivation, and dramatic video for the bell.

The viewing public, of course, is the dog.

The Pavlov Index of TV news combines the mayhem, fluff, and sports content in programs, adjusted for solution-oriented stories, to generate a single measure of emotion-laden conditioning for advertising.

Ninety-two stations scored over 50 percent on the Pavlov Index. That indicates that over half the newscast, excluding ads and weather, is based on high emotional arousal.

We propose that TV newscasts are masquerading as "news." Their function is not an informed public but an emotionally aroused audience that is susceptible to advertising. Emotion is honey for the advertising bee. If an audience is well primed and conditioned, advertising propaganda will go down like a sugar-coated pill. The public doesn't even taste it.

Most television stations are literally getting away with murder. One hundred news departments play variations on the theme, but it is mostly the same old song, the same old dog, the same old tricks. In mesmerized obedience, millions of Americans swallow without chewing.

Local news is the most profitable programming for television stations. News is cheaper to produce than drama or entertainment shows, and stations do not share advertising revenues from local news with the networks. It's a multibillion dollar industry.

Neil Postman has pointed out that the public ends up with emotions about current events, not opinions. Thirty-second clips about Bosnia or an earthquake in California can do little but give us a "feeling" about issues. Marketing experts call it "arousal," an absolutely vital ingredient to successful advertising. But just as sexual arousal is not love, mayhem, fluff, or sports arousal is not wisdom.

*Paul Klite is director of Rocky Mountain Media Watch.*

# TV VIOLENCE

**GEORGE GERBNER**

Humankind may have had more blood-thirsty eras, but none as filled with images of violence as the present, primarily because of television's obsession with crime. Yet, while violent crime rates remained essentially flat or declined in the last few years, television networks doubled the time given to crime news coverage between 1992 and 1993. TV Guide's 1994 survey showed a steep increase in stories of violence, especially in local television news.

TV's stress on crime and violence skews news priorities. As part of the Cultural Indicators television-monitoring project, we studied local news on Philadelphia television stations in the summer of 1995 and found that crime and/or violence items usually led news-casts and preempted balanced coverage of the city. Furthermore, only 20 percent of crime and violence on local news was local to the city and 40 percent was local to the area. As other studies have found, whites were more likely to be reported on when they were the victims and African-Americans when they were the perpetrators.

Violence is, of course, dramatic. However, a tragic sense of violence has been subsumed by "happy violence" produced on the dramatic assembly line. "Happy violence" is cool, swift, painless, and always leads to a happy ending, so as

to deliver the audience to the next commercial in a receptive mood.

*What Does It Mean?*
Violence is a demonstration of power. It shows who can get away with what against whom. It defines majority might and minority risk, one's place in the societal pecking order. Its principle consequence is the cultivation of the image of a mean world in which violence works, fear is rampant, and women and minorities are made to feel most vulnerable and dependent.

*Mean-World Syndrome*
The mean-world syndrome occurs when

television violence heightens a society's sense of danger and apprehension. Our surveys show that heavy viewers are more likely than

## Not In Our Town

Scandal. Murder. Conflict. Crisis. Day after day, the world beamed in through our TVs portrays the myriad problems of our society and our world at large. Imagine, instead, if the power of television was turned toward broadcasting stories about solutions, about how ordinary people address, and overcome, the issues affecting their lives and their communities?

*Not In Our Town* offers such a simple and inspiring story. Produced by the Oakland, California-based Working Group, the documentary tells the story of how the people of Billings, Montana, fought back when racist hate groups came to town. Fed up with the resulting rise in hate crime, the community took a

stand. The Painters Union formed a volunteer workforce to paint over racist graffiti; religious and civic leaders sponsored community watches, marches, and ecumenical services; and the local newspaper printed full-page menorahs that were displayed in the windows of nearly 10,000 homes and businesses.

Eager to test out the potential of collaboration, the Working Group (TWG) and the San Francisco–based Institute for Alternative Journalism (IAJ) launched the "Not In Our Town" (NIOT) campaign to amplify the impact of the video. Working to match the timing of the December 1995 PBS broadcast of the documentary, IAJ and CWG joined forces to create an innovative collaboration among media outlets, community organizations, organized labor, and public-television stations. This campaign was based on a

com-parable groups of light viewers to overestimate their chances of involvement in violence, to believe that their neighborhoods are unsafe, to state that fear of crime is a very serious personal problem, and to assume that crime is rising, regardless of the facts. Heavy viewers are also more likely to have bought new locks, watchdogs, and guns "for protection" (thus becoming a major source of handgun violence).

Viewers who see members of their own group underrepresented but over-victimized develop an even greater sense of apprehension and mistrust. Insecure, angry, mistrustful people may be prone to violence but are even more likely to be dependent on authority and suscepti-ble to deceptively simple, strong, hard-line postures and appeals.

*What Drives Media Violence?*
Despite the claims by television broadcasters that they "give the public what it wants," Nielson ratings for violent programs are consistently lower than for comparable nonviolent programs. So why is violence commercially successful, despite its lack of general popularity? The reason is that it "travels well" on the world market. What violent programs lose on ratings, they more than make up by grabbing the attention of younger viewers whom advertisers want to reach, and by extending their reach to the global market of private and government broadcasting systems hungry for cheap product.

Most program producers barely break even on the domestic market. They are forced onto the world market and into all forms of syndication, including cable and video sales, to make a profit. As the media companies merge, production and distribution are handled by one entity, and global marketing becomes the driving force behind TV and film production. Syndicators demand "action" (the code word for violence), because it "travels well." As the producer of *Die Hard 2* explained, "Everyone understands an action movie. If I tell a joke, you may not get it but if a bullet goes through the window, we all know how to hit the floor, no matter the language." (*Nieman Reports*)

*George Gerbner is founder of the Cultural Environment Movement.*

simple hypothesis: if independent media worked together, collaborating on and pooling resources and talent toward a shared goal, the impact could resonate well beyond any single effort.

The NIOT campaign carried the documentary's restorative message to communities across the land: From November 1995 through January 1996, hundreds of NIOT screenings and town hall meetings were held in more than 75 towns and cities; the program aired on more than 200 PBS stations. Alternative media played a key role in publicizing the campaign, with the involvement of over 25 weekly papers, many of which hosted local events, radio broadcasts like FAIR's CounterSpin, and the NIOT website, which helped spread word over the Net. The community-based elements of the NIOT campaign also helped catalyze an echo effect that resonated from the alternative to the mainstream media.

The campaign was so successful, in fact, that the Working Group produced a sequel, *Not In Our Town II*, featuring a number of communities that applied the model of Billings in their responses to hate and intolerance in their towns. Broadcast by PBS in December 1996, *Not In Our Town II* was followed by another NIOT campaign and ongoing activities around the country. Key to the future of independent media is finding ways to be heard amidst the onslaught of the monopoly-dominated media—the "campaign" model does just this by making media accessible and relevant to people's lives.

*Contact: Working Group, (510) 547-8484;*
*E-mail: wedothework@igc.org;*
*URL: http://www.igc.apc.org/an/niot/*

# A Day in the Life of Local TV News

On the night of September 20, 1995, the Rocky Mountain Media Watch analyzed 100 local TV newscasts from 58 United States cities. The evidence from this survey shows:

- Non-news is more prevalent than news.
- Crime stories dominate the majority of newscasts.
- Murder stories are out of proportion to reality.
- The Mayhem index is 42 percent.
- The Fluff index is 39 percent.
- Commercials are more frequent than on network programming.
- Copycat programming is rampant.
- Stations are prone to feeding frenzies on sensational stories.

Conversely, serious deficiencies are also endemic in newscasts:

- Many important topics are almost invisible on the news.
- Solution-oriented stories are infrequent.
- Women and minorities are underrepresented as on-air station personnel.
- People of color are stereotyped as perpetrators.
- Women are stereotyped as victims.

## Samples on the Pavlov Scale

| Rank and Call Letters | | City/State | Pavlov Index |
|---|---|---|---|
| 1 | WHDH TV | Boston, MA | 97.2 |
| 2 | KFOR TV | Oklahoma City, OK | 96.2 |
| 3 | KPRC TV | Houston, TX | 95.3 |
| 4 | WLKY TV | Louisville, KY | 93.4 |
| 5 | KNBC TV | Los Angeles, CA | 92.1 |
| 96 | KCRA TV | Sacramento, CA | 42.9 |
| 97 | WICD TV | Champaign, IL | 42.3 |
| 98 | KDNL TV | St. Louis, MO | 41.2 |
| 99 | KEZI TV | Eugene, OR | 40.5 |
| 100 | KTCA TV | Minneapolis, MN | 19.1 |

Note: A high ranking on the Pavlov Index indicates a preponderance of fluff and mayhem.

### Mayhem
Taken together as the "mayhem index," stories about crime, disaster, and war constitute more than half of the news.

### Fluff
"Fluff" is the relative amount of soft news, anchor chatter, teases, and celebrity items compared to the amount of news. Roughly a third of news is devoted to fluff.

## Making Peace

 In Detroit, Clementine Barfiled responded to the murder of her son by founding Save Our Sons and Daughters (SOSAD), a group that consoles families and steers children toward nonviolence; Chicago's Luis Rodriguez, a writer and poet, works with gang members through the organization Youth Struggling for Survival; Pam Butler of Palo Alto, California, was nearly killed by an abusive husband and went on to found a one-on-one big-sister program for victims of domestic violence. These are a few of the success stories featured in *Making Peace*, a four-part documentary series that spotlights successful community-based initiatives to heal the conditions that create violence.

Producer Tom Weidlinger envisioned *Making Peace* as an alternative to violence-saturated images on television that offer no solutions, let alone hope. *Making Peace* is intended to inspire more community groups to organize violence prevention programs. To that end, the producers also developed a workshop facilitator guide and an organizing kit to use these documentaries to stimulate discussion. These materials offer concrete suggestions for community outreach strategies, which include forums, training and recruiting, and organizing town meetings.

Contact: Films for the Humanities, Tel: (609) 275-1400.

# SHOULD THE COVERAGE FIT THE CRIME?

### JOE HOLLEY

What if a TV news operation refused to cover crime in the same old way? Would crime still make the same noise in the community? Would the station? Since the beginning of 1996, the ABC affiliate in Austin, Texas, KVUE-TV, a Gannett station, has been trying to find out. The station's experiment has not only given Austin viewers something of a choice, but it has forced the KVUE staff to reassess long-held assumptions about how to cover crime, or even whether to cover it. It has forced reporters, editors, and news directors to ask that more basic question: What is news?

In breaking the Pavlovian response to the squawking police scanner and the melodramatic visuals, a crime story must meet one or more of KVUE's five criteria to be aired:

*Does action need to be taken?*

*Is there an immediate threat to safety?*

*Is there a threat to children?*

*Does the crime have significant community impact?*

*Does the story lend itself to a crime-prevention effort?*

## COMMENT

*People worry about street crime because they don't want to go into a 7-11 and get shot up. In fact, corporate and white-collar crime is also violent crime and inflicts far more violence than street crime. For example, since the Occupational Safety and Health Act was passed, 200,000 American workers have died on the job. Compare that to the homicide rate, which is about 24,000 a year, that's street-crime homicide. Overall, the corporate crime and violence rate is far greater than the street-crime rate and yet the public perception is that street crime is the theme we should be more worried about. Now, why is that? That's because the media focuses on that. All the crime shows focus on street crime. Rarely do you get a story about corporate or white-collar crime.*
*— Russell Mokhiber, Corporate Crime Reporter*

*A KVUE Text Case*
Following is an example of how KVUE shapes the news:

*The crime:*
A murder/suicide at an apartment complex for married students at the University of Texas. A graduate student in engineering had shot his wife and four-year-old daughter and then turned the gun on himself.

*KVUE reporter's dilemma:*
There was no immediate threat to the community, the crime itself was solved, and there was really nothing to say about prevention. There seemed to be no significant community impact; the family was new to the apartment complex, and the neighbors barely knew them. The guideline about children? In this case, the child was dead.

*The coverage:*
The story focused on the immediate community's response to the tragedy. The residents of the apartment complex gathered at sunset on a playground and talked over what had happened, among themselves and with the reporter, who also listened as counselors talked to the residents about signs of domestic abuse, which was an issue in the investigation, and what they could do to prevent it.

The February 1996 ratings came out in mid-March. They were KVUE's best ever. The station increased its already-solid ratings lead for every newscast, reaching its highest numbers in a decade for its 10 P.M. show. (*Columbia Journalism Review*)

COMMENT

*What the press does with the sort of bleed-lead philosophy is take the most unusual and extraordinary crimes and present those to people as though they are the everyday ordinary experience of the streets. They take the most unusual crimes and make them the most ordinary ones. And this in turn leads to some real fear and distortion or public policy. It's very dangerous.*
— Bruce Shapiro, The Nation

# 2. Representation and Distortion

*Plus comment by* Rodger Streitmatter

*And profiles of* CEMOTAP, Community Journalism Cross–Training, FAIR, Yo!, CMBE, and "Red, Hot, and Cool."

ETHNICITY:     CHECK THE APPROPRIATE BOX

☐ American Indian or Alaskan Native     ☐ Asian or Pacific Islander     ☐ Caucasian White (Not Hispanic)

☐ Black (Not Hispanic)     ☐ Hispanic

# PAPER TIGER GUIDE TO TV REPAIR

**KIM DETERLINE**

Keep an eye on the following symptoms of faulty equipment:

*Is your equipment connected to establishment power sources?*
Be aware of the political perspective of the sources used in a story. Media often rely solely on "official" (government, corporate, and establishment think tank) sources. For instance, several years ago the media watch group FAIR found in a study of 40 months of *Nightline* programming that the most frequent guests were white males such as Henry Kissinger and Jerry Falwell and that progressive and public-interest voices were grossly underrepresented. This hasn't changed much.

**Scary but True...**

People of color, the vast majority of humankind, make up less than 11 percent of prime-time and 3 percent of children's program casts, and, unlike in life, are mostly middle-class. Latino/Hispanic persons, nearly 10 percent of the United States population make up about 1 percent of prime-time and half of that of children's program casts. The world of daytime serials is even more white than prime-time.

Although the United States census classifies more than 14 percent of the general population,

To portray issues fairly and accurately, media must broaden their spectrum of sources. Otherwise, they serve merely as megaphones for those in power.

*Does your set need color and gender adjustment?*
What is the race and gender diversity at the news outlet you watch compared to the communities it serves? How many producers, editors, or decision makers at news outlets are women or people of color? In order to fairly represent different communities, news outlets must have members of those communities in decision-making positions.

How many of the experts these news outlets cite are women and people of color? FAIR's survey of *MacNeil/*

29 percent of Latino/Hispanics, and 33 percent of African-Americans as "poor," and many more as low-income wage earners, on television they are virtually invisible: 1.3 percent of characters in prime-time, 1.2 percent in daytime, half that (0.6 percent) in children's programs, and 0.2 percent in the news.

As the 43 million disabled Americans struggle to gain rights of equal access, employment, and dignity, disability is visible in only 1.5 percent of prime-time programs. Those shown as disabled or mentally ill are most likely to be stigmatized and victimized. (Cultural Indicators)

*Lehrer*'s guest list during a six-month survey was 90 percent white and 87 percent male.

*Who controls the focus on your set?*
From whose point of view is the news reported? Coverage will often focus on how issues affect male politicians or corporate executives rather than those directly affected by the issue.

For instance, strike coverage is usually reported from the perspective of how it affects business and consumers rather than the workers. Abortion coverage often emphasizes the "tough choice" confronting male politicians and how it affects their chances for reelection.

*Are you picking up a double standard?*
Do media subject certain constituencies to a double standard? Strong, aggressive women leaders will often be described as "strident" or "shrill," while men with the same qualities will be described as "tough" or "outspoken."

*Do stereotypes interfere with your reception?*
Does coverage of the drug crisis focus on African-Americans almost exclusively despite the fact that the vast majority of drug users are white? Are gay men portrayed as "sexual predators" and lesbians portrayed as "man-hating"?

*Are unchallenged assumptions lodged in your receiver?*
In coverage of women on welfare, especially women of color, reporters tend to skirt over economic factors and jump to the women's sexuality (the age at which

a woman had her first child, for example) as the reason for her plight.

*Is manipulative language escaping through your screen?*

When media adopt loaded terminology, they help shape public opinion. For instance, media increasingly use the term "racial preference" to refer to affirmative action programs. A Louis Harris poll of 1,250 adults found that 70 percent said they favored "affirmative action" while only 46 percent favored "racial preference programs."

*Kim Deterline is director of* We Interrupt This Message, *an organization that trains social-justice groups to fight unfair media images of their issues and communities.* Paper Tiger *is a public access tv show.*

# NETWORK TV: LATINOS NEED NOT APPLY

### YVETTE DOSS

It would be hard to find someone who hasn't heard the unmistakable call of everyone's favorite Cubano: "Hey Lu-cy, I'm home!" Ricky Ricardo's call to his lovable, harebrained wife was a familiar sound to millions of Americans in the 1950s. In what was probably the only opportunity Americans had to hear a string of Spanish insults, millions tuned in to watch Ricky rant and rave weekly for nearly 10 years on prime-time television, watching him fulfill the role of the hot-tempered Latin lover they had come to expect of Latino stars since the early

days of film. Sure, Ricky was somewhat of a buffoon, but since he produced as well as starred in *I Love Lucy*, his character was a successful buffoon who owned his own nightclub, made Hollywood movies, and got to hang out with big-name actors.

What about the portrayal of other Latino characters on network TV? Their stories aren't nearly as rosy. From the very beginning, Latino TV characters have fallen into one of a very few number of stereotypical roles: the Latin lover, the lazy sombrero-wearing imp, the gun-toting bad guy. For women, the roles were even more limited: either the

pious rosario-toting mother of the bad guy or the Latin Lover's hot-to-trot female counterpart. From the early years of Zorro and the Cisco Kid to today, you'd think all that would have changed. In recent years, three shows starring Latinos—Warner Bros.' *Jackie* plus Fox's *House of Buggin'* and *Culture Clash*—have surfaced, raising the hopes of young Latino actors and directors everywhere. But all three went under after only a short time. Latinos are faring far worse in today's TV climate than they were during the *I Love Lucy* days. (*Latino Link*)

## CEMOTAP

Since its March 1987 inception at St. Alban's Congregational Church in Queens, the Committee To Eliminate Media Offensive to African People (CEMOTAP) has promoted a more accurate portrayal and understanding of blacks in New York–area media outlets. With its stated goal of "monitoring, confronting, changing or eliminating media that offends African people or that devalues or disrespects African achievement, history, culture, progress and personalities," CEMOTAP has evolved from a group of 10 individuals who were tired of seeing negative portrayals of blacks to a media organization that owns its headquarters, publishes a newsletter, sponsors letter-writing campaigns, supports a school in Kebi, Ghana, sponsors free biweekly forums, and, with the aid of its over 1,500 members, gives $1,000 donations to a different independent black school each month.

CEMOTAP's most noted campaign was one of its first, the "Postbuster," in which the group took on the once-liberal *New York Post*'s poor treatment and coverage of African-Americans with an active publicity campaign. Today, the group takes credit for aiding in the $300,000-a-week hemorrhaging the paper reportedly suffered as a result of their campaign.

For their final campaign of 1995, CEMOTAP organized a protest against a $150-a-plate black-tie dinner for WABC-AM radio talkshow host Jay Diamond, a well-documented purveyor of racial hatred. (Diamond is known for regularly presenting mock lethal-injection executions of black leaders he doesn't like.) As word spread that a number of prominent politicians had been invited to the tribute dinner, including the governors of New York and New Jersey, CEMOTAP took action and began raising awareness about the true nature of Diamond's show. On the night of the event, guests were greeted by some 300 demonstrators. Thanks to CEMOTAP, the dinner turned out to be less than the star-studded affair organizers had hoped for.

CEMOTAP activist Betty Dopson looks back to when she was first told that challenging the New York media was too daunting a job. "But there's nothing so big in the media that an average person couldn't handle it," she answered. So far, CEMOTAP's 1,500 "average" members have proved her right.
—Karen Carrillo, *Third Force*

Contact: CEMOTAP at: P.O. Box 120340, St. Albans, NY, 11412; (718) 322-8454.

## Community Journalism Cross Training

Millions of Americans don't get their news from *Time* or *Newsweek*. They don't read the *New York Times* or the *Washington Post*. They don't even watch Ted Koppel. They are America's ethnic minorities, they are sick and tired of the mainstream media's racial stereotypes, and they are increasingly turning to America's growing community press for information about the world they live in.

The ethnic and community press, defined as publications serving communities distinguished by either identity or geography, plays an increasingly important role as a vital source of news, discussion, debate, and opinion for their readers. The primary political role of most ethnic publications is to serve and defend the community that reads them.

Despite the growing audience in diverse communities, ethnic and community papers remain primarily small-scale operations that are often strapped for resources and cannot afford to pay for the advanced training and education routinely offered to mainstream journalists. Many of the writers and junior editors working for the ethnic and community press have little formal journalism training.

Faced with these obstacles, a 1995 experiment called the Community Journalism Cross Training (CJCT) brought together editors from ethnic publications in San Francisco to explore the possibilities for collaboration and mutual assistance. Sponsored by *Third Force maga-*

*continued on page 113*

# ISLAM: FUNDAMENTAL MISUNDERSTANDINGS ABOUT A GROWING FAITH

## SAM HUSSEINI

Approximately 5 million Muslims live in the United States. Islam will probably be the largest non-Christian religion in the country in the next century. Yet there's rarely a mention of Muslims in the media that doesn't have to do with violence.

The media is so full of reports on the "Islamic threat" from "radical Muslim terrorists" plotting "Islamic fundamentalist violence" that the average non-Muslim American could conclude that the "fundamentals" of Islam include a course in demolitions training. According to a 1995 *Los Angeles Times* poll, 45 percent of Americans agreed that "Muslims tend to be fanatics."

The media often identify Muslims by their religion—as in the AP headline "Muslims Convicted in [World Trade Center] Case." Would a headline read "Jews convicted"? Would anti-abortion militants be described as engaging in "Christian violence"? When reporting on "Islamic violence," how deep do these biases go?

"Fundamentalism" is a term borrowed from self-described Christian groups; it's not a Muslim term. But it implies that strict adherents to Islam use violence to advance their religion, while peaceful Muslims must be less observant. As a United States ally, the government of Saudi Arabia is usually described as "moderate," not "fundamentalist," even though it adheres strictly to Islamic law. (*EXTRA!*)

Microsoft Corp. issued a public apology in Spain and Mexico for a Spanish-language product that offered "savage" and "man eater" as synonyms for the word "Indian" in its thesaurus for Microsoft Word 6.0. Microsoft apologized in a press release issued in Mexico City and also took out newspaper ads in Mexico and Spain promising to make new software available for free. (Associated Press)

*continued from page 112*

zine and the Center for the Integration and Improvement of Journalism, CJCT drew editors from about 20 community publications, local newspapers, and small magazines, including the *Korea Times*, *Asian Week*, *El Tecolote*, *Third Force*, *Southern Exposure* (from Durham, North Carolina), *El Mensajero*, *Sun Reporter*, *Crossroads*, *City Sun* (New York), *El Andar*, *India Currents*, and so on.

In addition to offering concrete ways to support the people and publications in the ethnic press, the participants at CJCT found numerous opportunities to involve ethnic publications in wider progressive media/journalism and political projects. Collaboration on such projects serves to educate many of the writers and junior editors working for the ethnic and community press who are not familiar with the histories and current situations of communities other than their own. Exploring the similarities among various communities of color, the participants in CJCT realized they could pool their resources to expand their financial base while at the same time create a support network to provide inclusive reporting of their respective communities.

Out of CJCT, the Community Press Consortium was developed, in cooperation with the Center for Integration and Improvement of Journalism at San Francisco State University.

—Bill Mesler

*For more information, call (415) 338-7434.*

**Fairness & Accuracy In Reporting (FAIR)**

FAIR is the leader of national media watch groups, offering well-documented criticism in an effort to correct bias and imbalance. With a versatile and top-notch staff, FAIR focuses public awareness on the narrow corporate ownership of the press, the media's allegiance to official agendas, and insensitivity to women, labor, minorities, and public-interest constituencies. FAIR seeks to invigorate the First Amendment by advocating for greater media pluralism and the inclusion of public-interest voices in national debates.

The group has organized in support of alternative media and independent journalists facing attacks from both the conservative right and the corporate media, and continuously fights to save public broadcasting from both government attacks and corporate encroachment.

"FAIR doesn't just complain about how bad things are—we do something about it," says executive director Jeff Cohen. "We don't just mourn media bias—we organize."

FAIR also produces the nationally syndicated radio program *Counter Spin*, and publishes the monthly magazine *EXTRA!*

Contact: FAIR/*EXTRA!*, 130 West 25th Street, New York, NY 10001; Tel: (212) 633-6700; Fax: (212) 727-7668; E-mail: http://www.fair.org/fair.

# READING THE ETHNIC PRESS

**JOHN ANNER**

There is a thriving, diverse ethnic press emerging across the country, some of which is explicitly progressive in its politics. The opportunities for collaboration are numerous, and there needs to be a transfer of personnel, experience, understanding, and information between insular white progressives and their counterparts in the ethnic press.

Ethnic newspapers are vital sources of news, discussion, debate, and opinion for their readers. Many people of color (especially low-income people) read only their local ethnic newspaper regularly. This is particularly true when the paper is published in a language other than English and caters to immigrants. The primary political role of most ethnic publications is to serve and defend the community that reads them, and the oldest papers have names that reflect their connection to struggles for social justice (*Defender, Advocate, Crusader*, etc.).

The local newspapers are by far the oldest and most numerous of ethnic press outlets. Any major urban area in the United States has at least a few, and many highly diverse areas have dozens.

"IN THE NEXT HALF HOUR, MY WEALTHY WHITE CONSERVATIVE MALE FRIENDS AND I WILL DISCUSS THE ANNOYINGLY PERSISTENT BLACK UNDER-CLASS, AND WHY WOMEN GET SO EMOTIONAL ABOUT ABORTION."

By one estimate, there are over 100 ethnic newspapers (including community papers) serving communities of color in the New York metropolitan area, while a recent survey in the San Francisco Bay Area found between 40 and 50 publications that fit this description. The *New York Times* reports that there are 60 newspapers nationwide that reach the Vietnamese community alone, while in Los Angeles' various Latino communities there are at least 17 newspapers, tabloids, and free publications in Spanish and English targeted to Latino readers.

The universe of local ethnic newspapers is probably the best point of access to communities of color. The local newspapers are close to the people. They reach large percentages of their communities, they have their finger on the pulse of many of the most important debates and trends in their communities, and they are often the single most important print source of news, opinion, and analysis for that community.

*John Anner is the editor of* Third Force *magazine.*

**Scary but True...**

In two years' worth of PBS primetime programming, there were 27 hours of programs that "addressed the lives and concerns of workers as workers," compared with 253 hours focused on the upper classes. Of the 27 hours on working people, 19 were about *British* workers—leaving 20 minutes a month on United States workers. (City University of New York)

# BLURRY VISION OF WORKERS

## DON HAZEN

The representation of working people in corporate media has often reflected a negative bias, especially when it comes to covering unions. Strike coverage is usually the worst, where newspapers' corporate interests and hostility often appear unvarnished. This bias is worsened when the target of a strike is a media company, as is the case in the lengthy and tortured strike by six union locals against the Joint Operating Agreement (JOA) papers in Detroit, Gannett's *Detroit News* and Knight Ridder's *Detroit Free Press*. Despite the national ramifications, there was little coverage, particularly in Detroit.

Many in the movement for media reform are looking to organized labor to play a leadership role in battling the global media conglomerates. Analysis within labor appears to understand that the decline of unions can be directly traced to right-wing assaults against both unions and liberal social polices. These conservative attitudes are consistently delivered by the mainstream press to their viewers and readers.

Only unions and foundations have the resources to help fund public education about the consequences of media concentration and the attacks on public-interest journalism. Some unions seem ready to invest in independent media of their own, as the UAW has done by

investing in the United Broadcasting radio network. It often seems the case that much of the public doesn't distinguish between media that is designed to deliver audiences to advertisers and public-interest journalism, which at its best addresses the real needs of the people. Protecting journalism for the long haul, when its economic base is deteriorating, will be an uphill fight.

As Robert McChesney notes, in the 1940s there were approximately 1,000 full-time labor reporters and editors on U.S. daily papers. Today there are fewer than 10. These figures of course reflect both declining coverage of labor issues and the impact of the dramatically shrinking newspaper universe.

Coverage of unions may be improving however, reflecting the upsurge in union activism. The AFL-CIO's 1996 "Union Summer" program received wide notice in the mainstream press, suggesting that young people working with unions was a hip thing to do, and signaling the fact that young people today appear to have more positive attitudes toward unions than their slightly older brethren.

While media coverage of unions is still mixed, the notion that unions are more strategic and aggressive about their future—reflected mostly by the amount of resources invested in the '96 elections—means in certain media situations they are taken more seriously by the press as players, and 1996 was seen as a "turnaround" year for labor by a number of analysts. But this aggressiveness has also created a backlash.

As Jerry Ackerman wrote in the *Boston Globe*, unions "are also cleaning up their image in an economy in which working people are beginning to view corporate mergers and lay offs as an enemy far bigger than any so-called 'bad-boy' unions."

In the face of media corporations attacks on workers, represented by company downsizing and layoffs, many formally reticent media workers are turning to trade unions to protect their future. At the beginning of 1997, for example, after a long campaign, writers and editors at the Dow Jones Company, publisher of the *Wall Street Journal,* voted to affiliate with the Communications Workers of America (CWA). The Newspaper Guild's merg-er into CWA will no doubt provide more resources for organizing. Anger will also rise as media workers find themselves being undercut as media mergers increase pressure on the bottom line to pay for huge debts which provoke layoffs.

As McChesney notes: "Journalism, entertainment and communication workers' trade unions are on the front lines of the struggle for democratic media. These unions need to recognize that traditional campaigns to protect jobs and benefits in the short term may enjoy some success, but they do nothing to address the long-term trajectory of their industries which is resolutely anti-labor. In Canada and parts of Europe, communications unions are forming alliances with consumer and community groups, for example, to advocate a socially responsive vision of a non-market or at least well-regulated private telecommunication system. This is a model of progressive social unionism that may provide an escape route from the present downward spiral of U.S. communication unions, and is worthy of consideration by the labor movement as a whole."

*Don Hazen is the director of the Institute for Alternative Journalism.*

**Scary but True...**

Corporate influence in the newsroom accounts for some of the skew. Responding to a survey by the *Los Angeles Times*, 53 percent of newspaper editors admitted they usually take management's side in labor disputes; only 8 percent said they side with workers. (Janine Jackson)

# THE MEDIA'S STRIKE BIAS

### JANINE JACKSON

Contract negotiations that result, as most do, in safer workplaces or improved benefits for workers don't get much media coverage. Strikes, on the other hand, may get a story or two, at least in their opening days. Little wonder that some people think calling strikes is all unions do.

When strikes occur, press and TV reports affect how the public perceives them. Too often, these reports are skewed against striking workers and their interests.

Here's how *USA Today* described the 1992 UAW walkout at a GM plant in Lordstown, Ohio: "Analysts say the outcome of the Lordstown strike. . .will show whether GM can stick to its gut-wrenching plan to become a lean industrial powerhouse — or give in once again to the United Auto Workers union."

It's obvious where the paper thinks readers' sympathies should lie. But the use of unnamed "analysts" makes the opinion sound objective and neutral.

Like many strike stories, this article mentions the underlying issues only glancingly, toward the end of the piece.

*USA Today*'s approach is common through mainstream media: Workers who withhold their labor when negotiations fail are portrayed as "disruptive" and selfish—accusations virtually never directed at owners who exploit workers or close down plants in the interest of increased profits. Such moves are presented as management's prerogative, their motives unquestioned.

It's a common observation that unions make "demands" while management make "offers"; such weighted language came into play in coverage of the

Teamsters strike. Striking Teamsters, according to an Associated Press piece, sought to "cripple deliveries." Trucking companies, on the other hand, were "seeking the right" to hire lower-paid part-time workers, ship more by rail, and impose a no-strike clause.

The sources quoted in strike stories help determine who readers believe are out to "cripple" the system and who are merely "seeking their rights." Rank and file members are rarely heard from, although the *Charlotte Observer* did find one Teamster picket to say the strike was "the dumbest thing that could ever have come along." (The reporter neglected to mention the rank-and-file vote overwhelmingly supporting the action.)

Coverage of the truckers' strike was often self-contradictory, as media tried to depict the action as both destructive and ineffectual. Stories with headlines like "Strike isn't slowing freight" contended with those blaming strikers for layoffs and traffic tie-ups.

The emphasis on potential "damage" represents a "workers vs. consumers" approach that is common in strike coverage. A proposed rail strike in 1992, for example, led to numerous stories detailing ruined vacation plans and elephants unable to reach the circus. Of course, workers are consumers, too. And what of the damage to workers' livelihoods if they accept management demands without a struggle?

Teamster spokeswoman Cynthia Kain notes that some journalists seem to have their minds made up before they even start gathering the facts. One reporter began an interview by demanding, "Why are you on strike? You can't win!" Not surprisingly, the resulting article presented the strike as foolish, and contained none of Kain's comments.

Perhaps most ironic was the suggestion in many reports that strikes are anti-worker. A number of stories portrayed union workers (because they "demand" so much) as hurting the nonunionized. For example, virtually all accounts uncritically accepted trucking firms' claim that they had to cut "labor costs" due to increased competition from nonunion companies. But this explanation, Kain points out, omits the fact that the biggest unionized carriers are themselves the owners of their nonunion "competition." Whichever group of workers loses, the company wins.

Highlighting divisions within the union and within the workforce, press reports obscured the center point—the conflicting interests of workers and management.

Biased strike reporting turns the question of who is giving and who is grabbing upside down. The issue of pay rates, for example, would have looked rather different had press accounts mentioned the fact, included in Teamster background material, that the CEO of one of the truck companies (Consolidated Freightways) saw his own compensation leap 100 percent from 1992 to 1993—to $1,612,000. The average Teamster wage has dropped 21 percent since 1980. (*Solidarity*)

*Janine Jackson is co-host and producer of FAIR"s radio show,* Counter Spin.

---

**Scary but True...**

 Imagine that in reaction to Republican proposals to gut Medicaid, cut back on health-care benefits for the elderly, slash aid to dependent children, and give rich people a tax cut, somewhere between four and five million Americans went on strike and staged demonstrations in cities around the country.

Imagine that they shut down subway and rail service, postal service, hundreds of schools and day-care centers, and severely curtailed airline travel. Imagine these collective actions got the government to back off.

Pretty big story, huh? But wait—it didn't happen here (*tant pis!*). This happened in a foreign country where they don't even speak our language or anything, so who cares? American news executives and pundits alike know that we chuckleheads don't care about foreign countries at all—unless our vacation plans are at stake.

And so it was that during the same week that somewhere between 500,000 and 1.7 million French people took to the streets, *Newsweek* chose to put Elizabeth Hurley—supermodel and Hugh Grant's delightfully understanding girlfriend—on its cover. If followed up with its special "year in cartoons" issue.

Susan Douglas, *The Progressive*

# THE 1996 GOLDEN TURKEY AWARDS

**The Dispatcher,** the San Francisco-based newspaper for the Longshoremen's and Warehousemen's Union

### Darth Vader Memorial Helmet
**KATHY LEE GIFFORD**

...the daytime TV talk show host who was caught with her ethics down when it was learned that her Wal-Mart clothing line was made in overseas sweatshops. By the time a congressional hearing on child labor rolled around, Gifford had reinvented herself as a champion of the oppressed —although her testimony was largely confined to her personal "ordeal" in the hands of the media. In Oklahoma City for a Wal-Mart stockholders meeting, the wholesome– America's-sweetheart– wannabe blamed the fiasco on a "force of evil nature" hell-bent on discrediting her and Wal-Mart's success. May the force be with you, Kathy Lee, and others like you.

### Michael Milken Magic Marketeer of the Year
**JOHN STOSSEL**

...who insists that his job as correspondent for ABC's weekly television magazine *20/20*, is to explain "the magic of the marketplace." His April report slammed the Davis-Bacon Act, which requires prevailing union wages on federal construction projects, as an "outrageous example of how your tax money is being spent." He cited as a source a right-wing activist who declared that only "union thugs" benefit from it. Further, Stossel proselytized, the law hurts poor, unskilled workers because contractors won't hire "inexperienced strangers" at union wages. Great. Let's repeal the law and build a nuclear reactor next to your house, John.

### Excellence in Adolescent Indoctrination
**K-III COMMUNICATIONS**

...which owns Channel One, the commercial classroom television network appearing in schools near you. K-III, in turn, is 82 percent owned by KKR, the notorious leverage buy-out kings whose $25 billion purchase of RJR Nabisco (cigarettes and cereal, go figure) was the subject of the book Barbarians at the Gate. Channel One provides in-school news and commercials to a captive audience of 8 million students daily, with each 30-second ad selling for $200,000.

### Shut My Mouth Award
**ABC RADIO**

...which fired commentator Jim Hightower after he criticized ABC's massive media merger with Disney Corp. for concentrating "that much power in so few hands."

# MEDIA MYTHS ABOUT WELFARE

### FRANCES FOX PIVEN

The core argument in the assault on welfare by Democrats and Republicans alike is that it is a system of perverse incentives.

These arguments are by now so familiar that they have worn ruts in our minds. But all of them are based on myths. Here are some of the most common media-perpetuated myths, followed by their corresponding, harsh realities:

THE PRESS CONTINUES TO COVER THE HOMELESS

### Media Myth
Poor women have more children because of the "financial incentives" of welfare benefits.

### Reality
Repeated studies show no correlation between benefit levels and women's choice to have children. States providing relatively higher benefits do not show higher birth rates among recipients. The average family receiving Aid to Families with Dependent Children (AFDC) has 1.9 children—about the same as the national average. In any case, a mother on welfare can expect about $90 a month in additional AFDC benefits if she has another child—hardly an incentive.

Five million heads of families earn close to the minimum wage, which now falls short of the poverty line for a family of three. Fewer and fewer of these jobs pay health or pension benefits. If anything, it is increasingly the low-wage job with no mobility that is the trap. Welfare sometimes provides an opening —to go back to school or enter a good training program that would be impossible without some ensured income.

### Media Myth
We don't subsidize middle-class families, why subsidize low income ones?

"A family that works does not get a raise for having a child. Why then should a family that doesn't work?" columnist Ellen Goodman wrote in the Boston Globe.

### Reality
In fact, families do receive a premium for additional children, in the form of a $2,450 tax reduction. There are also tax credits to partially cover child-care expenses, up to a maximum of $2,400 per child. No pundit has suggested that middle-class families base their decision to have children on these "perks."

### Media Myth
The public is fed up with spending money on the poor.

### Reality
Contrary to claims from media pundits, the general public is not so hard-hearted. In a December 1994 poll by the Center for the Study of Policy Attitudes (CSPA),

80 percent of respondents agreed that the government has "a responsibility to try to do away with poverty."

Support for "welfare" is lower than support for "assistance to the poor," but when CSPA asked people about their support for AFDC, described as the federal welfare program that provides "financial support for unemployed poor single mothers with children," only 21 percent said funding should be cut, while 29 percent said it should be increased.

### Media Myth
We've spent over $5 trillion on welfare since the '60s and it hasn't worked.

### Reality
Conservatives and liberals alike use this claim as proof that federal poverty programs don't work. But spending on AFDC, the program normally referred to as "welfare," totals less than $500 billion from 1964 to 1994—less than 1.5 percent of federal outlays for that period.

To get the $5 trillion figure, "welfare spending" must be defined to include all means-tested programs, including Medicaid, food stamps, student lunches, scholarship aid, and many other programs. Furthermore, the poverty rate did fall between 1964 and 1973, from 19 percent to 11 percent, with the advent of "Great Society" programs. Since the 1970s, economic forces like declining real wages, as well as reduced benefit levels, have contributed to rising poverty rates.

### Media Myth
Anyone who wants to get off welfare can just get a job.

### Reality
Many welfare recipients do work to supplement meager benefits. And the lack of affordable child care and the low-wage, no-benefit jobs available to most AFDC recipients is no formula for lifting a family out of poverty.

Although it is almost never mentioned in conjunction with the welfare debate, the United States Federal Reserve has an official policy of raising interest rates whenever unemployment falls below a certain point—now about 6.2 percent. In other words, if all the unemployed women on welfare were to find jobs, currently employed people would have to be thrown out of work to keep the economy from "overheating."

*Based on an article published in* EXTRA! *and an excerpt from Frances Fox Piven's* Poorhouse Politics, *published in* The Nation.

---

### Scary but True...

 Women play one out of three roles in prime-time television, one out of four in children's programs, and one out of five of those who present the news. Even in daytime soaps, they fall short of the majority. They also age faster than men on TV, and as they age, they are more likely to be portrayed as evil and unsuccessful. (George Gerbner)

# WOMEN AND THE MEDIA

## SUSAN DOUGLAS

One of the major traits that defines womanhood in the 1990s is our daily war with all those media that we love and hate and that, after all these years, don't know what to do about us or for us, although they seem to have a better grip on what to do to us. It is easy for many of us to understand what an advertiser or a TV producer wants us to take away from this ad or that show, but that doesn't mean that women always, in fact, buy into and accept those meanings. We are fed up with ads that tell us we're too old, too fat, and too marked up in some way, but we feel, nonetheless, too old, too fat, and too marked up.

We are tired of blockbuster movies that glorify beefy, rippled men who speak monosyllabically and carry extremely well-endowed sticks, but we go to them anyway, nursing our fury and enjoying our catharsis. We get the bends as we escape the schizophrenic landscape of *Glamour* or *Vogue*, in which editorials, advice columns, and articles urge us to be assertive, strong, no-nonsense feminists while the fashion and beauty layouts insist that we be passive, anorexic spectacles whose only function is to attract men and who should spend our leisure time mastering the art of the pedicure.

We throw half-eaten bagels at Saturday morning kid's shows and commercials that train our daughters to be giggling, airheaded Valley Girls, but we go ahead and buy them Glitter Ken and the Fisher-Price toy kitchen on the theory that we played with Barbies and we came out OK—well, sort of.

We think that news programs must be getting less sexist because there are now famous women newscasters, but we also see how women's issues are either sensationalized (Have one more drink and you'll die of breast cancer) or trivialized (so what if a woman has to drive 300 miles to get an abortion, or a 16-year-old has to get permission from a father she never sees?), while women's voices about major areas of national policy are ignored. Most of all, the constant erasure of the contradictions that define our lives makes us crazy, since all the media, completely confused and conflicted about what to do about women, subtly acknowledge those contradictions while either pretending they don't exist or insisting they can be resolved, especially with a purchase or two.

What the mass media don't convey, and can't convey, is that feminism is an ongoing project, a process, undertaken on a daily basis by millions of women of all ages, classes, ethnic and racial backgrounds, and sexual preferences. And as they continue through this process, they have certainly taken note, with Susan Faludi's help, of a backlash filled with wishful-thinking pronouncements about the "death" of feminism and the heralding of a new "post-feminist" age.

But they have also taken heart in Roseanne and Murphy Brown, in Oprah and Nina Totenberg, and in the various defiant, smart, funny, and strong women they see on TV. Some of the sharpest and funniest columnists in this country are women—Molly Ivins, Katha Pollitt, Barbara Ehrenreich. On the other hand, women's voices are rarely heard in the news.

The only advice I have for women today is to purchase two things: extra slippers, for throwing at the TV set, and extra stationery, for writing letters to soda companies telling them we'll never buy their swill again and will organize boycotts if they keep pitting Cindy Crawford against older women and keep pitting us against one another. We can also reclaim the word "feminist" from the trash heap it's been relegated to by the media and remind them, and ourselves, that a woman who says "I'm not a feminist, but . . ." is a feminist. I agree with Susan Faludi, who said, "All women are feminists. It's just a matter of time and encouragement." And despite their best efforts to keep feminism a dirty word and women under their control, the media will continue, often inadvertently, to play a critical role in providing that encouragement. They are still our worst enemy and our best ally in the ongoing struggle for equality, respect, power, and love. (Excerpted from *Where the Girls Are: Growing Up Female with the Mass Media*).

*Susan Douglas is a professor of media studies at the University of Michigan.*

**Scary but True...**

 Fifteen percent of front-page newspaper references were to females in 1996, the second year in a row references to women declined.

 Male voices made up 85 percent of front-page references, 76 percent on key local pages, and 86 percent on key business pages. When females were covered as the main figure of a story, more than half were victims or perpetrators of crimes or alleged misconduct.

 Front-page bylines of women reached its highest number to date at 35 percent.

 Front-page photos of women remained at 33 percent, the same as 1995, a decrease from a high of 39 percent in 1994.

 Commentary written by women continued to decline, with women writing an average of 26 percent of opinion pieces on the op-ed or equivalent pages. Only 2 percent of op-ed pages had no male bylines, but 28 percent lacked female bylines.

 Less than 1 percent of the references in front-page political stories were to females; in those cases, they were mostly to wives and daughters.

*Source: "Marginalizing Women," a 1996 survey by Women, Men and Media.*

## Resource Lists of Women's Mags and Websites

 "Women don't live and die by hemlines," insists Grace Mirabella, founder of *Mirabella* magazine. True as this may be, the three leading themes of major women's magazines are fashion, sex, and health and fitness. Fortunately, there are alternatives to such amusing, though often mindless, airplane reading. Here are a few:

**MS.**
The grandmammy of feminist magazines, still going strong.
Subscribe: (800) 365-5232
Web:http://www.womweb.com/msnet.htm

**THE BODY POLITIC**
Monthly magazine focusing on the people and events involved the continuing struggle over reproductive freedom.
Subscribe: BodyPolitic@enews.com, or call (800) 403-6397
Web: http://www.enews.com/magazines/body

**ON THE ISSUES:**

**THE PROGRESSIVE WOMAN'S QUARTERLY**
A "feminist, humanist magazine of critical thinking."
Subscribe: (800) 783-4903
Web: http://www.igc.org/onissues

**WORKING MOTHER**
Essential reading for women who balance work and family.

To subscribe send name and address to: Working Mother, P.O. Box 5239, Harlan, IA 51593-2740
Web: http://www.womweb.com/wmlife.htm

One medium where there are fewer obstacles to women's voices is the do-it-yourself world of the Web. Type a query of 'feminist magazines' into your favorite search engine and you're sure to come up with a healthy list of websites. The content ranges from the whimsical to the pensive; here are a few worth visiting:

**WOMEN LEADERS ONLINE**
Dedicated to mobilizing women over the Net and stopping the "antiwoman" agenda of the radical right.
http://wlo.org/

**BRILLO**
"For today's cranky feminist"
http://www.virago-net.com/brillo/

**GEEKGIRL**
A "cyberfeminist zine" from australia
http://www.next.com.au/spyfood/geekgirl/

**GURL**
"Girl" culture on the web
http://www.tsoa.nyu.edu/gURL/

**CATT'S CLAWS**
A "frequently appearing" feminist newsletter; also available by E-mail.
http://www.city-net.com/~lmann/women/is/cattsclaws.html

# WHERE ARE THE FEMINISTS IN TALK RADIO?

**LAURA FLANDERS**

Radio relies heavily upon the imagination—the listener's and the speaker's. For my part, I picture that I am part of a rising tide of radio radicals, "speaking truth to power." I believe that the female audio warriors are out there, ranged against the bigots of Rush-radio. But that's not the reality.

I grew up listening to radio. The radio of my childhood was replete with soft-spoken British hosts. The women I remember were mellifluous story tellers on *Listen with Mother*, a daily dose of Nanny England—and a ghastly show. But tuning in to afternoon programming stateside almost makes me homesick for Nanny. At least she didn't directly threaten your life. Here, the typical lineup features Bob Grant (African-Americans are "savages"); Rush Limbaugh ("I like the women's movement—especially from behind"); and G. Gordon Liddy, whose only regret about Watergate is having been caught.

Women commentators barely have a toehold in this bad-boys club. We have always had to fight our way into the most lucrative areas of broadcasting. "The only women who are generally accepted are helpers," complains Carole Hemingway, a feminist with 20 year's radio experience in Los Angeles and New York.

The most widely heard women talk show hosts in the United States are therapist-entertainers: psychologist Joy Browne and psychotherapist Laura Schlessinger are heard on between 150 and 300 stations each. Along with their

shows, some of the most popular ones are those like Deborah Ray's *Here's to Your Health*, and the widely syndicated, cheerleader-voiced Laura Lee.

About 5 percent of the members of the National Association of Radio Talk Show Hosts (NARTSH) are women— or about 150 out of 2,000. Are these women wavelength warriors? Not really. The women who are playing in the Lim-

baugh-land of nationally syndicated "power" talk shows can be counted on one hand. In 1995, of the top 25 "most important hosts" cataloged by the trade rag *Talkers Magazine*, only five were female: Gloria Allred, Joy Browne, Blanquita Cullum, Victoria Jones, and Laura Schlessinger.

*continued on page 124*

NICOLE HOLLANDER © 1992

*continued from page 123*

Cullum's a female audio warrior, for sure, but not quite the teammate I had in mind. Mexican-American and a single mother, Cullum broadcasts on 45 high-powered stations across the country. Resolutely conservative, her show's easy listening for those on the right.

There are some liberals out there. At least three of the top 100 on the Talkers 1996 list considered themselves liberal— Allred of Los Angeles, Jones of Washington, DC, and Lynn Samuels of New York. Allred, who is a lawyer, lost her daily drive-time gig on KABC Los Angeles six weeks after she staged a protest at the 1995 NARTSH convention when G. Gordon Liddy received the annual free-speech award. She was replaced by a conservative man.

Where programmers are insulated from the constant demands of commercial advertising, the picture is a bit less bleak. National Public Radio boasts 50 women on the air, working as anchors, hosts, and correspondents. But increasingly, NPR is dependent on corporate underwriters, and a study published in 1993 by FAIR showed that the spectrum of opinion on the network barely differed from what you find in the commercial sphere.

The only network that rejects corporate underwriting is Pacifica Radio, where there are some genuine alternatives. In February 1996, Pacifica launched a new state-of-democracy program called *Democracy Now!*, hosted by intrepid investigative reporter Amy Goodman. Her program is entirely dependent on foundation funding and listener contributions.

Which brings us to economics. None of the big women's foundations have funded sympathetic media. And that's the real reason I don't hear many soulmates on the air.

Blanquita Cullum was launched with help from Holland Coors, of the conservative beer-brewing family. Beverly La-Haye, president of Concerned Women for America (CWA), uses her syndicated radio show to sell *Family Voice*, her magazine, and fund-raise for her group, which now claims 600,000 members (nearly three times the official size of NOW). Couldn't feminist financiers do the same? Why aren't they out there supporting the programs we need and building networks at the same time? (*EXTRA!*)

*Laura Flanders is cohost/co-producer of* CounterSpin, *the FAIR radio show.*

# SOMEBODY ELSE'S CHILDREN

### ROBIN TEMPLETON

Typically, the mainstream media recognize young people only in order to blame them for social ills like crime and unsafe sex. Meanwhile, the media rarely credit youth with the power to affect positive change or with relevant perspectives on crucial issues of the day. Unrealistic and unfair media coverage gives credence to myths about young people, keeping them locked out of policy debates that directly impact the future of young and old alike. Writer and media critic Mike Males

characterizes the scenario in his 1996 book, *The Scapegoat Generation*

"Unplanned pregnancies. HIV infection and AIDS, other sexually transmitted diseases. Cigarettes, alcohol and drug abuse. Eating disorders. Violence. Suicide. Car crashes." The 22-word lead-in to a *Washington Post* report sums up today's media image of the teenager: 30 million 12 through 19-year olds toward whom any sort of moralizing and punishment can be safely directed, by liberals and conservatives alike. Today's media

portrayals of teen employ the same stereotypes once [and still] openly applied to unpopular racial and ethnic groups: violent, reckless, hypersexed, welfare-draining, obnoxious, ignorant.

Following are several media stereotypes about youth:

**Media Myth**
Across the country, youth crime rates are rising disproportionately faster than those of adults.

**Reality**
Overall arrests for violent crime of juveniles and adults increased at essentially the same rate from 1965 to 1992. It's adults, not juveniles, who drive overall

crime rates: 81 percent of arrests are of people over 18 years old. (National Center on Institutions and Alternatives and Center on Juvenile and Criminal Justice, 1996)

Teenagers do not respond to poverty more or less violently than do grown-ups; teenagers just experience more poverty. Once the poverty factor is removed, "teen violence" disappears, and with it all the agonized why-why-why saturating the media and political landscape (usually fanned by experts who should know better) whenever the cameras roll another teen murder scene. (Mike Males, *The Scapegoat Generation*, 1996)

When youth appear on the news, it is most often as the victim or perpetrator of violence. In a recent media analysis, the single largest topic of stories involving youth was specific violent crimes, their aftermath in the courts, and the potential for violence. Meanwhile only 6 percent of all the stories about youth in this study featured youth accomplishments, and few of these stories were about local youth. (Berkeley Media Studies Group, 1995)

Six states account for more than half of the country's juvenile homicide arrests, and just four cities account for nearly a third of the juvenile homicide arrests. The problem is so site-specific

that fully 82 percent of the counties in the United States had zero known juvenile homicide offenders in 1994. Also, most arrests for juvenile crime are for nonviolent offenses. (Center on Juvenile and Criminal Justice, 1996)

**Media Myth**

U.S. cities are war zones plagued by gang-affiliated, gun-toting black and brown young men and the criminal justice system is too lenient on young offenders.

**Reality**

The violent crime rate for white juveniles increased 419 percent from 1965 to 1992, compared to 147.5 percent for African-American juveniles, although the African-American juvenile arrest rate was substantially higher during this entire period. (National Center on Institutions and Alternatives and Center on Juvenile Crime and Justice, 1996)

**Media Myth**

Teenagers are sex-crazed and irresponsibly promiscuous.

**Reality**

The strange logic of the modern media's attack on adolescents is nowhere stranger than its portrayal of "teen" sexuality. Consider its jargon: When a child is born to a father over age 20 and a teenage mother, the phenomenon is called "children having children." When an adult pays a teenager for sex, it is "teenage prostitution." (Mike Males, *The Scapegoat Generation*, 1996)

*continued on page 126*

*continued from page 125*

Sixty percent of the women raped in the United States are under the age of 18. (National Victims Center)

## Media Myth

American kids are spoiled materialists. For instance, *CBS Evening News* recently covered a new disease facing the country: spoiled children. "It has been called 'affluenza,'" related CBS correspondent Bob McNamara, "an American disease caused by too much money, too many material things and too few limits, and it has some parents worried that their generosity may be creating a generation of cash-happy kids...American kids are cashing in, commanding everything from designer clothes ...to elaborate birthday parties."

## Reality

McNamara neglects to mention the fact that the United States has the highest rate of child poverty in the industrialized world, with 22 percent of all children living below the official poverty line. The number of U.S. children living in poverty increased by 2.2 million between 1979 and 1990. The child poverty rate among whites increased from 12 to 16 percent, among Latinos from 28 to 38 percent, and among African-Americans from 41 to 45 percent. (U.S. Government Statistics)

## Media Myth

Young Americans, characterized as "Generation X," are apathetic and apolitical.

## Reality

High-school-aged people in 1991 were nearly two-and-a-half times more likely to participate in a political demonstration than high-school-age people in 1968. (*Harper's* Index)

*Robin Templeton, formerly of UNPLUG, is program associate at the Institute for Alternative Journalism.*

## Here's Lookin' at YO!

What does it take to get the media to look like you, to respect your voice, to recognize your existence? In the case of a group of young people in the California Bay Area, it took creating media by and for themselves. The bimonthly newspaper *Youth Outlook (YO!)* was founded in 1991 through self-determination and in direct response to cutbacks in high school journalism classes and censorship on campus. *YO!* is also a model response to the systematic exclusion of young people's perspectives and voices from the mainstream and progressive media.

"What's different about *YO!*," explains associate editor Andrea N. Jones, "is that those who are generally the subjects in the media do the speaking." *YO!*'s journalistic approach is to position young people as experts. The quality of the newspaper proves this position effective. *YO!* covers complex social issues like spirituality, drug use, and sexuality with a level of integrity and an absence of sensationalism that "adult" media would do well to emulate.

Unlike most media opportunities for youth, *YO!* pays its writers and artists. It's also widely expanding the scope of its audience. *YO!* recently launched a sophisticated Web page, instantly broadening its "circulation" nationally and internationally. In its hometown, *YO!* involves incarcerated youth in the process of publishing through a writing program called "The Beat Within," which it runs in conjunction with the San Francisco Youth Guidance Center. —Robin Templeton

*Contact: 450 Mission Street, Room 506, San Francisco, CA 94105; phone: (415)243-4364; website: www.pacificnews.org/yo/*

## Ideas in Action... MCEA

"Start the Presses," a student guide published by the conservative think tank Madison Center for Educational Affairs (MCEA), makes apparent the right wing's dedication to preserving its power and prestige for the long haul:

MCEA wants to supply you with intellectual ammunition and publishing support. It has designed the Collegiate Network to help its members achieve excellence in their writing and appearance and stability in their finances... Even though you do not yet belong to the Network, you should not hesitate to make use of the toll-free line as you set up your organization and start planning your first issue.... Your primary source of revenue will be *local advertising*.... Your secondary source of revenue will be *private donations*, including MCEA grants, as well as alumni who you identify as sympathetic to your cause. MCEA may also know friendly benefactors in your area and can help you make important contacts with your *alumni*. The Collegiate Network is a powerful *practical* resource for your publication...it connects you with like-minded people who can offer you support and who are excellent contacts for internships and jobs in politics and media.

## What's the Progressive Press Doing to Invest in the Future?

If media are to be democratized, young people must be included in every step of the process. Some of the things we can do to guarantee the inclusion of youth in the independent, progressive media include:

* mentoring
* paid internships
* supporting youth media through subscriptions and ads
* publishing/broadcasting youth's opinions
* including youth on advisory boards and panels

—Robin Templeton, Institute for Alternative Journalism

*See the Resource Directory for a short list of youth media resources.*

# OUT OF THE CLOSET AND INTO THE HEADLINES

## THE GAY AND LESBIAN ALLIANCE AGAINST DEFAMATION (GLAAD)

Accurate, balanced, and diverse images of lesbians, gay men, bisexual, and transgender people have been largely missing from most forms of mass communication in the United States. Traditionally, the few projects that included portrayals of lesbians or gay men were mostly negative or stereotypical, while bisexuals and transgender people simply never appeared.

Societal disapproval, institutionalized discrimination, and ignorance have always played a major role in the entertainment industry's inaccurate portrayals of gay people. In Hollywood, this has historically meant the restriction of honest, open lesbian and gay imagery on the silver screen. The Production Code of 1930 banned all mention of homosexuality from films. While the ban was lifted in 1961, it gave rise to portrayals that were stereotypical, frequently treating gay men and lesbians as sick or perverse.

In 1968 the code was abolished in favor of the current ratings system, and while things have improved, the same old stereotypes still show up. Movies tend to be about the "problem" of homosexuality or of AIDS rather than

*continued on page 128*

### Ideas in Action... Fair Coverage

A fair press cannot exclude groups of people because they might hurt media profits but claim to reflect society.

A fair press cannot overrely on official sources, who have their own axes to grind, and claim to offer objective news.

A fair press cannot preclude members of minority groups from covering their own communities because editors fear they will be any more biased than another reporter.

A fair press cannot exclude minority voices from the ranks of newsroom management and claim to support equality and justice.

A fair press cannot perpetuate derogatory stereotypes and consider itself an accurate source of news.

A fair press must find ways to reflect all segments of society.

—From *Straight News: Gays, Lesbians and the News Media,* by Edward Alwood.

*continued from page 127*

about people who happen to be lesbian, gay, bisexual, or transgender. Hateful imagery of gay people still shows up in comedies as a mean-spirited attempt at cheap laughs.

Within the news media the story has been much the same. Where once journalists, editors, and reporters ignored lesbians and gay men unless there were being demonized or stereotyped, gays are now becoming more and more recognized as citizens whose lives are worth covering.

Recently, great strides have been made toward more accurate and inclusive representation. By the early 1990s, mainstream films and television programming were beginning to include realistic and positive lesbian and gay characters. It has been critical that some popular figures, such as actors Amanda Bearse, Dan Butler, and Mitchell Anderson; recording artists k.d. lang, Melissa

Etheridge, Elton John; directors John Schlesinger and Gus Van Sant; and industry leader David Geffen, have come out and speak publicly about their lives.

Like Hollywood, news media representation has improved due to increased visibility by gay people nationwide, combined with a growing and increasingly media savvy political movement. Members of the media have begun to come out, and the National Lesbian and Gay Journalists Association represents their issues and concerns.

As we continue to struggle for civil rights we have become the target of increased homophobia and violence. Our enemies not only wield baseball bats but also place antigay referendums on ballots, attack us at local school boards, and deny us the right to legal marriage and open service in the military. On the positive side, all these issues have gained national media attention and demand greater comprehension and sensitivity in the press.

## COMMENT

*Ironically, it seems certain that the lesbian and gay press will benefit from the hard times facing general-interest news outlets, with the genre continuing to grow both in number of publications and total circulation. For as the captains of the American media shift from appealing to the masses to appealing to specialized audiences, affluent gay people clearly will be very desirable. What is not so clear is to what degree this phenomenon will benefit the [gay and lesbian] movement. How much are gay civil rights hastened by gay people learning how to bleach their teeth and decorate their homes? Such material is not likely to persuade Congress to create federal protection for lesbians and gay men who have been fired from their jobs. What's more, as the lifestyle magazines lure major advertisers to their pages, they make life more difficult for local news-oriented publications that provide high-quality news content, as the big companies prefer to place their ads on slick paper than on newsprint. Out (a national gay glossy magazine) boasts a circulation of 100,000; the largest of the newspapers, the* Bay Area Reporter, *struggles to maintain a third of that figure. The competitive world of the media today, whether aiming for a broad audience or a narrow audience, continues to be defined by the survival of the fattest.*

—Rodger Streitmatter, author of *Unspeakable: The Rise of the Gay and Lesbian Press in America*

---

**Scary but True...**

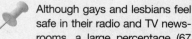 Newspapers are largely hospitable to gays and lesbians but they also harbor a palpable undercurrent of bias. On coverage of gay issues and concerns, the nation's newspapers get a grade of "mediocre" (1990 ASNE survey)

 Although gays and lesbians feel safe in their radio and TV newsrooms, a large percentage (67 percent) have heard derogatory remarks about people of same-sex orientation. In addition, statistics show a higher degree of satisfaction at work and with coverage among employees at public stations versus commercials stations.

A 1996 survey by ASNE, representing all daily newspaper journalists, indicates that despite the increase in quantity of articles about gays and lesbians, a large percentage considered the quality of coverage as "poor."

—NLGJA and the Radio and Television News Director Foundation

## Red, Hot and Cool

 *Red Hot and Cool: Stolen Moments* is a documentary about AIDS in the African-American community, including commentary by leaders like Cornel West and music from artists including Herbie Hancock and Digable Planets. Perfect for broadening the often narrow demographic focus of public TV? PBS didn't think so: It told producers of the program (which was funded by the Independent Television Service) that the show lacked "a broad impact" and that it was unlikely to "hold audiences or draw a significant viewership." Isn't PBS designed to air programming that won't necessarily get high ratings, and isn't that why they've been running *Masterpiece Theater* all these years? "They say they want to broaden their audience base, but they really don't want to do what they need to do to make it happen," *Red, Hot and Cool* executive producer John Carlin told *Variety*. "Public television is like one of those apparent contradictions, like jumbo shrimp."

Contact: the Red Hot organization at (212) 343-0043; 73 Spring Street, Suite 602, New York, NY 10012.

For more information on utilizing independent video and/or public television for community campaigns, contact:

Independent Television Service at (612) 225-9035, ext. 226; 190 E. 5th Street, Suite 200, St. Paul, MN 55101; Fax: (612) 225-9102.

# Media Makers: A List of Contacts
### Noncommercial Gay TV, Radio, Publications and Websites

**In The Life** is an hour-long bimonthly newsmagazine that airs on 70 PBS stations across the country. Contact ITL at (212) 255-6012.

**Dyke TV** is a weekly half-hour newsmagazine produced by and for lesbians and is on public-access stations in 61 cities. Contact Dyke TV at P.O. Box 55, Prince Street Station, New York, NY, 10012, (212) 343-9335.

**This Way Out** (TWO) is a weekly syndicated radio program currently on 85 stations in the United States and Canada. Contact TWO at P.O. Box 38327, Los Angeles, CA 90038-0327; (213) 874-0874; E-mail: tworadio@aol.com.

**Network Q** is a weekly half-hour "on-the-road" program available to public TV stations via satellite. Contact Network Q at (800)368-0638, or through the Southeastern Arts Media and Education project, 1083 Austin Ave., #203, Atlanta, GA 30307, (404) 523-4600.

**Gay Cable Network** (GCN) produces six weekly half-hour shows aired on lease-access and public-access stations in New York, plus a national interest *Gay America* newsmagazine in eight U.S. cities. Contact GCN at (212) 727-8850.

There are more than 2,600 publications serving the gay and lesbian community, including newsletters, tabloids, newspapers and glossy magazines (according to *Unspeakable: The Rise of The Gay and Lesbian Press in America*, Rodger Streitmatter, Faber and Faber, 1995). Numerous established publications lead the pack, including Out, (212) 334-9119; Advocate, (213) 871-1225; Washington Blade, (202) 797-7000; Bay Area Reporter, (415) 861-5019; Windy City Times in Chicago (312) 397-0025; and Gay Community News in Boston, (617) 262-6969. Additional titles include:

* *Transgender*, published by IFGE, P.O. Box 229, Waltham, MA 02254-0229, (617)899-2212; E-mail: ifge@world.std.com.

* *Anything That Moves,* about bisexual issues and people, 1360 Mission St., #200, San Francisco, CA 94103; E-mail: qswitch@igc.apc.org.

* *InsideOut*, published for queer youth, P.O. Box 460268, San Francisco, CA 94146; E-mail: insideout5@aol.com.

* *POZ*, featuring news on AIDS and HIV, 349 W. 12 St., New York, NY 10014; E-mail: pozmag@aol.com.

* *COLOURS,* published for the black gay and lesbian community, 1108 Locust St., 1 Floor, Philadelphia, PA 19107, (215)629-1852; E-mail: colours@critpath.org.

\* *Girlfriends,* published for hip lesbians, HAF Enterprises, 3415 Cesar Chavez, Ste. 101, San Francisco, CA 94110, (415) 648-9464; E-mail: staff@gfriends.com.

Among the scores of irreverent zines serving the queer community are Diseased Pariah News, (510) 533-3412; E-mail: dpnmail@netcom.com; Girljock, P.O. Box 882728, San Francisco, CA 94188-2723, (415) 282-6833; E-mail: girljock1@aol.com; and RFD (for rural queers and other radical fairies), Short Mountain Collective, Rt. 1, Box 84A, Liberty, TN 37095

## Select Queer Cybermedia

**Digital Queers** (DQ) works with gay, lesbian, bisexual, and transgender non-profit activist groups to use digital technology more effectively. Contact DQ at 584 Castro St., #560, San Francisco, CA 94114, (415) 252-6282; E-mail: digiqueers@aol.com, http://www.dq.org.

**AIDS Treatment News**, a highly respected and comprehensive AIDS newsletter, is now online through Immunet at http://www.immunet.org/atn, and at its own master site of AIDS links, http://www.aidsnews.org.

**PlanetOut**, a queer global megasite featuring news, entertainment, chat rooms, countless community and political groups, and more. Highlight is PopcornQ, an on-line home for gay and lesbian film fans and professionals. Contact PlanetOut at (415) 547-2800; http://www.planetout.com.

**Queer Resources Directory**, the "mother of all gay/lesbian/bisexual/transgender information pages on the Internet," is a megalibrary of information including political, social, organizational, sexual, and legal issues and calendar of events; http://www.qrd.org//QRD.

## Center for Media & the Black Experience

The Center for Media & the Black Experience (CMBE) is a media-monitoring non-profit group that empowers the black community with tools and techniques to understand the media and create its own independent media. As a response to the skewed reporting in the predominantly white media, CMBE encourages content that more accurately reflects the black experience.

In its on-line publication, HYPE, CMBE confronts such issues as the European media's reaction to the crowning of a black woman as Miss Italy, America's obsession with Buckwheat from *Our Gang*, and a porno movie called *Malcolm XXX*. CMBE also distributes a list, "Twelve Questions to Take With You to the Movies," an annual report that cri-tiques the way dictionaries handle the words "black" and "white" and other race-related listings, and an on-line list of resources pertaining to blacks and the media.

Contact: Yemi Toure, Center for Media & the Black Experience, 4357 Luxembourg Drive, Decatur GA 30034, Tel/Fax: 770-322-6653 E-mail: ytoure@mindspring.com. HYPE is at http://www.webcom.com/nattyreb/hype.

# 3. Incredible Shrinking Media: Radio

## RABID RADIO

### DON HAZEN

Corporate mergers that involve TV stations get a lot of press, but the enormous transformation in the radio industry has received scant attention beyond the business pages. For decades, the rule was that one company could own no more than five AM and FM stations in a single market. The Telecommunications Act changed all that, allowing one company to own as many as eight stations in one market.

Into the breach stepped Westinghouse, recent buyer of CBS. While in the process of trying to separate the industrial parts of the company from its growing media holdings, the new media giant, according to *Media Week*, in one fell swoop became the biggest radio company in the world, swallowing Infinity Broadcasting, owner of 43 stations for approximately $5 billion. Westinghouse's total largesse: seventy-nine stations in 17 markets, 64 of the stations in the top-ten markets, including six of the 10 highest-billing stations in the country.

Because the West-inghouse holdings were so dominant in three markets, waivers had to be secured from the FCC to allow them to temporari-ly enjoy holdings beyond even the most generous provisions of the law.

As a result of the merger, the future of right-wing and shock radio in the United States is more secure as well. Infinity, which itself had been consoli-dating for years, syndicates G. Gordon Liddy—the same G. Gordon Liddy who has counseled listeners on how to shoot federal law-enforcement agents—as well as shock jock Howard Stern.

As Jeff Cohen observes: "Travel around the country and you'll find radio stations whose talk-show line ups offer one conservative after another; on some stations, Rush Limbaugh sounds like a liberal compared with those he shares the air. Add to that the abolition by Reagan of the Fairness Doctrine, which has made it next to impossible to challenge 'all right, all the time' radio."

Limbaugh is heard daily on roughly 650 radio and 350 TV stations. His radio audience is about 20 million people. Limbaugh is the first and only person in the history of U.S. television allowed 30-minute partisan monologues to attack his political enemies without any counterpoint.

*—Don Hazen is the director of the Institute for Alternative Journalism.*

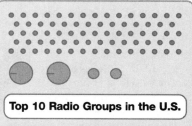

### Top 10 Radio Groups in the U.S.

| Rank/Group or Firm | Listeners | Stations |
| --- | --- | --- |
| 1. CBS Radio | 42,809,800 | 79 |
| 2. Evergreen | 19,907,800 | 42 |
| 3. Jacor | 15,381,400 | 113 |
| 4. American Radio | 14,128,800 | 93 |
| 5. Chancellor | 12,671,400 | 51 |
| 6. Clear Channel | 12,191,600 | 101 |
| 7. ABC Radio | 11,715,400 | 21 |
| 8. SFX | 10,232,200 | 75 |
| 9. Cox | 7,880,300 | 41 |
| 10. Emmix | 7,181,900 | 16+ |

Source: Who Owns What (Arbitron Ratings Company), February 3, 1997

# RADIO HISTORY

### ROBERT MCCHESNEY

Historically, the rise of crucial new communication technologies like broadcasting have generated national public debate. It was as a result of such debate, for example, that a system of public broadcasting was established. When radio broadcasting emerged in the 1920s, few thought it had any commercial potential. Many of broadcasting's pioneers were nonprofit organizations interested in public service. It was only in the late 1920s that capitalists began to sense that through network operation and commercial advertising, radio broadcasting could generate substantial profits. Through their immense power in Washington, these commercial broadcasters were able to dominate the Federal Radio Commission. As a result, the scarce number of air channels were effectively turned over to them with no public and little congressional deliberation on the matter.

It was in the aftermath of this commercialization of the airwaves that elements of United States society coalesced into a broadcast reform movement that attempted to establish a dominant role for the nonprofit and noncommercial sector in United States broadcasting. These opponents of commercialism came from education, religion, labor, civic organizations, women's groups, journalism, farmer's groups, civil libertar-

ians, and intellectuals. The reformers attempted to tap into the intense public disdain for radio commercialism in the years before 1934, when Congress annually considered legislation for the permanent regulation of radio broadcasting. These reformers argued that if private interests controlled the medium and their goal was profit, no amount of regulation or self-regulation could overcome the bias built into the system. Commercial broadcasting, the reformers argued, would downplay controversial, pro–working class, and provocative public-affairs programming and emphasize whatever fare would sell the most products for advertisers.

The reform movement disintegrated after the passage of the Communications Act of 1934, which established the Federal Communications Commission (FCC). The 1930s reformers did not lose to the commercial interests, however, on a level playing field. The radio lobby dominated because it was able to keep most Americans ignorant or confused about the communication policy matters then under discussion in Congress through their control of key elements of the news media and their sophisticated public-relations aimed at the rest of the press and the public. In addition, commercial broadcasters became a force that few politicians wished to antagonize; almost all of the congressional champions of broadcast reform in 1931–1932 were defeated in their reelection attempts, a fate not lost on those who entered the next Congress. With the defeat of the reformers, the industry's claim that commercial broadcasting was inherently American went on to set the context for the development of subsequent communication technologies including facsimile, FM radio, and television in the 1940s.

*Robert McChesney is the author of* Corporate Media and the Threat to Democracy.

# PROGRESS IN PROGRESSIVE RADIO

### SEETA GANGADHARAN

In the last decade, there has been a marked expansion in the quality and diversity of programming available to the range of noncommercial and community radio stations. Hard-hitting point-of-view shows as well as successful ethnic efforts offer a contrast to some of the very popular but more mainstream offerings of National Public Radio.

Progressive radio—distinct from public and commercial radio—"has a mandate to put out issues which don't normally survive in a commercial climate," says Peggy Law, executive producer of the National Radio Project.

Following is a list of nationally syndicated progressive programs:

**Alternative Radio** Boulder, Colorado
David Barsamian, Director

Alternative Radio spans the "progressive left," featuring interviews with the likes of Noam Chomsky and Ralph Nader. This weekly half-hour show is produced by David Barsamian and broadcast on community stations.

**FAIR CounterSpin** New York
Laura Flanders and Janine Jackson, Executive Producers and CoHosts

*continued on page 136*

Chairman: Michael Jordan, 59

Michael Jordan has transformed Westinghouse, long known for its industrial operations and household appliances, into a major media company over the past several years. In November 1996, he announced plans to spin off the company's industrial businesses by creating a separate company while maintaining a leaner, meaner media company. That company is anchored by CBS, bought for $5.4 billion, and Infinity Broadcasting (the largest radio network in the country), purchased for about $5 billion.

According to the *Washington Post*, Jordan plans to parlay Westinghouse's radio and television holdings into profitable advertising packages, saying the combination is critical to building "a dominant advertising force in the marketplace."

**FMR Corp. (6.5%),** parent company of Fidelity Investments, mutual funds manager

**Nuclear power plant design and maintinance:** Energy Systems (49% of the world's nuclear plants use Westinghouse engineering)

**Westinghouse Pension Management**

**Waste disposal** (including hazardous and radioactive):

Resource Energy Systems
Scientific Ecology Group
Westinghouse Remediation Services
GESCO
(This branch of the company also operates 4 government-owned nuclear facilities, including Savannah River, installed reactors in Sea Wolf, the navy's new nuclear submarines, and refueled the U.S.S. Enterprise, the first nuclear aircraft carrier. It also recently won a contract to dispose of 2,253 tons of stockpiled chemical weapons at an Army base in Anniston, Alabama.)

**WPIC Corporation** (insurance, communications, financing)

**Mobile refrigeration:**
Thermo King

**Parts for electric power plants:**
Power Generation

**Bankers Trust**

**Brandywine Asset Management**
(investment advisors)

**Communications and information:**
Telephone, network and wireless communications systems; security systems

**Group W Satellite**
Communications
(satellite distribution of TV programming)

# Westinghouse/CBS

**Cable:**
CMT: Country Music Television (33% owners with Gaylord Entertainment)
Home Team Sports (a regional network in the mid-Atlantic)
TNN: The Nashville Network (does marketing for this Gaylord-owned network)

**CBS Network News**
*Up to the Minute*
*CBS Morning News*
*CBS News Sunday Morning*
*60 Minutes*
*CBS This Morning*
*CBS Evening News With Dan Rather*
*Face the Nation*
*48 Hours*

**CBS**

**TV stations:**
KCNC-Denver
WFOR-Miami
KYW-Philadelphia
KUTV-Salt Lake City
WWJ-Detroit
WCCO-Minneapolis
WFRV-Green Bay, WI
KCBS-Los Angeles
WCBS-New York
WBBM-Chicago
KPIX-San Francisco
KDKA-Pittsburgh
WBZ-Boston
WJZ-Baltimore

**CBS Radio** (21 FM stations; 18 AM stations; 1,900 stations carry some CBS programming, about 450 carry *CBS News*)

*continued from page 133*

**CounterSpin** highlights investigative independent journalism and explores corporate influence on media, religious right, pundits' bloopers, sexism, racism, and homophobia in media coverage.

**National Radio Project**
Portola Valley, California
Peggy Law, Executive Director

**Making Contact** offers 29 minutes of unconventional wisdom, promoting "activism and determination" over "cynicism and passivity." Weekly forays include interviews with human-rights advocates to discussion of rising commercialism.

**National Native News** Anchorage, Alaska, Nellie Moore, Host

National Native News is a daily five-minute news program focussing on Native American political or informational news.

**Native America Calling**
Albuquerque, New Mexico
Harlan Mckosato, Associate Producer

An electronic talking circle, Native America Calling is a live weekly, one-hour call-in radio program broadcast to most tribal stations nationwide.

**Pacifica Network News** Washington, DC
Julie Drizin, Director

Pacifica Network News broadcasts a daily half-hour program which moves beyond the usual NPR public-media diet and focuses on labor, the American left, and more.

**RadioNation** New York

RadioNation, hosted by contributing editor Marc Cooper, is a weekly radio magazine review of news, politics, and culture. Writers and editors of *The Nation* magazine such as Katha Pollitt, Cornel West, and Molly Ivins are featured guests.

**Radio Bilingue** Fresno, California
Talk-show news program *Línea Abierta* and the short newscast program *Noticiero Latino* serve the Spanish-speaking community. Using the airwaves, these shows contribute to the cultural heritage and political education of Latinos.

**Radio for Peace International** Costa Rica
The only American left short-wave radio station, produces its own radio program titled **Far Right Radio Review**, and broadcasts out of its station based in Costa Rica.

**Second Opinion** Madison, Wisconsin
Matthew Rothschild, Host

Second Opinion, the half-hour show of *The Progressive,* features in-depth interviews with leading writers, scholars, and activists, including Edward Said, Barbara Ehrenreich, and Jane Slaughter.

**Women's International News Gathering Service (WINGS)** Austin, Texas
Frieda Werden, Executive Director

WINGS produces a half-hour show on women's news, rights, activists, and analysts. They also provide a radio training center in conjunction with Women's Access to Electronic Resources.

*Check the Resource Rolodex for contact information.*

---

## The Lowdown on Hightower

When the Disney Corporation laid off populist radio host Jim Hightower after his searing criticisms, he had no intention of being a former radio host.

Hightower's back on the air, broadcasting live from the Chat & Chew café located high atop Threadgill's World Headquarters in downtown Austin, Texas. He continues the kind of honest, no-nonsense hell-raising that got him unplugged from ABC in the first place.

Hightower's show airs live weekdays at noon (EST). The two-hour show is provocative, humorous, and outspoken, questioning a system that pays corporate CEOs tens of thousands of dollars an hour while knocking down the wages, hopes, and aspirations of America's workaday majority. The United Broadcasting Network and its affiliates bring Hightower's made-in-America populism to millions of listeners trying to make ends meet and wondering why neither political party speaks to them.

The call-in number for Hightower Radio is 800-TALK-YES. Hightower is the author of *There's Nothing in the Middle of the Road But Yellow Stripes and Dead Armadillos.*

# HOW PACIFICA AND KPFK ARE TRYING TO CATCH UP TO THE RADIO REVOLUTION

### JOE DOMANICK

Los Angeles Pacifica's KPFK station manager Mark Schubb and all of Pacifica are struggling to resurrect a station whose influence and avant-garde status is as dead today as the time when terms like "the left" and "counterculture" actually meant something. KPFK is struggling to regroup, as Rush Limbaugh continues to broadcast on 650 radio stations with 20 million listeners.

The political muscle of Limbaugh and his imitators flowed from a radio revolution that KPFK—along with its parent network, Pacifica, and a fragmented left—had completely missed.

As had the Democratic party, organized labor, the progressive foundations, and media-savvy Hollywood liberals. The new satellite-transmission technology, the FCC's repeal of the Fairness Doctrine, the increasing time commuters spend in automobiles, discontent with the homogeneity of mainstream political discourse, and the dismantling of federal regulations restricting monopolistic ownership—all had set the stage for the transformation of a flaccid medium into a powerful new political force. From 1990 to 1995, the number of talk-radio shows rose from 360 to more than 1,100 nationwide, as talk radio became to politics what television is to mass culture: transmitter, reflector, arbitrator, and trendsetter.

Today, as a shrewd, energized conservative moment continues to choke America's airwaves with proselytizing talk shows, Mark Schubb is battling to catch up with that revolution, trying to restore to its former glory a station that was once at the heart of the antiwar, civil rights, environmental, and women's movements.

Faced off against Schubb are a cadre of current and former KPFK employees and programmers. Threatened by change, they are deeply suspicious of Schubb and Pacifica's attempts to move away from narrowly focused, locally based programming toward national network shows, and of the network's current drive to double its humiliatingly small listenership. They are waging a bitter ideological battle to stop that from happening.

According to a recent yearlong study of talk radio conducted by the Annenberg School for Communication in Philadelphia, 18 percent of the adult population listens to talk radio, which is both highly political and highly skewed toward the right wing. (And according to a Times-Mirror study, a remarkably high proportion of talk-radio listeners are registered voters.)

Standing out from this very stacked deck, KPFK remains the only alternative to commercial and corporate-sponsored radio in Los Angeles, and the only progressive broadcast voice in LA, period. Which is why its fate is important.

Some important questions, as Marcos Frommer (a host of KPFK's morning program "Up For Air,") points out, are: How can Pacifica reach out to people in their 20s? How can it possibly compete with MTV? How do you attract people who are open and frustrated and sense that something's wrong, who feel that the economic system is unfair?

"Well, first of all," he continues, "you don't sit around and talk about left, left, left. People don't relate to that. You have to be able to craft a populist message that says it doesn't matter whether you're left or right, it's where you are on the economic ladder. Whose side are you on? Are you on the side of Wall Street, which literally cheers when AT&T lays off 40,000 workers? Or are you one of those laid-off workers?" (*LA Weekly*)

# RADIO STATIC

### NORMAN SOLOMON

Since the landmark Telecommunications Act of 1996 became law, a frenzy of radio deals has sent profiteers laughing all the way to the bank. Meanwhile, the victims—the American people—remain clueless.

The new law has opened the floodgates by lifting limits on how many radio stations a single firm can own.

The *Wall Street Journal* reports that "the telecommunications legislation has triggered a gold rush of the airwaves." Since President Bill Clinton signed the Telecommunications Act, radio mergers and buy-outs have been worth an average of half-a-billion dollars each week. A lot more than money is at stake. Those airwaves will be carrying whatever is most profitable—even if it's sleaze, hate talk, or misinformation.

Infinity Broadcasting, now owned by Westinghouse, has finalized a new five-year contract with its brightest syndicated star, the proudly crude Howard Stern. Now, Infinity plans to premiere "The Howard Stern Radio Network"—described by *Advertising Age* magazine as "24 hours of talk and music from jocks picked by Mr. Stern."

In the craven new world of megaradio, it doesn't matter that Stern often denigrates women on the air. Commercial success qualifies him to judge who else should be promoted on national radio.

America's 10,200 commercial radio stations don't provide much diversity. With few exceptions, the "news" and "public affairs" range from inadequate to pitiful.

Even many "public" stations have become homogenized. Political reporter Cokie Roberts sounds about the same whether she's reporting for National Public Radio or the Disney-owned ABC network. Despite more lengthy coverage and a more erudite style, the gist of NPR news increasingly resembles what's on commercial networks.

Yet radio is still enriching the lives of many listeners. Some independent-minded broadcasters are sticking to their mission.

Consider what one man named David Barsamian has accomplished. Ten years ago, with no money but lots of determination, working out of his home in Boulder, Colorado, he started a national program called *Alternative Radio*, featuring speeches by people rarely heard in mass media.

Today, *Alternative Radio* is a mainstay on more than 100 noncommercial radio stations, which receive the weekly hour-long program via satellite. The speakers are articulate, committed to progressive social change—and quite unlike what we usually hear on the radio.

In this high-tech era, radio retains the positive power to break through clichés that divide or confuse us. Unadorned, the sound of the human voice can resonate

Norman Solomon is a syndicated columnist and co-author of *Through the Media Looking Glass: Decoding Bias and Blather in the News.*

## Micro Radio Broadcasting: License? We Don't Need No Stinking License

 Imagine that you've finished a new issue of your zine. You take it around to all the local music stores and comic shops, hoping they'll stock it, but they keep asking the same question: "Where's your Federal Zine License?" If you're lucky (or corporate) enough to have one, you still have to watch it. Any slip up, any foul language, any deviation from the reams of government regulations, and you'll be banned from publishing for years with fines running in the tens of thousands of dollars.

Sounds like a funny scenario, but it's only a slight exaggeration of the way the federal government has been dominating radio for the last 80 years.

The system, as set up by the Federal Communications Commission, makes it impossible for the neighborhood broadcaster to legally operate. The FCC refuses to consider any license applications for stations under 100 watts, when most microstations operate in the .5- to 30-watt range. The FCC can prosecute and fine radio pirates for broadcasting without a permit. Even if small-wattage broadcasters were allowed to apply, the application fee is $2900. The same amount of money could build several microstations. The message is clear: Radio belongs in the hands of corporate broadcasters.

However, a few brave activists are challenging the FCC monolith. A couple of year ago, Mbanna Kantako from Springfield, Illinois, began broadcasting to Springfield's African-American community through neighborhood station WTRA, now known as Black Liberation Radio. With radio equipment that cost only a few hundred dollars and the help of his sons and neighborhood youth, he went on the air with community news, recorded speeches, and music programming. It wasn't until years later, when some kids in Mbanna's project were beaten up by local police and Mbanna allowed the youth to tell their story on the air, that the FCC and local cops showed up to shut the station down. Mbanna is still broadcasting though, and the $750 fine against him has not been collected.

Stephen Dunifer set up Free Radio Berkeley in 1993 to push the federal government for acceptance of community radio. It wasn't long before the FCC tuned in and slapped a $20,000 fine against him for unlicensed broadcasting. When the fine did not halt the broadcasts, the FCC filed a separate lawsuit seeking an injunction against the station.

"Unlicensed broadcasting creates chaos and anarchy on the airwaves." This old argument that the radio dial will be filled with electronic babble if microbroadcasters are allowed free access is just an FCC scare tactic. Low-wattage stations, like any other broadcasters, want the clearest signal possible, so it only makes sense that they transmit on a frequency not in use. (In January 1995, Judge Claudia Wilken handed down a decision denying the FCC injunction on constitutional grounds, forcing the FCC to reevaluate its policies—a breakthrough for microbroadcasters, their strongest victory to date.)

Microbroadcasters are sprouting up everywhere across the country. In the San Francisco Bay Area alone there are at least five stations that broadcast to their surrounding neighborhoods. The diversity and range of programming rivals the best college or alternative stations, and having a station set up just down the block gives the community a sense of empowerment. There's a much closer relationship between broadcaster and listener than you will ever find on any coast-to-coast Top-40 program.

—Christopher Becker, *Factsheet Five*

*Check the Resource Rolodex to find out how to contact Free Radio Berkeley.*

# Access

## Part IV

# INTRODUCTION

**JULIE WINOKUR**

In today's media, there is a wide discrepancy between who gets to make the news and the rest of us. This chapter looks at the people behind the scenes and in front of the camera—the ones who literally make the news—versus the people whose stories appear on screen.

The right wing, so busy crying elitism when it scapegoats the media, never owns up to the fact that it dominates the mainstream press. The notion that the media is an exclusive club isn't far from the truth, but the political, racial, and gender elitism of the press isn't liberal at all. It's predominantly white, male, and conservative.

This is evident on newspaper staffs, where the racial makeup doesn't reflect the demographics of the country, and in front of the camera, where women are still more often seen than heard. The authoritative figures that mainstream media appoint as our pundits belong to a club that wouldn't have most of us as its members.

Between the pundits and the rightwing think tanks, the conservative agenda has created an "echo chamber," notes Jeff Cohen, that firmly dominates public discourse. The reverberation is then amplified as fewer and fewer corporations own more and more newspapers. The profits that drive these papers don't take into account diversity or the responsibility for creating an informed citizenry.

That job is left to the independent press and the voices of public-interest journalism. Although the public harshly criticizes the press for irresponsibility, jaded views, and skewed reporting, there are still journalists who believe in a more noble calling, a drive to tell stories that have personal meaning and provide information that's useful for the people. These independent voices represent the savior of a profession reeling under the forces of both public opinion and commercial pressure.

# 1. Behind The Scenes

# THE UNBEARABLE WHITENESS OF PUBLISHING

### JAMES LEDBETTER

Writers and editors exercise tremendous control over a range of social and policy discussions, including the debate over affirmative action. Yet as an industry, publishing is whiter than most. And most popular magazines are as bad or worse than even the industry standard. "I was hired as senior associate editor at *Premiere* two years ago because Spike Lee insisted on having black journalists on his set," says writer and editor Veronica Chambers. "It was ridiculous, but I got a job. Before that, they didn't even have black cleaning people or black secretaries there."

According to Charles Mann Associates, a research firm that analyzed 1990 census data, the whitest occupation in New York (of those jobs with more than 500 workers) is "author." Almost 93 percent of New Yorkers who call themselves authors are white. The fifth whitest occupation—84.73 percent, just a shade darker than firefighter—is "reporter/editor."

Perhaps this comes as a surprise. After all, one of the most enduring American legends of the last decade or so is that the media is left-wing. (It used to be amusingly surreal to hear the media denounced as left-wing by the right-wing commentators who run most of the shows on the electronic media; by now it's routine.) And since, the conventional logic continues, the media is the enforcer of the left-wing's political correctness, it is probably overflowing with blacks, Latinos, Asians, and the white leftists who do their bidding. What else would you expect, since the media and publishing worlds are headquartered in New York City, the Minority Mecca?

At a time when surveys show that black readers are buying almost 160 million books a year, federal figures show that blacks number 3.4 percent of the managers, editors, and professionals who choose the nation's popular literature. (*New York Times*)

It ain't necessarily so. In fact, it ain't even remotely close.

It is the best estimate of more than a dozen magazine staffers I have interviewed that minority representation in the magazine industry in New York—including such black-targeted titles as *Essence*—hovers around 8 percent. That figure includes administrative and financial staff; the editorial makeup is estimated at 5 percent.

Making the question of publishing's glass ceiling more urgent is the fact that, of all marginalized groups, people of color are the last to pull a winning ticket in what Lani Guinier calls America's "oppression sweepstakes." When Andrew Sullivan was appointed editor of the *New Republic* in 1991, it was a breakthrough: a gay white man could edit a national political magazine without—in the eyes of all but the most squeamish observers—turning the magazine into a gay-specific sheet. With Tina Brown editing the *New Yorker*, white women, too, have "proven" that they can run a large-circulation general interest magazine. There have been no comparable publishing breakthroughs for blacks, Latinos, or Asians.

By comparison to magazines, most of New York's daily newspapers have done a decent job of increasing numbers of people of color in their workforces, even at high levels. Progress at the *New York Times* has been achingly slow, but the paper now boasts of a black op-ed columnist (Bob Herbert) and a black assistant managing editor (Gerald Boyd). Although the *Times*'s total minority representation is an iffy 13.7 percent—compared, say, to a surprising 18 percent at the *Wall Street Journal*—the paper of record has also shown itself willing to give prominent beats covering more than "minority" issues to reporters of color, such as James Dao in the Albany bureau, or Mireya Navarro on AIDS.

Under the best of circumstances, the print media's domination by whites would be a stain of dishonor. In today's political climate, the persistence of whiteness leaves the press ill-equipped to raise persuasive challenges to the accelerating attack on civil rights. It also corrodes credibility: the arrogance and denial that accompany discussion of race in publishing shed light on why the public holds the media in only slightly higher regard than it does used-car salesmen. (*Village Voice*)

*James Ledbetter is the media critic for the* Village Voice.

# WHO'S MAKING WHAT NEWS

### FARAI CHIDEYA

Looking at the many African-American television anchors on local stations and reading the strong black columnists who have joined media's comfortable upper ranks, it would be difficult at first to see just how skimpy the African-American presence in the media is. The reality? Although progress has been made, television and print media are still unwilling or unable to hire and retain black journalists—and are especially bad on pro-

moting people into positions where they actually can influence the news America sees and reads.

According to the American Society of Newspaper Editors, only 5 percent of reporters in the United States are black and 3.1 percent of newspaper managers are black. Forty-five percent of all newspapers do not employ any nonwhite reporters. And even major metropolitan dailies often employ shockingly few

*continued on page 144*

*continued from page 143*

reporters of color. For example, less than 15 percent of the staff of the *New York Times* is nonwhite, though the city is "majority-minority." Only 19 percent of the *Washington Post's* staff is nonwhite, though the District of Columbia is 66 percent black. Both of these prominent papers are national in distribution and scope. But their small rosters of nonwhite journalists contribute to the alienation of many readers in the cities in which they're based.

Three decades ago, following the Watts riots, Lyndon Johnson's Kerner Commission lambasted news organizations for being "shockingly backward" in not hiring, training, and promoting more African-Americans: "For if the media are to comprehend and then to project the Negro community, they must have the help of Negroes. If t he media are to report with understanding, wisdom, sympathy on the problems of the black man—for the two are increasingly intertwined—they must employ, promote and listen to Negro journalists." Those words were prophetic when they were first written and are still crucially important now. Unfortunately, it seems that the media will only show us the real face of black America when we compel it to do so. (Excerpted from *Don't Believe the Hype: Fighting Cultural Misinformation About African Americans*)

*Farai Chideya is a reporter for ABC News.*

Of 1,515 daily newspapers (53,711 newsroom employment), 45 percent of newspapers employ no ethnic minority journalists; 92.3 percent of all newsroom managers are white; 7.7 percent of all newsroom managers are ethnic minorities.

**Ethnic Composition of Newspaper Jounalists**

89.51 percent are white

5.38 percent are African-American

2.95 percent are Hispanic

1.83 percent are Asian-American

0.33 percent are Native American

Source: American Society of Newspaper Editors 1994 employment survey

## Unity

Almost 6,000 journalists of color, journalism students, news-industry leaders, and other supporters convened at Unity '94, a historic gathering in Atlanta, Georgia. The gathering was prompted by several undeniable trends affecting the news industry: the changing demographics in America; mounting criticism of racial stereotypes and inadequate coverage of minority communities; media-industry surveys revealing sluggishness in meeting diversity goals; and the emergence of a whole new generation of professional journalists of color in print and broadcast.

The Unity '94 Coalition included the Asian American Journalists Association, the National Association of Black Journalists, the National Association of Hispanic Journalists, and the Native American Journalists Association. Its overall objective was to "inspire and motivate the nation's media companies to fully embrace diversity."

Unity-related projects included News Watch: A Critical Look at Coverage of People of Color, which offers analysis and suggestions from a multicultural team of writers and researchers who reviewed representations of minorities in newspapers, magazines, television, and radio.

Unity '99, the second joint convention, will take place July 7–10, 1999, in Seattle, Washington, and will focus on more cross-cultural interaction. In the meantime Unity '99 will build momentum during the intervening years with projects devoted to workplace retention, education and recruitment, and coverage.
—Diane Yen-Mei Wong, with assistance from Connie Rivera

For more information on Unity '99, contact Connie Rivera, Unity '99 Program Coordinator, at (206) 828-4293; 428-10th Avenue NE, #E-201 Kirkland, WA 98033.

Black journalists see less opportunity for advancement and more racial backlash in the newsroom than other minority journalists, and more than a quarter want to leave the business, according to a 1994 survey of 760 members of minority journalists groups.

 Hispanic journalists are the most critical of the way their community is portrayed, with 70 percent saying the news media are doing a poor or very poor job. Sixty-two percent of Asian-American journalists, and 58 percent of black and Native American journalists give the media such low marks. (*Washington Post*)

 Minority participation is severely limited in journalism education. In the 1990s, fewer than 5 percent of all journalism and mass communication educators are minorities; if one counts only those that are tenured, the number drops significantly. Courses to teach students how to cover underrepresented communities are virtually nonexistent. (Mercedes Lynn de Uriarte, associate professor of journalism and Latin American Studies at the University of Texas)

 In 1978, the newspaper industry set a goal that by the year 2000, American newsrooms should be as racially diverse as the American population. While newspapers have made some progress toward the goal, executives say they still have a long way to go. The American Society of Newspaper Editors, which requires members to submit annual figures on minority employment, reported that 10.49 percent of journalists at daily newspapers in 1993 were African-American, Hispanic, Asian-American, or Native American. The figure is up from 3.95 percent in 1978. (*New York Times*)

 At a time when major houses are rushing to satisfy the burgeoning Hispanic market with new imprints, Spanish romance novels, and self-help primers, Hispanics make up 1.8 percent of the professional and executive work force in publishing, according to the latest federal figures. There are so few Hispanic employees, in fact, that it's not unusual that a major publishing house like HarperCollins, a unit of the News Corp., runs its new Libros line of Hispanic literature without a Hispanic editor involved in the project. (*New York Times*)

# 2. Who Gets to Speak

## COMMENT

*It is in the three main opinion-shaping forums — talk radio, TV punditry, and op-ed pages — that progressive views are smothered. The most widely-distributed columnists (100 to 300 newspapers each) are largely right-wing: George Will, James J. Kilpatrick, William Safire, William Buckley. The most distributed columnists who aren't on the right tend to be centrists: writers like David Broder and the late Mike Royko. Progressive columnists are underexposed.*

*The same goes for progressive TV pundits. In national debates on TV each day, you hear fire-breathers on the right like Bob Novak and Mona Charen — but the other side is generally represented by moderates like Al Hunt of the* Wall Street Journal. *Or Mark Shields, a centrist whose promotional material describes him as being "free of any political tilt." After representing the "left" on CNN's Crossfire for more than six years, Michael Kinsley described himself to a* Washington Post *reporter as a "wishy-washy moderate."*

*— Jeff Cohen, executive director of FAIR*

# ADVENTURES IN PUNDIT LAND

### JILL NELSON

As average consumers become increasingly alienated from the overwhelming task of ingesting, digesting, and understanding what is going on in their community or state, not to mention the world, it is not surprising that as a culture we have become more dependent on those eminences known as pundits. These people are essentially interpreters of information, and in recent years they have proliferated, defining

for Americans not only what is news but, just as dangerously, what it means and what we should think about it. Not very long ago, being white and being male were requisites for eligibility for pundit status. More recently, in a largely cynical bow to diversity and demographics, the world of pundits has expanded a few inches to include some women, some people of color, and an occasional voice to the left of the far right, although all of the above are few and far between on the punditing circuit.

Pundits who are female, of color, left of center, or all of the above often function as sane voices in an insane wilderness, doing their best to get a word in edgewise before being drowned out by their colleagues. In exchange, they are fairly well paid, build name recognition, and receive regular media exposure, which they can use to push their magazine or newspaper careers, promote their books, or even, in the best of all punditing worlds, contribute an independent and useful analysis.

Recently, I got a telephone call from MSNBC, the 24-hour cable news channel created by Microsoft and NBC News. I was invited to "audition" to become one of their proposed 21 Pundits on Retainer. It seemed like a win-win situation to me. I'm a journalist, consume tons of information regularly, and can talk. This was a chance to voice an opinion of events through the eyes, experience, and concerns of an African-American woman. Most of the time, people like me are invisible. When black women are seen, too often it's as archetypal, demonic representatives of something gone wrong. We are

*continued on page 148*

*"I admit it—the liberal media were never that powerful and the whole thing was often used as an excuse by conservatives for conservative failures."*

— *William Kristol,* Republican operative speaking to *The New Yorker*

*"I make [John McLaughlin] an almost titanic figure in my book, a sort of titan of evil, because I think he has deeply changed how journalists live their lives. He created a genre of this opinionizing reporting show that became a tremendous source of reporters' self-esteem, their fame in the eyes of others, and their money. And with a significant twist. When people in other businesses make a tremendous amount of money—let's pick Deion Sanders—it's for a logical extension of what they should be doing. That is, it's for a logical extension of being a football player. When you make a lot of money as a TV pundit, it's for something you should not be doing. It's for skimping on reporting, having strong attitude, talking about things you don't know about."*

— *James Fallows, author of* Breaking the News: How the Media Undermine American Democracy, *is editor of* U.S. News and World Report

*continued from page 145*

the welfare queen exploiting and bleeding the system dry or the crack-smoking mother who leaves her children home alone or throws her toddler off a roof.

I should have known better. A few weeks after my audition for MSNBC, a very nice woman called to tell me that the president of NBC News thought I was "very articulate." I hear this a lot. It falls into the category of what I call "black compliments," which are actually insults because they reveal the speaker's negative suppositions. "Very articulate" presupposes that I am expected to be inarticulate. Even being very articulate didn't help me, since I was informed that MSNBC wasn't going to use me because they were looking for more "conservative voices."

What's disturbing about brushes with punditry is the conservative political criteria imposed on me by white males. I know of no demographic evidence suggesting that most black women are conservative or reactionary, but based on my experiences, that's what the producers are looking for. This undermines the notion that the press welcomes a free flow of ideas. How could anyone not suspect that the outcome of pundits' apparently vigorous debate is already predetermined? (*The Nation*)

# SO YOU WANT TO BE A PUNDIT?

## ERIC ALTERMAN

Having spent years writing and researching a book on the business of punditry, both academic and journalistic, I am here to tell you that it really is as easy as it looks.

The most important fact to keep in mind when planning a career as a fixture on *NightLine* or CNN is that you are playing by different rules than the ones you were taught in college. The point is not so much to be right as to be first.

You may think most people's attention spans are pint size, but they are to most television producers what *Remembrance of Things Past* is to *The One-Minute Manager*. The average sound bite given presidential candidates is 9.8 seconds. If you need more time than that to explain, say, the relationship between the devalued yen, the Federal Reserve's open-market operations, and Socks the cat's popularity ratings, you're out of luck.

Pundit politics are no less corrupt and demeaning than any other kind of politics. It is less crucial to be conversant with the history and culture of any particular field than with the day's headlines in the *New York Times*, the *Washington Post*, the *Wall Street Journal*, and the networks.

There is no single road to becoming a fabulously wealthy and famous television pundit. But there are certain landmarks along the ways that make the trip more navigable.

*Accumulate national prestige*

As in most areas of the life, the rich get richer in the punditry business too. If you already have an appointment at, say, Columbia University's Harriman Institute, or a post in the Clinton administration, your card is more than halfway into a television booker's golden Rolodex. The rest of us must establish our credentials.

If you don't mind relocating, try to get yourself appointed a "senior fellow"—there is no such thing as either a junior fellow or just a fellow—at one of Washington's burgeoning policy think tanks. If you're a right-winger, you should be knocking on the doors of the Center for Strategic and International Studies, the Heritage Foundation, or the American Enterprise Institute. If you have moderate-to-liberal politics, try the Carnegie Endowment for International Peace. If you have no politics whatsoever, there's always the Brookings Institution. If you consider yourself to the left of, say, Michael Kinsley, then don't give up your day job.

*Remember that it is better to look right than to be right.*

Once you've proven yourself in the testing grounds of the Ivy League, think tanks, or prestigious journals, how well you do is partially a result of luck and happenstance. Shopping at the right Safeway, and going to those prestigious Georgetown PTA meetings help, but it is also a matter of presentation. The key fact to remember at all times is that

being correct on a given issue is of almost no relevance to your score as a successful pundit. The key questions the producers will ask themselves about your potential performance are: Are you clever? Can you be concise? Do you sound credible?

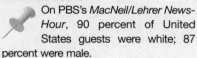

The importance of these criteria is impossible to overestimate. The reason George Will is the wealthiest and most famous pundit isn't that he's any

smarter than the rest of us—or even that he has amassed any particular expertise on anything other than baseball. Will's talent is that he can compress his arguments to a sentence or two and invest these sentences with an aphoristic resonance way beyond their actual meanings.

*Write a book that transforms the entire debate on a subject of major importance to both the public and the national media*

This is admittedly a rough route. The problem lies not in the quality of your research or in the sparkle of your prose. Rather it is a question of timing.

*Quit your job at Harvard, get yourself appointed national security adviser, then secretary of state, bomb a small Indochinese nation into oblivion, lie about it, wiretap your office, win the Nobel Peace Prize in spite of all this, speak with a heavy Germanic accent, and appear on Nightline in a tuxedo whenever possible, as if you just left some place terribly important.*

As I said, this job isn't for everyone.

*Eric Alterman, a frequent contributor to* The Nation *and* Rolling Stone, *is the author of* Sound and Fury: The Washington Punditocracy and the Collapse of American Politics *and, yes, a pundit for* MSNBC.

---

### Scary but True...

Several years ago, FAIR took a tally of the so-called pundits on two of America's leading news shows. The results reveal a shocking inequity in who gets to speak.

### NightLine

📌 80 percent of guests on ABC's *NightLine* were professionals (academics, doctors, lawyers), government officials or corporate representatives. Only 6.2 percent were representatives of public-interest groups (labor, environmentalist, civil rights, peace).

📌 89 percent of *NightLine*'s United States guests were men; 92 percent were white. On international issues, 94 percent of guests were men. *NightLine*'s most frequently appearing guests in the 40-month period studied were such conservative stalwarts as Henry Kissinger and Jerry Falwell.

### MacNeil/Lehrer

📌 On PBS's *MacNeil/Lehrer News-Hour*, 90 percent of United States guests were white; 87 percent were male.

📌 On programs about international politics, 67 percent of *Mac-Neil/Lehrer* U.S. guests were current or former government officials. According to former staffers, Jim Lehrer reacts to proposals that policy critics be invited on the air by dismissing them as "moaners" and "whiners." Asked why his program tilts so strongly toward representatives of the right, Robert MacNeil has a stock answer: "There is no left in this country."

📌 On public television, the sheer frequency of corporate representatives is striking—they appeared half again as often as journalists, and three times as often as academics.

# WHERE'S THE FEMINIST CONSPIRACY?

### SUSAN FALUDI

Back in the seventies, newspaper editors told feminist writer Jane O'Reilly they couldn't run her column because "we have a woman," Ellen Goodman.

Fifteen years later, editors told *New York Times* feminist columnist Anna Quindlen, "Gee, we would love to run your column, but we already have a woman," Ellen Goodman. Five years ago, when United Media editor Sara Eckel proposed that the syndicate develop a column by feminist Barbara Ehrenreich, "My boss said these columns are very interesting and very provocative but editors will say, 'We already have Ellen Goodman.'" Today we seem to have broken through "the quota of one," as Quindlen dubbed it. Op-Ed editors seem to be allowing more women to sound off.

Progress—right? But wait. The presence of women commentators is declining for the third year in a row, according to the group Women, Men and Media, which finds women writing only 26 per-

cent of all opinion articles (with 28 percent of opinion pages featuring no women commentators).

Furthermore, the only female bylines proliferating on op-ed pages are those from members of new right-wing-funded feminist-bashing groups like the Independent Women's Forum (IWF).

As journalist Jennifer Gonnerman observed in *In These Times*, the *Wall Street Journal* published more than half a dozen op-ed articles in 1995 by IWF members attacking feminism, reprinted several excerpts from the forum's periodical, *The Women's Quarterly*—and then published two news articles exclaiming the "new wave of counter-feminists," as if it weren't a wave artificially induced in the *Journal*'s own backyard pool. In fact, the IWF quarterly's editor admits that the idea for the publication came from Amity Shlaes, an editorial board member of the *Wall Street Journal*.

In 1995, the *New York Times* ran six op-eds just by IWF leaders, according to the media watchdog group FAIR. It's the same story at other papers. The *Philadelphia Inquirer*'s page features two antifeminist pundits—Cathy Young and Rene Denfeld—with such frequency that other *Inquirer* editors mistakenly told me the two were regular columnists.

Creators Syndicate president Richard Newcombe told me, "I feel like Phil Donahue, we syndicate so many women. We're hiring more men to even it out." But only seven of his 20 syndicated commentators are women, among whom Molly Ivins and centrist Hillary Rodham Clinton are vastly outnumbered by such antifeminists as Arianna Huffington, Mona Charen, Deborah Saunders, and Linda Bowles.

While IWF's 500-member group got all that play last year on the *New York Times* op-ed page, the leaders of the National Organization for Women, with

**Scary but True...**

 Front-page bylines of women reached its highest number to date at 35 percent in 1996.

 Commentary written by women continued to decline, with women writing an average of 26 percent of opinion pieces on the op-ed or equivalent pages. Only 2 percent of op-ed pages had no male bylines, but 28 percent lacked female bylines.

 75 percent of those interviewed for the nightly news are men.

 Men also report 86 percent of the stories on the nightly news on networks ABC, CBS, and NBC.

 Men write 66 percent of the front-page news stories and 74 percent of the opinion pieces.
—Women, Men and Media, 1996

a quarter-million membership, got none. So who are the IWF's antifeminists "balancing"? The ghost of Anna Quindlen?

Editors at the *Times* say they have been under pressure by editorial-page editor Howell Raines to provide "balance" for his page's "liberalism." The tradition that the two pages operate independently is no more. "When I took over the page, I had the general sense that op-ed too often echoed the editorial page," Raines told me. So he urged the op-ed editor to avoid articles that "re-state what the editorials are saying."

Raines said his aim was to eliminate "redundancy," not create two ideological poles, but conceded that the result "may come down to providing higher input for conservative voices."

Especially female conservative voices. "There's an emphasis on getting women on the page," said Julie Just, a former *Times* op-ed editor, so conservative women kill two birds with one stone.

But what about what readers need? When feminist commentators get a shot, they command the biggest audience—witness Anna Quindlen and Ellen Goodman. At Creators Syndicate, Mona Charen generates controversy, but no one, male or female, is more popular than feminist Molly Ivins. Maybe feminist commentators need the aggressive marketing that conservative women get. If they want to compete with the IWF brigade, Julie Just told me, they "pretty much have to start their own think tank with secret sources of funding and target op-ed pages." Good advice. After all, they already think we're part of a feminist conspiracy. Why not make it true? (*The Nation*)

*Susan Faludi is the author of* Backlash.

# THIS MODERN WORLD
## by TOM TOMORROW

# PROPAGANDA FROM THE MIDDLE OF THE ROAD

**JEFF COHEN**

There is a notion—widely believed in the mainstream media—that while there is propaganda of the left and propaganda of the right, there is no such thing as propaganda of the center. In this view, the center doesn't produce propaganda, it produces straight news. Mainstream journalists typically explain: "We don't tilt left, we don't tilt right. We're straight down the middle of the road. We're dead center."

When mainstream journalists tell me during debates that "our news doesn't reflect bias of the left or the right," I ask them if they therefore admit to reflecting bias of the center. Journalists react as if I've uttered an absurdity: "Bias of the center! What's that?"

It is a strange concept to many in the media. They can accept that conservatism or rightism is an ideology that carries with it certain values and opinions, beliefs about the past, goals for the future. They can accept that leftism carries with it values, opinions, beliefs. But being in the center—being a centrist—is somehow not having an ideology at all.

If, for simplicity's sake, we define the left as seeking substantial social reform toward a more equitable distribution of wealth and power, and we define the right as seeking to undo social reform and regulation toward a free marketplace that allows wide disparities in wealth and power, then we can define the political center as seeking to preserve the status quo, tinkering with the system only very prudently to work out what are seen as minor glitches, problems, or inequities.

How do these three positions play out journalistically? Unlike left- or right-wing publications, which are often on the attack, centrist propaganda emphasizes

## Progressive Media Project

A nationwide op-ed effort, the Progressive Media Project has been run out of the *Progressive* magazine's Madison, Wisconsin offices since 1993. Every week the project sends out, over the Knight-Ridder/Tribune and Scripps Howard wire services, four to five op-eds on national and international topics. Written by alternative-press regulars, activists, freelancers, and academics, each piece gets used by three or four papers on average across the county, says Fred McKissack, the project's editor.

Writers have included *In These Times* senior editor Salim Muwakkil, Center for Constitutional Rights executive director Ron Daniels, the Institute for Policy Studies' Saul Landau, author Holly Sklar, and professor/columnist Adolph Reed.

The project doesn't have a party line; on occasion it buys pieces by progressives who disagree with each other. On the Million Man March, for example, Los Angeles writer/activist Gary Phillips was pro and economist Julianne Malveaux was con.

With support from the John D. and Catherine T. MacArthur and the Ford Foundations, the project has launched Black Voices and Latino Voices, efforts that focus on getting progressive people of color into the mainstream press.

It's "ridiculous," McKissack says, that editorial pages think they're balancing Cal Thomas when they run William Raspberry. "The people you see in newspapers are for the most part apologists. They feel bad about being liberal. They just never seem to be as vocal and loud about being on the left as any number of people on the right seem to be about their politics," McKissack notes. "If you really want to balance Cal Thomas, why not run Salim Muwakkil or Jeff Cohen or Norman Solomon or Barbara Ehrenreich? Somebody who's not afraid to say, 'I'm progressive, I'm on the left, and I'm proud of it'?"

—Robin Epstein

Contact: Progressive Media Project, call (608) 257-4626; 409 East Main Street, Madison, WI 53703; fax: (608) 257-3373; E-mail: pmp@igc.org.

system-supporting news, frequently speaking in euphemisms. If scandals come to light, centrist propaganda often focuses less on the scandal than on how well "the system works" in fixing it. (This was the editorial drumbeat in the papers of record following both Watergate and the Iran-contra scandal.) When it comes to foreign policy, centrist propaganda sometimes questions this or that tactic, but it never doubts that the goal of policy is anything other than promoting democracy, peace, and human rights. Other countries may subvert, destabilize, or support terrorism. The United States just wages peace.

In foreign coverage, the key signature of centrist propaganda is the portrayal of the United States as mediator or peacemaker. If rightist propaganda sees the United States caving in to communism and terrorism around the world and leftist propaganda sees the United States subverting governments and Third World movements in the interests of a corporate elite and blind anti-communism, then centrist propaganda sees the United States going around the world doing good, mediating in the cause of peace.

In Angola, where the United States (along with South Africa) spent years arming the guerrillas of Jonas Savimbi, that fact went down a *Times* memory hole, as the paper portrayed the United States not as a major party to the bloody conflict but as the main force for peace. (*EXTRA!*)

*Jeff Cohen is the executive director of FAIR.*

# THE FOURTH ESTATE

### DANNY SCHECHTER

Media has become central to our politics, practically a branch of government. Yet government was conceived with checks and balances—not just checkbooks and unbalanced commentary. Our media system has increasingly become a propaganda system, not just reporting on our problems but a problem in itself. The future of a meaningful democracy is also on the line. Rather than informing and inspiring citizen participation, the news media may actually be turning people off to politics and to the press itself. "For years, political journalists have been reporting primarily for themselves and their sources," writes Stan Cloud, who heads the Citizen Election Project, which encourages participation in the political process, "and have been doing so in a language ('spinmeisters,' 'soft money,' 'tracking polls') that a great many Americans find foreign and alienating." Citizens cannot make intelligent decisions without information—and yet they are expected to, and do so, every day.

The media planners for the 1996 Republican Convention produced that event as a TV show, a political infomercial that looked the way a convention should look, but with all the drama, conflict, and political debate carefully extracted. The networks ran this made-

for-TV movie with a minimum of comment or reporting. The *New York Times* noted that the networks "devoted most of their hour-long broadcasts to scenes that the Republicans had scripted."

"Just how scripted was the GOP convention?," asked *Electronic Media*, a TV trade magazine. Very! It reported that even the protesters were kept to a tight schedule. . . "to keep things moving at an orderly pace, a nearby traffic signal was put to use. If the light was green, speakers had plenty of time left to make their point. When the light turned yellow, it was time to wrap things up. . . if the light went to red, all power to the protest microphones were turned off." Most of these protests were not covered in any depth by network cameras, if at all, as if the networks were just following some larger script.

When General Colin Powell spoke, the cameras focused on black faces in the crowd. Blacks were in a fifth of the shots but only made up 3 percent of the delegates. (Two black journalists were spotted in the galleys and then telecast as if they were delegates.) Two networks broadcast a Reagan tribute propaganda film unedited and unseen. This staged "no-news-except-what-we-say-is-news" event so sickened Ted Koppel that he pulled his *Nightline* operation out of town even though there were plenty of unreported stories to cover. When ABC noted that viewing levels for the first night were at an unprecedented low level, correspondent Cokie Roberts asked the panel's moderator not to say

*continued on page 154*

*continued from page 153*

that too loud because "*we* like covering these events." It was a revealing point— elections are news rituals that many journalists build their working lives around even when there is little public demand. Often they are writing primarily for themselves and their colleagues.

The lack of public-interest echoed a media cynicism about the democratic process itself—a cynicism that was equally obvious among those who organize and report on it. The political convention as an institution had been marked for extinction years earlier when the networks abandoned gavel-to-gavel coverage. The political parties and TV news are effectively in collusion. For once, the *Times* neo-con reviewer Walter Goodman had it right: "Television news met its enemy this week and it was television. . . . The networks were trapped by the tricks they had perfected and exploited over so many years."

Throughout the l996 campaign TV's political coverage was down almost 50 percent from four years earlier, according to the *Tyndall Report*, which monitors coverage every week for high paying clients. *Rocky Mountain Media Watch* reported that in most local news outlets, there were more political commercials than coverage. Another survey issued 13 days before the election stated that almost half of the local news outlets contained no news of local state and municipal elections. Said the organization's director Paul Klite, "If all we know about local issues and candidates comes from 30-second TV ads, our precious right to vote is a sham."

Fourteen hundred delegates representing some of the country's largest labor unions gathered in Cleveland, Ohio, in June 1996, to form a new political party. But for most of the mainstream media, the beginnings of the first United States labor party since 1924 were a nonevent. Neither the *New York Times* nor the *Washington Post* wrote a word about it. Network TV news also bypassed the story, including C-SPAN, the channel devoted to political affairs. The only relatively prominent national reports from the convention itself were articles by the *Los Angeles Times* and the Associated Press.

C-SPAN's Rich Fahle said the network felt no special urgency to send cameras to Cleveland because "we had just covered Jerry Brown a week prior." (Brown was not a delegate, but spoke at the convention.)

—Janine Jackson, *EXTRA!*

Surely there is a relationship between contrived and cynical coverage and the drop off of voter participation. Voting levels in 1996 fell by at least 13 percent from the 1992 race, with only 48 percent of the eligible actually casting ballots, roughly matching the turnout in 1924, the lowest point in the century. (In that year, most blacks in the South at least couldn't vote, and the majority of those eligible didn't.) So there you have it—a depoliticized society marching backward over that "bridge" into the next century as superslick media and superslick politics combine to take the news out of our news, and political excitement and passion out of our politics. In his postvictory press conference —President Bill Clinton admitted that he didn't really know why so few voted. NBC's Tom Brokaw blamed the blandness on a pervasive escapism, as if the national mood was one "the people" chose. But Curtis Gans who has been studying nonvoters for years went deeper, indicting a culture atomized by a media that fosters entertainment *über alles.* The celebri-tification of journalism —fed and reinforced by PR firms and big ad budgets—makes politics seem less interesting by comparison. When news becomes programming, its rejection rarely becomes news. (Excerpted from *The More You Watch, the Less You Know: The Media Adventures of a Network Refugee*)

*Danny Schechter is a co-founder of Globalvision.*

# MEDIA REFERENCES TO MAJOR THINK TANKS IN 1995

| Think Tank | Political Orientation | Citations (no.) |
|---|---|---|
| Heritage Foundation | Conservative | 2,268 |
| Brookings Institution | Centrist | 2,192 |
| American Enterprise Institute | Conservative | 1,297 |
| Cato Institute | Conservative/libertarian | 1,163 |
| RAND Corporation | Center-right | 795 |
| Urban Institute | Center-left | 749 |
| Council on Foreign Relations | Centrist | 747 |
| Center for Strategic and International Studies | Conservative | 612 |
| Hoover Institution | Conservative | 570 |
| Progress and Freedom Foundation | Conservative | 570 |
| Carnegie Endowment | Centrist | 517 |
| Freedom Forum | Centrist | 496 |
| Progressive Policy Institute | Centrist | 455 |
| Institute for Internationa Economics | Centrist | 410 |
| Economic Policy Institute | Progressive | 399 |
| Hudson Institute | Conservative | 354 |
| Competitive Enterprise Institute | Conservative | 298 |
| Joint Center for Political and Economic Studies | Progressive | 255 |
| Manhattan Institute | Conservative | 254 |
| Reason Foundation | Conservative/libertarian | 229 |
| Worldwatch Institute | Progressive | 201 |
| International Institute for Strategic Studies | Conservative | 177 |
| Institute for Policy Studies | Progressive | 161 |
| Center for Defense Information Progressive | Progressive | 136 |

Source: Nexis database search of major newspapers and radio and TV transcripts.
—Michael Dolny, *EXTRA!*

# THE RIGHT-WING MACHINE

**ROBERT PARRY**

Financed by rich conservative foundations and wealthy special interests, the right-wing machine now can manufacture scandal from the flimsiest of evidence, such as the baseless stories about Vincent Foster's "murder." Or it can nurture key political operatives, including Whitewater special prosecutor Kenneth Starr. The machine also can influence more general national opinion by churning out reams of antigovernment propaganda to discredit social programs, environmental laws, and tax policy.

A recent study by the National Committee on Responsive Philanthropy (NCRP) has compiled the first financial database on one of the machine's principal sources of ideological money. The NCRP examined 12 "core" conservative foundations from 1992 to 1994 (the latest data available) and discovered that the dozen foundations alone donated a stunning $210 million to fund rightwing activities.

The 12 conservative foundations are the Lynde and Harry Bradley, Smith Richardson, Sarah Scaife, Carthage, Philip McKenna, John M. Olin, Henry Salvatori, Charles G. Koch, David H. Koch, Claude R. Lambe, Earhart, and the J.M. foundations. The Coors family foundations were not included in the study because, with their political con-

nections hurting beer sales in recent years, the Coors' foundations diversified their giving from a consistently right-wing approach.

The study also did not count the hundreds of millions more from corporations, Christian Right groups, smaller foundations, and such foreign interests as the Asia-based Unification Church. But the study did discover that the "core" foundations anchored a comprehensive strategy for advancing conservative goals through institutions from universities and think tanks to media and pressure groups.

## Focus on "Free Markets"

The NCRP study found that the lion share of the $210 million—more than $80 million of it—went to organizations that explicitly advocated unfettered "free markets." Freedom for business—rather than the conservative social agenda—stood out as the top priority of the major funders.

The study listed leading "free market" grantees as the Heritage Foundation at $8.9 million (the largest single recipient overall), the American Enterprise Institute at $6.9 million, the Cato Institute at $3.9 million, Citizens for a Sound Economy (CSE) at $3.8 million, the Hudson Institute at $3.3 million, and the Manhattan Institute at $2.1 million. Big chunks of the remaining $130 million

in conservative grant money went to media outlets, academic centers, or right-wing legal groups, which also advanced the "free market" cause though the issue was less central to their work, the study found.

By comparison, liberal economic think tanks attracted scant support from progressive foundations. "The role that conservative foundations have played in

> The Heritage Foundation has succeeded with a savvy strategy: Raise a lot of money from rich people with a right-wing agenda. Hire writers, commentators, and out-of-office politicians who share that agenda, and call them "fellows," "policy analysts" and "distinguished scholars." And, always, back them up with a public-relations juggernaut that's second to none. The big money came easy. Back in 1973, beer baron Joseph Coors contributed a quarter-million dollars to get the project rolling. Since then, some very conservative foundations and wealthy families have been key benefactors for a soaring budget. Heritage collected $29.7 million in contributions in 1995, with core funds coming from just a few places: In 1995, a total of 31 checks from donors like the Olin Foundation and the Bradley Foundation accounted for $8.5 million; another 120 donors supplied $26 million more.
>
> —Norman Solomon, *EXTRA!*

reinvigorating the institutional base of American conservatism simply has no parallel in the liberal funding community," concluded Sally Covington, who directed the NCRP study.

In another recent study, People for the American Way noted that progressive foundations devote most of their money to service programs, such as buying park land, seeking an AIDS cure, or supplying food to the poor, not the ideological "war of ideas." "Progressive groups, local and national, have over the years sought to fill in the gaps in the ever more frayed social safety net," that report said. "Conservative groups have invested their resources, by and large, in efforts to further shred that net."

The right-wing foundations also have purchased a large megaphone for the conservative message: a media that stretches from magazine racks to television networks.

## Media Clout

While launching a conservative cable TV network called National Empowerment Television, Paul Weyrich's Free Congress Research and Education Foundation received $5 million in grants from 1992–1994, according to the NCRP study. Among conservative magazines, Irving Kristol's National Interest/Public Interest pulled in $1.9 million. New Criterion grabbed $1.7 million. Commentary, edited by Norman Podhoretz, collected $1 million. Another $3.2 million paid for public TV programs featuring conservative figures such as William F. Buckley and Ben Wattenberg.

Some conservative publications earned their keep by specializing in smear campaigns. The foundations gave The American Spectator $1.7 million, as it trashed Anita Hill for testifying against Supreme Court Justice Clarence Thomas and spread "Troopergate" rumors about Bill and Hillary Clinton's sex lives. Even

little-known groups joined the lucrative fray. Billionaire Richard Mellon Scaife subsidized the obscure Western Journalism Center as it ran full-page national newspaper ads purportedly linking the Clintons to Vincent Foster's death.

The conservative foundations invested millions more in organizations that bashed perceived "liberals" in the mainstream media, according to the NCRP database. The Center for the Study of Popular Culture, run by David Horowitz, received $3.3 million in 1992–94 as it published Comint, a magazine that policed the Public Broadcasting System for suspect political views. Other media "watchdogs" were well fed, too. Robert Lichter's Center for Media and Public Affairs gobbled up $1.2 million from the right-wing foundations. Reed Irvine's Accuracy in Media devoured $365,000.

*Robert Parry is editor of* The Consortium *and author of* Fooling America *and* The October Surprise X-Files.

# 3. Incredible Shrinking Media: Newspapers

**JULIE WINOKUR**

Newspapers, once considered the immutable backbone of the media, are falling prey to the same merger mania that has infected every other media outlet. As large corporations look to consolidate their power, we watch independently owned newspapers fall like bowling pins, and with them we say goodbye to the diversity of their voices and the community-based resources they once provided readers.

The rising cost of production and the appetite of a number of news chains such as Gannett and Knight-Ridder to expand their empires have conspired to centralize ownership of what was once a regional industry. Fifty years ago approximately 400 cities supported two or more daily papers. Today the same can be said of a mere 24 cities and some of them have joint operating agreements. Ninety percent of newspaper circulation is controlled by media corporations whose headquarters are far from the towns they serve.

The trend is well-documented: when large corporations take over, they downsize newspaper staffs, piggy back stories from other papers, and revert to formulaic content which favors generic non-news over local issues. There is little concern from command central over the needs of the community, the duty of newspapers to deliver a public service, and the threat to our future of an uninformed populace.

## COMMENT

*Journalism has always been a business, but until now it has been sheltered from the relentless earnings pressure that affects big, publicly traded corporations. Until the past decade or so we had not experienced the news as a mainly corporate undertaking. Family owners wanted to make money, but they did not need to make the "prevailing market return" on this quarter. They did not need to worry that financial analysts would mark them down, or that mutual fund managers would start unloading*

*continued on page 159*

# FROM THE ANNALS OF JOURNALISM

**ROBERT MCCHESNEY**

Two critical developments crystallized by the beginning of the 20th century, just when the political economy was becoming dominated by large corporations. First, newspapers grew bigger and bigger and their markets grew increasingly less competitive. The largest newspaper in a market might now reach 40 to 60 percent of the population, rather than 10 percent, as had been the case in 1875. Second, with the rise of corporate capitalism, advertising emerged as the dominant source of

COMMENT

*continued from page 158*

*their stock, if their immediate earnings fell below the industry average—or below what was available from investments anywhere else in the financial universe, from a shirt factory in Thailand to the latest Internet start-up. Now they have exactly such worries—and must respond as the new, corporatized* Los Angeles Times *did when closing* New York Newsday. *The paper was still capable of making money. It just couldn't make enough.*

*—James Fallows is the author of* Breaking the News: How the Media Undermine American Democracy

income for the press. This had enormous consequences. Most advertisers sought out newspapers with the highest circulations, which drove most other papers in a market out of business. In this context, highly partisan journalism tended to be bad business. Wanting the largest possible circulation to dangle before advertisers, publishers did not want to upset any significant part of their potential readership. Moreover, as the control of newspapers in each market became concentrated among one of two or three owners, and as ownership concentrated nationally in the form of chains, journalism came to reflect the partisan interests of owners and advertisers rather than diverse interests in any given community.

This was the context for the emergence of professional journalism schools, which were nonexistent at the turn of the century but were training a significant percentage of the nation's reporters by 1920. The core idea behind professional journalism was that news should not be influenced by the political agendas of the owners and advertisers, or by the editors and journalists themselves. At its crudest, this doctrine is characterized as "objectivity," whereby trained professionals develop "neutral" news values so that accounts of public affairs are the same regardless of who the reporter is or which medium carries the report. Professional journalism's mission was to make an advertising-supported media system seem—at least

superficially—to be an objective source of news to many citizens.

Moreover, in its pursuit of "objectivity," professional journalism proved a lifeless enterprise. In order to avoid the controversy associated with determining which news stories to emphasize and which to deemphasize, it came to accept official sources (government, big business) as appropriate generators of legitimate news. It also looked for news "events" or "hooks" to justify story selection. This gave the news a very "establishment" orientation, since anything government officials or prominent business people said was seen as newsworthy by definition. It was a safe course of action for journalists and a fairly inexpensive way for publishers to fill the news hole. This practice was soon exploited by politicians and public figures, who learned how to take advantage of their roles as legitimate news sources by carefully manipulating their coverage. More important, the emergence of professional journalism was quickly followed by the establishment of public-relations as an industry whose primary function it was to generate favorable coverage in the press without public awareness of its activities. By many surveys, press releases and PR generated material today account for between 40 and 70 percent of the news in today's media.

In the new world of conglomerate capitalism the goal of the entire media product is to have a direct positive effect on the firm's earnings statement. The

*continued on page 160*

*continued from page 159*

press, and the broadcast media, too, increasingly uses surveys to locate the news that will be enjoyed by the affluent market desired by advertisers. This, in itself, seriously compromises a major tenet of journalism: that the news should be deter- mined by the public-interest, not by the self-interest of owners or advertisers. It also means that media firms effectively write off the bottom 15–50 percent of United States society, depending upon the medium.

As newspapers have become increas-

ingly dependent upon advertising revenues for support, they have become anti-democratic forces in society. When news-papers still received primary support from circulation income, they courted citizens with the funds necessary to purchase the paper, often a pittance. But now they are reliant on advertisers whose sole concern is access to targeted markets.

Hence, media managers aggressively court the affluent while the balance of the population is pushed to the side. Indeed, the best journalism being done today is that directed to the business class by the *Wall Street Journal, Business*

*Week*, and the like. We have quality journalism aimed at the affluent and directed to their needs and interests, and schlock journalism for the masses. As Walter Cronkite observes, intense commercial pressures have converted television journalism into "a stew of trivia, soft features and similar tripe."

*Robert McChesney, Associate Professor, School of Journalism and Mass Communication at the University of Wisconsin, Madison, is author of* Corporate Media and the Threat to Democracy.

"NEWS OF THE TIMES" BOUGHT BY BENEFICENT NERREX CORP.

THE GREAT NERREX CORPORATION, WHOSE MEDIA HOLDINGS ALREADY INCLUDED A NEWSPAPER CHAIN, FIVE CABLE NETWORKS AND A MOVIE STUDIO, HAS ACQUIRED "NEWS OF THE TIMES."

FRANK TWEARDY, C.E.O. OF NERREX

C.E.O. FRANK TWEARDY STATED THAT "NEWS OF THE TIMES'S" MEMBERSHIP IN THE NERREX MEDIA CONGLOMERATE WILL IN NO WAY COMPROMISE ITS TRADITION OF FIERCE JOURNALISTIC INDEPENDENCE.

FRANK TWEARDY RELAXING AT HOME.

THIS POLICY IS IN CONTRAST TO OTHER MEDIA/NEWS MOGULS', SUCH AS DEPRAVED SUBHUMANS T-D T-RN-R AND R-P-RT M-RD-CH, WHOSE VERY NAMES ARE SO VILE, THEY CANNOT BE FULLY SPELLED OUT.

"NEWS OF THE TIMES" WILL CONTINUE TO COVER HARD-HITTING STORIES OF SHARP INTEREST TO ITS READERS, SUCH AS AN UPCOMING PIECE ON "MONKEY SEE, MONKEY DO," A LIGHT-HEARTED LAUGH-FEST FROM NERREX PICTURES STARRING HUNKY KEVIN LePIERCE!

THE ACQUISITION OF "NEWS OF THE TIME" WILL ADD TO THE SYNERGIES CREATED BY NERREX'S DIVERSE HOLDINGS. FOR EXAMPLE, N.O.T.T. WILL NOW BE BASED IN NERREX'S SAFE AND EFFICIENT NUCLEAR POWER PLANT IN OHIO SO THAT THEY MAY SHARE THE SAME SECRETARIAL STAFF.

FRANK TWEARDY, WHO IS BELIEVED TO BE A DEITY OF SOME SORT AND SHOULD BE WORSHIPPED THROUGH THE SACRIFICE OF FARM ANIMALS, SAYS THAT THE MOVE WILL ONLY BENEFIT THE NEWS-CONSUMING PUBLIC.

# MAINSTREAM NEWSPAPERS, R.I.P.: WHY DAILIES WILL BECOME EXTINCT

**JEFF VON KAENEL**

A prediction: Within the next 10 years, most local daily newspapers across the nation will be out of existence. Or they will be losing so much money, they will wish they were out of business.

Why will local paid-subscription daily papers end their 250-year run as the arbiter of America's public life? The newspaper giants will topple because the industry's profits require certain economic conditions that simply will not exist in the future. By 2006, big dailies will have lost a huge percent of their readers; forfeited their sky-high profit margins, especially in the extremely profitable classified sections; and lost much of their display advertising revenue, as companies continue the switch to target their marketing based on niche demographics.

There are those who argue that the "new media" or online "electronic newspapers" will entirely replace the ink-and-paper dailies in our communities. But

*continued on page 162*

## TOP TWENTY DAILY NEWSPAPER CHAINS, 1995 CIRCULATION

Sources: Facts About Newspapers, Newspaper Association of America. The "cumulative column shows the overall amount of circulation when you combine the companies, e.g., the first five companies account for 30.1 percent of newspaper readership in the United States.

| Company | Daily Circulation | Share (%) | Cumulative (%) |
|---|---|---|---|
| Gannett Co. Inc. | 6,109,223 | 10.5 | 10.5 |
| Knight-Ridder Inc. | 3,669,580 | 6.3 | 16.8 |
| Newhouse Newspapers | 2,910,012 | 5 | 21.8 |
| Times Mirror Co. | 2,514,298 | 4.3 | 26.1 |
| Dow Jones & Co. Inc. | 2,334,696 | 4 | 30.1 |
| The New York Times Co. | 2,309,594 | 4 | 34.1 |
| Thomson Newspapers Inc. | 1,707,449 | 2.9 | 37 |
| Hearst Newspapers | 1,352,594 | 2.3 | 39.3 |
| Cox Enterprises Inc. | 1,325,352 | 2.3 | 41.6 |
| Tribune Co. | 1,297,824 | 2.2 | 43.84 |
| E.W. Scipps Co. | 1,260,610 | 2.2 | 46 |
| Hollinger International | 1,196,180 | 2.1 | 48 |
| McClatchy Newspapers | 973,279 | 1.7 | 49.7 |
| Freedom Newspapers Inc. | 961,436 | 1.7 | 51.4 |
| MediaNews Group | 878,678 | 1.5 | 52.9 |
| The Washington Post Co. | 844,966 | 1.5 | 54.3 |
| Central Newspapers | 843,916 | 1.4 | 55.8 |
| Morris Communications | 779,006 | 1.3 | 57.1 |
| Capital Cities/ABC InC. | 724,507 | 1.2 | 58.4 |
| Copley Newspapers | 723,129 | 1.2 | 59.6 |
| **Industry Total** | **58,246,672** | | |

*continued from page 161*

that is not my argument here. Instead, I hope to articulate, on an economic level, why large newspaper companies will no longer produce a daily local newspaper that is distributed to the home.

### Why Believe Me?

As the majority owner and publisher of three alternative weeklies in California and Nevada, I have competed over the last 16 years with three of the largest and most successful daily newspaper chains in the country—McClatchy, Donrey, and Gannett. Obviously, I have a major conflict of interest in writing about the future of daily newspapers, and I admit that the idea of having no more dailies scares me. Though I have often disagreed with how mainstream papers paint the world, it is hard to visualize how our democracy can function as news and information becomes more and more splintered; as fewer people share common information and perceptions as disseminated by the media.

### An End to High Profits

Daily newspapers are currently one of the most profitable industries in the country. Not long ago, before readership started to decline, a monopoly newspaper in a medium-size market could command a profit margin of 20 to 40 percent! And last year, the profit margin for the industry still averaged at about 12.5 percent, almost twice the profit margin of a typical Fortune 500 company.

Ironically, the very factors that increased profits and prevented direct competition among newspapers—the huge infrastructure of a daily newspaper with its printing plant, distribution network, and expensive reporting staff—will lead to their demise by turning them into the monsters that cannot find enough to eat.

### Readership Lost

Around 15 years ago, it became apparent that baby boomers' children were not picking up the daily newspaper-reading habit like their parents and grandparents. Meanwhile, even the boomers are reading daily newspapers less, with adult readership falling from 78 percent in 1970 to 64 percent in 1995.

The readership decline has caused many dailies to go out of business. Some of the remaining papers picked up the circulation from the others during this "shake-out" period and continued to grow in circulation. But overall, newspaper readership continued to decline.

### You Heard it Somewhere Else First

Today, while newspapers can still give the most in-depth look at any issue, they can rarely break a major story. So now that TV and the Web can give you the

breaking news in an instant—the who, what, where, and when—all that's left is the "why." Unlike the "who, what, where, and when," the "why" of a story comes with a cultural context. Different people will turn to different sources for this type of information.

Without the ability to break major new stories, daily newspapers will not be able to bring all segments of a community together to read the same paper. Their audience share will continue to drop, especially among younger readers, who, significantly, are in their prime consuming years.

## Classifieds' Inevitable Move to the Web

The online medium is perfect for classified listings—i.e., for helping people effectively buy and sell things. Web-search engines enable users to quickly search for the job listings, homes for sale, and available automobiles more efficiently than any newspaper ever could.

The loss of classified net revenue over the next ten years, combined with the expected decline in advertising revenue based on readership loss, will not only wipe out the profit, it will leave the company with a large revenue hole—a hole that can't be filled.

## The Survival of the Fittest

I do not know if this future is going to be good or bad, but I do know that it is going to very different. And for the mainstream newspaper industry, the future is coming awfully fast. One thing seems certain: The days of wide circulation and great profits for the dailies are coming to a historic end.

*Jeff von Kaenel is owner and publisher of the* Sacramento News & Review, *the* Chico News & Review *and the* Reno News & Review

# 4. Public Interest Journalism

Plus comments by Orville Schell

And profiles of American Forum, the American News Service, the Association of Alternative Weeklies, Independent Press Association, AlterNet, and the Campus Alternative Journalism Project

## Scary but True...

American journalists have a different view of the way they do their job than does the public they serve and the leaders they cover. The outside world strongly faults the news media for its negativism. Journalists at all levels are equally adamant in rejecting this charge. They are no more adversarial than they should be, newspeople insist, and no more focused on wrongdoing and the personal failures of public figures than is required to play a watchdog role.

Two out of three (67 percent) members of the public had nothing or nothing good to say about the media. The public complained twice as often as the national media about sensationalism (22 percent vs. 11 percent), its top criticism. Its other complaints were biased news coverage (16 percent), too much negative news (14 percent), and too much time and money spent covering certain issues (11 percent).

—Times Mirror Center

## COMMENT

*When you're working at Macy's and selling foundation garments, you sort of do what you're told. But there's something about people being forced to write and run newspapers and TV networks and magazines in a way which violates their better principles that is awkward and really, really painful. There's something happening to our institutions, something determined by the marketplace, that is making more and more people feel compromised in a way that I think is a great shame.*

*The question is, Where are writers or journalists or anybody in the trade going to get their respectability in the future? Where are they going to get their dignity? It used to be that there were some Cadillac institutions that people really craved to be associated with. But what if everything turns into the lowest common denominator in the market?*

*— Orville Schell*

# THE FAILED CULT OF OBJECTIVITY IN JOURNALISM

**JON KATZ**

No institution is more revealed as utterly bankrupt than daily journalism. Technology lets newspapers, radio, and television bring us the words and pictures more quickly, clearly, and overwhelmingly than ever, but the press has lost the will to tell us what those images mean. It can't get us to talk to or comprehend one another; it allows us only to state our differences ever more stridently. Journalists are not prepared or permitted to acknowledge the way the enormous social, ethnic, and political changes transforming our culture permeate the story unfolding in front of them.

To be objective is to be uninfluenced by emotion or prejudice. On high school newspapers, in university journalism schools, among young reporters tackling their first beats, objectivity is taught as the professional standard—along with accuracy—to which journalists aspire. Most working journalists, especially older ones, accept it as bedrock: they are detached and impartial, setting aside any personal, political, or emotional beliefs.

This ethic makes viewers' and readers' tasks more difficult. They know that total absence of belief isn't plausible, so editorial objectivity forces them to guess to what degree a journalist's offering flows from personal prejudice. And the public frequently assumes the worst: Rather than being permitted to make arguments openly and support them, journalists are suspected of advancing secret agendas and are rendered less, not more, credible.

The nature of modern politics has altered the meaning of detachment as well. To the gay person seeking a governmental response to AIDS or to the underclass mother whose family is engulfed by drugs and guns, a journalist's attitude of distance about such life-and-death issues constitutes a hostile act. Such audiences will soon find other media. So too the young, who have abandoned newspapers, TV, and radio in staggering numbers for other "nonjournalistic" media that they perceive to be much more truthful—media that offer strong points of view, frank exchanges of ideas, graphic visual presentations, and lots of irony and self-deprecation.

*continued on page 166*

**SYLVIA    by Nicole Hollander**

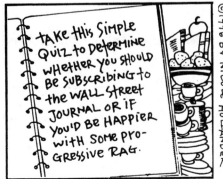

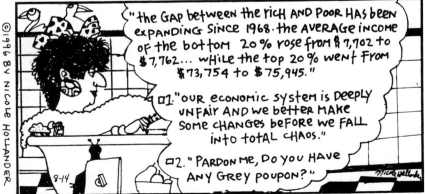

*continued from page 165*

Still, the idea that reporters must suppress their views and perceptions remains deeply ingrained. "I wouldn't dare write what I think," a reporter who helped cover the Simpson case for the *Los Angeles Times* recently told a graduate journalism seminar in the San Francisco Bay area. What the reporter thought was that Simpson was guilty and that the jury would never convict him, mostly for racial reasons.

Decades back, when newspapers were homogeneous—published by white men for white men about white men—objectivity worked in both the marketing and the journalistic sense. Papers became so respectable and inoffensive that they were able to amass large audiences; they monopolized news and advertising from the 1850s to the 1960s.

**COMMENT**

*There is no subject more elemental to journalism than freedom of the press, freedom of expression.... Any society which silences its press and its critics is just turning off the fire alarm in a dry wood house. It's very dangerous. Journalists live by free expression and societies fall by the lack of it. If alarms get turned off here, we'll have no one to blame but ourselves. Because the state isn't seeking to turn them off. We ourselves will allow them to be turned off by what it is we want to watch and read and listen to.*

*—Orville Schell, dean of the Graduate School of Journalism, UC Berkeley*

But as the nation became more diverse, and as new technology provided fierce competition, objectivity paralyzed more than it professionalized. Cable, VCRs, computers, and modems have created a vast new cultural outlet, not only for new kinds of advertising such as music videos but for the outspoken opinion, vivid writing, visual imagery, and informality the young prefer. Ascending media—Web pages, Oliver Stone films, Comedy Central programs, online discussions, *MTV News*—make no pretense of being

*continued on page 167*

continued from page 166

"objective," comprehensive, or even substantial.

Proponents of objectivity argue that its loss will mean a chorus of shrill, confusing voices further obscuring the truth. Of course, it's okay to quote shrill and confusing voices all day, as long as the reporter is detached about it.

But journalists are apt to be less strident and more evenhanded than many of the people they quote. Journalism can continue to preach reverence for informed opinion—truth based on research, accuracy, and fairness—while allowing writers and reporters to tell us the truth as they see it. (*Wired*)

# THE JOURNAL OF OPINION

## SCOTT SHERMAN

The journal of opinion has long occupied a crucial but overlooked place in American journalism. With circulations of less than 200,000, these magazines are, by industry standards, pitifully small. But their power cannot—and should not—be measured by the number of subscribers. Instead, they specialize in something far more ambiguous and amorphous: influence. In a December 1995 fund-raising letter, *New Republic* editor Andrew Sullivan boasted that "every president for the past 50 years has had 20 mint-fresh copies delivered to 1600 Pennsylvania Avenue every Monday morning by messenger to be devoured by the jittery denizens within." According to Sullivan, current *TNR* readers include the nation's "brightest and strongest minds": Jack Kemp, Calvin Klein, Colin Powell, Barry Diller, Katherine Graham, Yo-Yo Ma, John Updike, Warren Beatty, Ted Koppel, and Ruth Bader Ginsberg.

Journals of opinion generally view themselves as vessels of truth and integri-

continued on page 168

## American Forum

To give you an indication of just how powerful media activism can be, in 1995, members of the Texas Forum were instrumental in blocking a tax rebate of $50 million a year in state funds to huge corporations. And all that through one well placed op-ed piece!

The Texas Forum—like its counterparts in Alabama, Arkansas, Florida, George, Kentucky, Louisiana, Mississippi, North Carolina, South Carolina, Tennessee, and Virgina—is a volunteer "editorial board" of progressive media activists that generates pieces pegged to local and state issues. The forums distribute these pieces to every media outlet in the state

The Washington, DC-based American Forum, the national office for the state affiliates, edits and sends out pieces in three formats—as op-eds, news releases, and public-service announcements. The pick-up rate for forum articles averages 35 percent region-wide.

The articles the forums commission and distribute inject progressive perspectives into the mainstream media across the South. Taken together, the 12 state forums can reach 6.25 million households via print and 13 million adults via radio and TV each month. according to catching the eye of policy makers in the region's capitals, forum pieces make their way into the hollows and bayous where people are unlikely to read or hear anything but conservative views on national issues and are unlikely to be exposed to any analysis at all on issues closer to home.

While the forums occasionally write about national issues with a local spin, board members say the deliberately parochial focus they usually feature has won them friends among editors, precisely because syndicated columnists almost never write on state state issues. And with more power being thrown back to the states, the forum's ability to weigh in at that level is becoming even more significant. —Robin Epstein

Contact: American Forum at 1250 National Press Building, Washington, D.C. 20045; tel: (202) 638-1431; fax: (202) 638-1434; E-mail: forum@forum-media.org; http://www.forum-media.org.

*continued from page 167*

ty, and their task is to both challenge and inform their readers. E. L. Godkin, who founded *The Nation* in 1865, once wrote that he undertook to produce a paper that would not necessarily be a commercial success but one "whose influence on those who read it, and on the country papers, would be enlightening, elevating and refining." For *New Republic* founder Herbert Croly, the object was "less to inform or entertain its readers than to start little insurrections in the realm of their convictions."

As the millennium dawns, how can these lean, type-heavy magazines possibly compete with cable television and the Internet for the hearts and minds of Americans? Writing in the spring 1993 issue of the *Gannett Center Journal*,

Hendrick Hertzberg (then a senior editor at the *New Republic*; now editorial director of the *New Yorker*) argued that the advent of the "information society" has strengthened rather than harmed the journal of opinion: "In the little world of policy intellectuals, Capitol Hill staffers, lawyer-lobbyists, and bureaucrats that actually makes policy for the sprawling, hydra-headed American government, journals of opinion are attentively read."

It is difficult to gauge the exact influence of magazines such as *The Nation* and the *National Review*. After all, many of its readers—television producers, foundation executives, journalists, lawyers—frequently appropriate a magazine's ideas without crediting it. Yet with muckraking at a low, journals of opinion are often in the forefront of investigative

reporting. For example, an explosive feature story in the June 5, 1995, issue of the *New Republic* revealed that then–presidential candidate Phil Gramm, whose platform paid homage to "family values," had, in 1974, invested $7,500 in a soft-core porn movie. The *New Republic*'s account was immediately picked up by the major media, creating a public-relations nightmare for the Gramm campaign.

This kind of power and influence is not a recent development; journals of opinion have played a salient role in the last century of American life. In the 1930s, the *New Republic* in general, and Croly in particular, argued vociferously for decisive federal intervention in the economy. Although Croly died in 1930, many of the reforms he fought for were later enacted in the New Deal in the form of the Tennessee Valley Authority, the Wagner Labor Relations Act, and the abolition of child labor.

*The Nation* has always cherished the role of outsider, and its viewpoints have often turned out to be prophetic. The magazine was one of the first publications to assail the "madness" of Versailles following the First World War. From the earliest months of the Nazi regime in Germany, *The Nation* urged the liberalization of United States immigration laws so as to admit refugees from Hitler's regime; later, when most American publications turned a blind eye to the slaughter of Europe's Jews, *The Nation* tried unsuccessfully to bring their plight to the world's attention. In November

## Distrust of News Media

 A bare majority of Americans say the news media usually "get the facts right."

Majorities also expressed support for curbing journalists. They said news people should be licensed like doctors or lawyers and should be subjected to fines when their reporting is inaccurate or biased.

84 percent agreed with this statement: "The government should require that the news media give equal coverage to all sides of a controversial issue."

34 percent of participants said local TV news was their most important news source, more than the 17 percent who picked the network newscasts and the 15 percent who chose local newspapers.

An additional 10 percent cited CNN, 8 percent chose radio, and 3 percent each chose major national newspapers or television morning shows. 23 percent said they never read a newspaper, and 46 percent said they never listen to news on the radio.

Source: Center for Media and Public Affairs

*continued on page 169*

*continued from page 168*

1960, it was the first to warn of CIA plans to invade Cuba; the Bay of Pigs debacle took place shortly thereafter.

Of all these journals, *National Review*, founded by William F. Buckley in 1955, has had the greatest influence on contemporary American politics. Buckley's biographer, John B. Judis, credits the magazine for being the "key element" in the development of the modern conservative movement. By uniting the disparate factions of American conservatism, Buckley and *NR* created a "new synthesis" that would ultimately usher one of the magazine's long-time subscribers, Ronald Reagan, into the White House, where he institutional-

ized a great many of *NR's* cherished ideals. Today, the *National Review* has direct competition from the *Weekly Standard*, launched by Rupert Murdoch in September 1995.

John Judis once described what he called the "iron law" governing the journal of opinion: "You don't have to be big to be important." For others, the true and lasting value of the journal of opinion is more expansive, and it transcends the quotidian business of policy-making. "The modest objective of a weekly magazine," observed E. L. Doctorow, "transforms in time into a kind of narrative depicting an awesome journey of the national spirit."

*Scott Sherman is a New York-based writer.*

# PUBLIC JOURNALISM

## SUSAN NALL BALES

Public journalism is a new way of covering the world that contributes to a "better, richer political dialogue." It is also a way of exploring what it would mean for advocates and journalists to challenge the libertarian principles increasingly espoused in public debate today. To get there, Jay Rosen, director of the Project

*continued on page 170*

---

### American News Service

If you think the world is going to hell in a handbasket, you've been reading stories from the wrong wire service. Defying the old adage that "no news is good news," the American News Service concentrates on "solution-oriented" journalism. With a team of 20 journalists nationwide, ANS produces stories that focus on coalition-building and problem solving in such diverse arenas as crime, education, environment, race relations, and community development.

Founded in 1995, ANS is the brainchild of Frances Moore Lappé (of *Diet for a Small Planet* fame) and Paul Martin Du Bois. With an extensive roster of

community activism between them, Lappé and Du Bois determined to swim upstream in a media world that magnifies the negative and downplays the positive. By focusing on such subjects as community-based job-training programs, local efforts at mediation, and citywide initiatives to discourage negative campaigning, ANS helps to promote what Lappé and Du Bois call "living democracy." Shining the spotlight on grassroots success stories, ANS aims to shift public perception away from murder and mayhem and toward the hopeful glimmers we all know are out there.

Providing stories to more than 1,000 media subscribers, ANS features can be seen in the *Washington Post*, *ABC's*

*World News Tonight*, and *Life*. Here are a few sample stories:

*Breast Cancer Survivors Now Part of the Cure*

*Citizen Take on Campaign Finance Reform*

*A Strategy to Defuse Racial Tension*

*College Students Find Ways to Help the Homeless*

*Men Join Fight Against Domestic Violence*

Contact: American News Service at RR 1 Black Fox Road, Brattleboro, VT 05301; tel: (800)654-6397; E-mail: ans@americannews.com

*continued from page 169*

on Public Life and the Press at New York University, asserts, will take a fundamental reinventing of the values and art of journalism. Journalists "will have to change their lens on the political world and learn to see politics anew, as a discussion they have a duty to improve. . . . The horse race, insider baseball, the gotcha question, the feeding frenzy, the cult of toughness—these ought to be seen as unsustainable practices."

Rosen suggests that citizens examine the composition of news closely, to see how we think differently about the way we tell ourselves what is going on in our country. He says that in addition to setting the public agenda, journalists also participate in (1) defining their dominion; (2) the art of framing; (3) the capacity to publicly include; (4) the positioning effect; and (5) shaping a master narrative. Public journalism offers advocates a progressive vision of news (what others make) and of public storytelling (the news we make ourselves). To better understand the premise of public jour-

nalism, in the following analysis its approach is contrasted with the libertarian approach to journalism, which is so prevalent today.

## Dominion

*Public journalism's definition*: Dominion is the art of defining what journalism is about, its ultimate goals, what it "covers," and to what end. And public journalism, says Rosen, asks journalists "to include in their dominion the problem of making public life go well."

*The libertarian frame*: The news is simply what's new. It is about individuals who, through their own pluck or luck, rise or fall in the society. There is no systemic, historic, or thematic interpretation to explain the plight of certain social groups. The responsibility for correcting negative situations resides with those individuals, their families, or with charity. News is driven by the market, by what people find "interesting." It is not required to serve a higher "public" purpose. In this scenario, the media takes no responsibility for the effects of violent programming. The public can vote with its dial.

## Framing

*Public journalism's definition*: Journalism schools don't teach this, but still it's true: "Facts can't tell you how they want to be framed," writes Rosen. "Journalists decide how facts will be framed, and that means making decisions about which values will structure the story. . . . Done well, framing in journalism should proceed from and support certain val-

THIS MODERN WORLD — by TOM TOMORROW

LET ME READ YOU SOMETHING, BIFF: "A NEWSPAPER MUST AT ALL TIMES ANTAGONIZE THE SELFISH INTERESTS OF THAT VERY CLASS WHICH FURNISHES THE LARGER PART OF A NEWSPAPER'S INCOME..."

"THE PRESS IN THIS COUNTRY IS...SO THOROUGHLY DOMINATED BY THE WEALTHY FEW...THAT IT CANNOT BE DEPENDED UPON TO GIVE THE GREAT MASS OF THE PEOPLE THAT CORRECT INFORMATION CONCERNING POLITICAL, ECONOMICAL AND SOCIAL SUBJECTS--"

"--WHICH IT IS NECESSARY THAT THE MASS OF PEOPLE SHALL HAVE IN ORDER THAT THEY VOTE...IN THE BEST WAY TO PROTECT THEMSELVES FROM THE BRUTAL FORCE AND CHICANERY OF THE RULING AND EMPLOYING CLASSES."

WHO ARE YOU QUOTING, SPARKY? SOME LEFT-WING WACKO?

ACTUALLY, BIFF, THAT WAS WRITTEN AT THE TURN OF THE CENTURY BY E.W. SCRIPPS, FOUNDER OF THE FIRST MODERN NEWSPAPER CHAIN.

WELL, HE WOULDN'T GET VERY FAR IN JOURNALISM TODAY WITH AN ATTITUDE LIKE THAT.

NO, I SUPPOSE HE WOULDN'T...

web: http://www.well.com/user/tomorrow ... Email: tomorrow@well.com ... TOM TOMORROW©1-10-96

ues, and these are public values: the values of conversation, participation, deliberative dialogue, public problem-solving; the values of inclusion, individual responsibility, cooperative and complementary action; the values of caring for the community, taking chart of the future, overcoming the inertia of drift; finally the value of hope, understood as a renewable resource."

Framing is a simple concept. It asks of each news story: What was left in the story and what was left out? Public-journalism proponents would ask of each frame whether or not it contributes to "democracy and the flourishing of public life."

*The libertarian frame*: Libertarians frame news with the notion of a nation of disconnected individuals, whose circumstances are seen as random events. This undercuts the need for government or even collective responses. The libertarian response to the plight of individuals is to hold them responsible for their situation.

### The Capacity To Publicly Include

*Public journalism's definition*: "By selecting whom you include in a discussion," says Jay Rosen, "you're making a statement about what kind of discussion people require, and what's worth knowing.... By choosing whom to include, the press tells us whose voices count, whose lives are relevant, whose concerns are central."

*The libertarian frame*: The libertarian notion is one of complete free will. The individual has the ability to choose or to reject any idea, on his own. . . . The indi-

vidual is a consumer and a lone protagonist. But he is not part of a broader collective, nor is he responsible for others except inasmuch as he chooses to be. He has no responsibility to inform himself of others who are different from him. He does not feel compelled to "argue" or engage in discussions with people different from him, because he is free to choose his own individual course.

### Positioning

*Public journalism's definition*: "News stories position us in a wide variety of ways —as spectators or as participants, as insiders or as outsiders, as voters, as consumers, as fans, as victims, as celebrants.

The libertarian frame: You do not "need" any kind of news; news is a commodity. The news has no obligation to present people in any way whatsoever,

except to sell advertising.

To suggest that the reader is a learner, a stakeholder, and has a "need to know" certain aspects of the news is to create a responsibility for the news media that is decried by libertarians.

### Master Narrative

*Public journalism's definition*: "By master narrative," Rosen writes, "I mean . . . the Big Story that lends coherence and shape to all the little stories journalists tell. In the Bible the master narrative— the story that produces all the other stories—is the theme of creation and redemption, or the fall from grace and search for salvation. A master narrative is not a particular story journalists write; it is the story they are always writing

*continued on page 172*

### Association of Alternative Weeklies

 The 106 members of the 19-year-old Association of Alternative Newsweeklies (AAN) are always outspoken, often outrageous—and outstandingly successful, with annual industry revenues of approximately $250 million in 1995 alone. More than 13 million people now count themselves as readers of AAN papers each week.

When AAN was founded in 1978, 30 papers belonged to the group and the overall circulation was less than a million. Today, these papers, which serve com-

mitted local readerships in small towns and big cities alike, have a combined circulation of more than 5.5 million and often offer the only alternative to the corporate media fare of the dailies.

While daily newspapers are downsizing, AAN papers continue to grow. In fact, alternative newsweeklies are one of the few truly healthy segments of the publishing industry. More important, each works to strengthen diversity and independent voice as a counter to corporate media.

AAN can be reached at (202)822-1955; 1001 Connecticut Ave., NW, Suite 822, Washington, DC 20036; http://aan.eline.com.

*continued from page 171*

when they tell the stories they typically tell. In election-coverage, the master narrative is winning."

*The libertarian frame*: The master narrative is the individual on the frontier —free to protect, defend, and provide for himself and his family. Anyone not in the picture is an outsider. The bonds of community are entirely voluntary and can be relinquished at any time. The body politic is to be viewed as a constraint on individual freedoms and to be used only as a last resort.

**Taking Back The Territory**

Says Jay Rosen: "Doing public journal- ism means asking yourself:'How do we tell the story of this community in a manner that invites citizens to join the story as informed participants?' That's the challenge for public journalism as a narrative art."

*Susan Nall Bates is with the Benton Foundation.*

---

**Independent Press Association**

 Founded at the first annual Media & Democracy Congress, the Independent Press Association (IPA) was created to give progressive periodicals and community-based publications a much-needed sense of community and base for networking. The IPA creates opportunities to share intellectual as well as material resources among members, provides a vehicle for marketing and other efforts, and offers a mutual support network for independent press editors, publishers, writers, and artists.

Alternative Press Index
The Amicus Journal
Buffalo Commons
Build Magazine
Bulletin of the Atomic Scientists
Catalyst
Chicago Reporter
City Limits
Country Connections
Crone Chronicles: A Journal of Conscious Aging
Cultural Survival Quarterly

E Magazine
Earth Island Journal
EcoNews
EXTRA!
Food and Water Journal
Grassroots Fundraising Journal
High Country News
Hip Mama
HUES
In These Times
Infusion: Tools for Action and Education
Labour/Le Travail
Labor Research Review
Lambda Book Report
Latin American Perspectives
Lumpen
The Mother is Me
MOUTH Magazine
NACLA: Report on the Americas
The Neighborhood Works
New Moon
New Politics
Off Our Backs
The Progressive
The Progressive Review
RaceFile
Race, Poverty & the Environment
Rachel's Environmental & Health Weekly
Ragged Edge

Rethinking Schools
SageWoman
Shelterforce
Sierra
Social Justice
Social Policy
Southern Exposure
The Sun
Teen Voices
Terrain: Northern California's Environmental Magazine
Third Force
Tikkun
Turning the Tide
Utne Reader
Who Cares
Women's Education des Femmes
The Women's Review of Books
The Workbook
Working People
World Watch
Yes! A Journal of Positive Futures
Yoga Journal
Z Magazine

For information, contact IPA at P.O. Box 191785, San Francisco, CA 94119-1785; phone/fax: (415) 896-2456; E-mail: indypress@igc.org

# A ZINE PRIMER

### SETH FRIEDMAN

I've read probably 50,000 zines in the last ten years.

I discovered music fanzines back in the '70s, and just never grew out of them. Five years ago, I restarted *Factsheet Five* magazine, which catalogs and reviews thousands of zines in each issue. Zines (short for fanzines) contain writing that's unlike anything else in the mainstream: more opinionated than newspaper editorials, more personal than magazine articles, more topical than books.

Although zines can be anything from darkly xeroxed handwritten poetry to slickly printed full-color music magazines, what unites all zine publishers is their passion for communication. Zine makers are driven to publish their ideas purely for the sake of communicating, generally with complete disregard for money or profits.

Most people publish zines just for the joy of it, but occasionally professional writers start up zines as an outlet for their more creative impulses. Instead of restricting themselves to "objective" news reporting or informative magazine articles, zines give writers the freedom to write from a more personal, opinionated perspective.

This quirky personal writing is what draws people to zines. Open up one zine and you'll find someone waxing eloquently about his collection of beer-bottle openers; while in another someone will be writing about her abusive husband and recent divorce; and in a third you might find a hateful rant about Rush Limbaugh and his legions of "dittoheads."

*continued on page 174*

## AlterNet

 The Institute for Alternative Journalism (IAJ), established in 1983, exists to enhance democracy and broaden public debate. Over the years, it has developed numerous projects to help extend the reach of independent media, including the creation of AlterNet in 1987.

AlterNet is the nation's only news service and information clearinghouse for the alternative press and is aimed at strengthening independent and alternative journalism and improving the public's access to that journalism. The more than 140 papers, commentators, radio programs, and online publications in the network reach six million people each week and often offer the only alternative to the corporate media fare of daily newspapers and broadcast news.

One of AlterNet's primary goals is also to help news outlets cover issues overlooked or ignored by the mainstream press and provide a forum for a diversity of voices. The service has facilitated the syndication of thousands of stories in the alternative press by some of the best independent writers in America today, expanding the reach of public-interest and independent journalism and helping dozens of new, independent papers make it through their difficult first year.

AlterNet's broader goal is to function as a conduit for publicly accessible independent news and information. AlterNet not only facilitates greater information sharing among independent media, but provides the connective tissue binding the alternative media world together. Today, major sources of information for journalists, think tanks, academics, researchers, business, and the general public are tied to corporate media and contain little or no contributions from noncommercial and independent media. A respite for those fed up with the commercial, AlterNet offers a way to find the news you need from a source intent on serving the public-interest and making independent voices heard.

Visit AlterNet's "hub" of independent journalism at http://www.alternet.org and check out the best weekly stories and opinions, resources for journalists and activists, related job listings, and links to a vast network of the best noncommercial journalism and content online.

Contact: IAJ at 77 Federal St., San Francisco, CA 94107; Tel: (415) 284-1420; Fax: (415) 284-1414; E-mail: congress@igc.org.

Most typical is the small, digest-sized zine, created by folding several sheets of standard-size writing paper. This convenient booklet format allows the publisher to produce a publication that's compact and easily carried around or sent through the mail.

This is where the power of the United States mail comes in. Zine publishers make use of a sprawling network of publishers and readers, all connected through the United States postal system. It's through this network that the unsuspecting reader might pick up a single innocuous-looking zine and then be exposed to an entire world of bustling activity. (Excerpted from *The Zine Reader* )

*Seth Friedman is editor of* Factsheet Five.

# WRITERS' RIGHTS

### JONATHAN TASINI

Why should the public care about the struggles of freelance writers?

The media conglomerates are taking away the livelihood of writers, driving them out of business. If writers cannot get their fair share and make a decent living, it will mean fewer contributors to our arts and sciences and a decline in independent voices, making our society culturally poorer.

We are not talking about a privileged class. Most working writers, who earn their living from licensing their copyrighted works, earn less than $7,000 per year from their writing; they do not have health insurance or pensions. Their fees for print use have been declining in real terms over the last 15 years.

The situation has gotten far worse with the growing power of the media companies. In December 1993, 11 writers sued the *New York Times*, Time, Inc., and others, arguing that the media companies were illegally using their work in the electronic world. Essentially, they took what had been given them to use in print form and, without permission, placed the work on databases, CD-ROMs, and other formats. In fact, the lawsuit highlights the mission of the media companies: reap as much money as possible even at the expense of impoverishing our culture, whether by stealing from writers and/or failing to provide people with a broad set of choices of information.

Writers are now asking for a fair share. For example, the Journalism Committee of the National Writers Union (NWU) came up with a fair resolution, recommending that writers be paid a minimum of 15 percent of the original print fee (i.e., the First North American Print Rights fee) for use of a writer's work in a single electronic outlet for a period of up to one year. An additional licensing fee would be paid for each specific electronic use of the original work for each year that it is used.

For example, if a writer is paid $1,000 for the print version of her story, she should be paid at least an additional $150 for the use of her story for one year on a

*continued on page 175*

*continued from page 174*

World Wide Web edition of the publication. She should be paid another $150 if her story is included as part of a database service such as Magazine Database Plus on Compuserve or at a magazine's electronic location on America Online. The National Writers Union even created a solution: the first-ever transaction-based licensing system for freelance writers, called the Publication Rights Clearinghouse (PRC); it's a sophisticated method to make sure writers' works can be used easily, while also guaranteeing writers get the pay they deserve for the use of the works they create.

Will paying writers their fair share mean higher prices for the public? It doesn't have to be that way. The NWU's position is that the writers' fair share should come from the profits of the companies, not by raising prices and taking more money from the pocketbooks of average people.

Moreover, the NWU has always seen its mission as protecting writers and participating in the broader struggle over how our society is shaped. As the debate over the information revolution has raged in the past several years, the NWU has worked to form coalitions with librarians, advocates of freedom of expression, unions, and other representatives of the public-interest, all in an effort to guarantee that every sector of society share in whatever benefits flow from new technologies.

*Jonathan Tasini is president of the National Writers Union.*

## Campus Alternative Journalism Project

 The Center for Campus Organizing (CCO) is a clearinghouse dedicated to increasing the base of progressive activism within the United States. The center promotes political action and participation by helping campus activists develop organizing skills, create alternative media, and form local organizations. In addition, the group is dedicated to building the links between campus activists and other progressive organizations needed to sustain progressive efforts over the long haul.

In the fall of 1994, CCO launched the Campus Alternative Journalism Project (CAJP) to serve the thousands of students who are making progressive social change through alternative media. The CAJP provides training, information and support to grassroots student papers, as well as a sense of being a part of a larger movement. While CAJP concentrates on print media—that is, newspapers, magazines, and newsletters—student journalists in other media will find the services helpful.

In addition to CAJP's flagship *The Alternative Journalism Internship Guide*—featuring more than 120 internships for young people—the group published in 1996 *Afflict the Comfortable, Comfort the Afflicted: A Guide for Campus Alternative Journalists*. The guide aims to advise student activists in starting a new paper, train new staffers, stimulate new ideas, and serve as a general reference resource.

For more information, contact Campus Alternative Journalism Projects at Center for Campus Organizing, P.O. Box 748, Cambridge, MA 02142. For a free subscription to the Campus Alternative Journalism E-mail network, send a message to canet@pencil.math.missouri.edu

# STORYTELLING

## SUSAN NALL BALES

This is about storytelling—how public interest journalists tell stories to citizens, how advocates tell stories to journalists to convey to citizens, and how we tell stories to each other to try to make sense of what is happening to our families, neighbors and people we don't know.

A different kind of story is needed. Media advocates need to pioneer a new kind of talking back, a values-based style of storytelling whose big story is about overcoming boundaries between people to engage in common problem-solving. Many progressives have operated on the assumption that we need to promote streams of human interest stories—mostly, as it turned out, about victims.

These stories are intended to make the point that real people are suffering, but they do so within currently accepted journalistic practices that undermine public resolution of social problems. Now there is new scholarship to suggest these stories do a disservice to progressive ideals and detract from the bigger story we are trying to tell about our common destiny. It's time to reexamine our tactics.

We need to ask ourselves, What is the story behind the story—the BIG story that we tell ourselves over and over about our experiences as Americans? How are values embedded in the commentary and how do those values either help us solve problems together, as communities or as a country, or break us down into individual problem-solvers, a nation of individuals only loosely tied together?

This is also about a new kind of journalism—public journalism—that we can use to inform and support our work. Ernie Pyle was a pioneer of public journalism back in the 1930s and '40s, when he wrote a nationally syndicated column. The way Pyle approached telling stories—interpreting Americans to themselves and helping them see their country and its values up close and personal - is an art we must recapture if we are to find a public voice for progressive ideas. In the end, journalism is far too important to be left to the journalists. It's time to take back the territory of public storytelling.

Ernie Pyle's language and vision are as fresh as if the dateline were yesterday. The populist distrust of government, but the strong insistence nevertheless on connectedness and mutual responsibility. The yearning for words devoid of politics, that real people can understand. The emotional connection to Americans' basic sense of fairness, told from the perspective of "the little guy." This has always been the challenge of progressives in this country, to personalize the impacts of policies in ways that bring home the consequences to real people we recognize as part of "us."

### Ernie Pyle, March 16, 1939

ENTERPRISE, ALABAMA—This is a New Deal story, so if you don't like the New Deal you won't see any sense in it.

When the government took a hand here in 1935, six out of ten school children in the county had hookworm. Every other baby died at birth. One mother in every ten died in childbirth. The average mentality was third-grade. One out of ten adults couldn't read or write. Three-fourths of the farmers were tenant farmers. Most of them had never been out of debt in their lives. They averaged only one mule to three families.

And this is in Coffee County, which stands third among all the counties of Alabama in the value of agricultural products. These figures are not the scandalous revelations of some smart Brain Truster from the North. They are from a survey, made by Southerners. Sure, you'll find wealth and grace and beautiful homes in the South, homes are pretty and people as fine as anywhere in the world. But you drive the back roads, and you won't see one farm home in a hundred that would equal the ordinary Midwest farmhouse.

Coffee County has become a sort of experimental station in Alabama. Not by design, especially, but because the government people and the local agencies got enthusiastic, and it just grew up under them.

Federal, state, and county agencies all have a hand. To prevent overlapping, they are coordinated under a council, with the county school superintendent as chairman. They say it's the only thing of its kind in America.

These agencies cover most everything from typhoid shots to fruit-canning. They're like agencies in your home territory, only the need is greater and I suspect they are a bit more enthusiastic. The work is climaxed in the Farm Security Administration, which actually owns thousands of acres of land and plants these down-and-out farmers on its acres.

I wish there were something to call these things besides "projects." The idea of a project makes the farmers contemptuous, makes Republicans snort with rage, brings sneers from the townspeople. A project is Brain Trust—experimenting, regimenting people.

What they're doing here isn't a project, anyway. They aren't setting up a "settlement." Nobody is forced to do anything. The six hundred farmers on FSA are scattered over a county twenty-five miles square. What they're doing is simply a general and wide-stretching process—starting almost from zero—of trying to get people to live better.

# The Next Frontier

## Part V

**T**he production and sale of information have become major sites of profit making. What had been in large measure a social good has been transformed into a commodity for sale. In particular, the commercialization and privatization of government information has become a paradox. Unarguably, it has been of great benefit to affluent users who now have access to the kind and amounts of data that would have been unimaginable only a few years ago. For the rest of the population, the vast majority, the quality and the availability of information leave a lot to be desired. In the domain of general government information, the supply has been curtailed severely. The American Library Association notes that "since 1982, one of every four of the government's 16,000 publications has been eliminated."

— *HERBERT SCHILLER, author,*
Information Inequality

# INTRODUCTION

## JAY WALLJASPER

The dawning era of the information age offers extraordinary potential for promoting global democracy and international understanding. Yet, as we have seen with automobiles and nuclear power, there are often unintended consequences of revolutionary new breakthroughs, especially when the political and economic circumstances governing these changes are downplayed in public debate. There's only one side to this story in most media reports: the bright future awaiting humanity as unlimited access to information through new technology works wonders in every facet of modern life from human rights to pet grooming.

When information itself becomes the chief commodity of international business, what happens to poor people and developing nations who can't pay the price? What are the implications for children and education? Free expression? Privacy? And quality, in both information and entertainment? *(Utne Reader)*

# 1. Democracy for Whom?

## THE INTERNET AND THE DIGITAL REVOLUTION

**ROBERT MCCHESNEY**

The rise of a global commercial media system is only one striking trend of the 1990s. The other is the rise of digital computer networks in general, and the Internet in particular. The logic of digital communication is that the traditional distinctions between telephony and all types of media are disappearing. Eventually, these industries will "converge," meaning firms active in one of them will by definition be capable of competing in the others. The present example of convergence is how cable and telephone companies can now offer each other's services. The Internet has opened up very important space for progressive and democratic communication, especially for

activists hamstrung by traditional commercial media. This alone has made the Internet an extremely positive development. Yet whether one can extrapolate from this fact to see the Internet becoming the democratic medium for society writ large is another matter. The notion that the Internet will permit humanity to leapfrog over capitalism and corporate communication is in sharp contrast to the present rapid commercialization of the Internet.

Moreover, it will be many years before the Internet can possibly stake a claim to replace television as the dominant medium in the United States, and much longer elsewhere. This is due to bandwidth limitations, the cost of computers and access, and numerous, often complex, technical problems, all of which will keep Internet usage restricted. Rupert Murdoch, whose News Corporation has been perhaps the most aggressive of the media giants to explore the possibilities of cyberspace, states that establishing an information highway "is going to take longer than people think." He projects that it will take until at least 2010 or 2015 for a broadband network to reach fruition in the United States and western Europe, and until the middle of the 21st century for it to begin to dominate elsewhere.

It is also unclear how firms will be able to make money by providing Internet content—and in a market-driven system this is the all-important question. Even the rosiest forecasts only see Internet advertising spending at $5 billion by 2000, representing only 2 or 3 percent of projected U.S. advertising spending that year. The media giants have all established websites and have the product and deep pockets to wait it out and establish themselves as the dominant players in cyberspace. They can also use their existing media to constantly promote their online ventures, and their relationships with major advertisers to bring them aboard their Internet ventures. In short, if the Internet becomes a viable commercial medium, there is a good chance that many of the media giants will be among the firms capable of capitalizing upon it. The other "winners" will probably be firms like Microsoft that have the resources to seize a portion of the market.

While the media firms do not face an immediate or direct threat from the Internet, such is not the case for computer software makers and telecommunication firms. The Internet is changing the basic nature of both their businesses, and both industries are turning their attention to incorporating the Internet into the heart of their activities. The eventual mergers and alliances that emerge will have tremendous impact upon global

*continued on page 180*

## Ideas in Action...Influencing the Universal Access Debate

Universal access provisions of the Telecommunications Act are still being defined. Your input, especially at the state level, can make a difference. Here are a few of the best sources to turn to according to the Center for Media Education.

*The Public Utility Commission (PUC) staff:*
The public information office at the PUC should be able to send you a schedule of upcoming proceedings and background information. Ask if the commission has formally issued a "notice" that it intends to take action on key issues such as universal service or alternative regulation. Formal proceedings generally have a timetable for soliciting comments, conducting studies, and holding hearings. Plan your efforts around that schedule.

*Consumer Advocate's office:*
Most states have an official designated to represent the public-interest in proceedings at the PUC and other agencies. A meeting with the staff person assigned to telecommunications is an important early step that could yield valuable information and insights.

*Consumer groups:*
Your state's principal consumer groups are likely to be actively involved in telecommunications issues. Since these groups usually have telecommunications expertise, you should enlist their help early on.

*Identifying key corporate players:*
The main player in any commission proceeding is the utility being regulated, which usually means a Baby Bell company. The other corporate players will be its competitors, which may include long-distance companies planning to offer local phone service. Cable companies may also be involved in the proceedings.

*Enlisting allies:*
Consumer, education, and disability groups already involved in telecommunications policy are potential allies. They include:

Consumer groups such as the Consumer Federation of America, Consumers Union, Citizen Action, and the PIRG (Public Interest Research Group) network

Education and library organizations such as Council of Chief State School Officers, the National School Boards Association, the National Education Association, the American Library Association, and Libraries for the Future

Groups representing the disability community

Hospitals, child care centers, colleges, and universities

Contact: The Center for Media Education at 1511 K Street, NW, Suite 518, Washington, DC 20005; phone: (202) 628-2620; Fax (202) 628-2554; E-mail cme@cme.org; http://www.cme.org/cme.

*continued from page 179*

media as media firms are brought into the digital communication empires. This is speculative; it is also possible that the Internet itself will eventually be supplanted by a more commercially-oriented digital communication network.

Long ago—back in the Internet's ancient history, like 1994 and 1995—some Internet enthusiasts were so captivated by the technology's powers they regarded "cyberspace" as the end of corporate for-profit communication, because there people would be able to bypass the corporate sector and communicate globally with each other directly. That was then. Perhaps the most striking change in the late 1990s is how quickly the euphoria of those who saw the Internet as providing a qualitatively different and egalitarian type of journalism, politics, media and culture has faded. The indications are that the substantive content of this commercial media in the Internet, or any subsequent digital communication system, will look much like what currently exists. Indeed, advertisers and commercialism arguably have more influence over Internet content than anywhere else. Advertisers and media firms both aspire to make the Internet look more and more like commercial television, as that is a proven winner commercially. In December 1996 Microsoft reconfigured its huge online Microsoft Network to resemble a television format. AT&T's director of Internet services says the Internet may become the ultimate advertising-driven medium: "If it's done well, you won't feel there's any tension between the consumerism and the entertainment." Frank Beacham, who in 1995 enthused about the Internet as a public sphere outside corporate or governmental control, lamented one year later that the Internet was shifting "from being a participatory medium that serves the interests of the public to being a broadcast medium where corporations deliver consumer-oriented information. Interactivity would be reduced to little more than sales transactions and E-mail."

*Robert McChesney is the author of* Corporate Media and the Treat to Democracy.

*A 1995 study by the Rand Institute stated that without government intervention to close the widening gap, the nation will soon be experiencing "information apartheid." The cost of being online is a major factor in the underrepresentation of some communities on the Net, but the lack of relevant information contributes to the lack of participation. According to the Rand study, approximately 13 percent of African-American, Latino, and Native American households have computers, compared to 31 percent of white and 37 percent of Asian-American households.*

*— River Ginchild,* Third Force

## Ideas in Action...
## The Little WiRed Schoolhouse

If computers are the "new basic" of American education, and the Internet the blackboard of the future, then why is it that there is no clear road map for fully wired schools and technological literacy? According to the Center for Media Education, linking schools and libraries to the information highway requires the following components if access is to be meaningful.

## Hardware
The first step is to supply schools with a sufficient number of multimedia-ready computers, ideally one for every five students. The ratio is currently one computer to every 38 students.

## Infrastructure
Beyond computers, classrooms need both an Internet connection and local area networks (LANs) to be fully up to speed. For many schools, basic hurdles must be cleared first, including the improvement of electrical wiring and the removal of asbestos.

## Trained teachers
Right now, nearly half of all teachers have had little or no experience with computers, and only a small minority have the training needed to integrate networked computers fully into classroom teaching. Only 18 states require training in technology for teachers seeking certification, and only five require technology as a subject of in-service training.

## Maintenance and upgrades
Fully 85 percent of today's school computers are unequipped to handle multimedia, and there is little reason to expect that the existing trend toward rapid "obsolescence" in the microcomputer market will end anytime soon.

## Skills for the future
According to the Department of Labor, nearly half of all jobs now require some form of computer and/or networking capability, roughly double the number just ten years ago. By the year 2000, 60 percent of all jobs will require technical skills that only 22 percent of the United States population currently has. The implications for students who will enter the workforce in the next century are clear: those lacking computer skills will be at a decided disadvantage, both in competing for jobs and in advancing their careers.

—Center for Media Education

# 2. Incredible Shrinking Media: The Internet

## BLAND AMBITION

### JON KATZ

Like it or not, we are all now living in a Microsoft world. But journalists have a tough time grasping the downside of this and making it clear to the many millions of Americans who have no idea that control of a vast percentage of their information world is falling into one pair of hands.

The media created by Jefferson, Paine, and the founders of American journalism derived its strength from a moral imperative: It supported individual rights, challenged authority, and gave expression to disenfranchised individuals. The tragedy of Microsoft isn't that it seeks to take over our lives or define our culture or define our values as Wal-Mart does. The real problem with this kind of company assuming so powerful a position in the information world is that it has no discernible values or morals beyond creating the Next Big Thing.

Here's the big irony: Gates is now the most powerful person in American media, and he has no apparent philosophy of or vision for media at all, other than controlling the machinery that distributes it. He isn't a populist, as William Randolph Hearst initially was, or a revolutionary, as Thomas Paine was, or an advocate of impartial and thorough journalism, as Adolph Ochs was, or a proponent of the potential of commercial broadcasting, as William Paley was. It isn't clear how he feels about investigative reporting, journalistic ethics, the role of political coverage in American life, or the quality of writing in mass media. It isn't even clear he's thought about these issues at all.

As a media company, Microsoft has yet to do even one outstanding, brave, radical, or particularly creative thing. Which, if Gates is to inherit the media earth, may be scarier than even censorship or bias. (*Wired*)

*Jon Katz is a contributor to* Wired.

# MICROSOFT MORPHS INTO A MEDIA COMPANY

**DENISE CARUSO**

Whether by design or by circumstance, Microsoft is holding all known pieces to a puzzle that could snap together into a new breed of media company, a "technomedia" company that not only creates media but also controls the entire value chain of delivering it. Though the company continues to assert that software for personal computers is its primary business, over the past few years Microsoft has methodically placed significant amounts of capital, staff, and corporate resources into building its media capacity.

The best example of Microsoft's growing strategic commitment to media is its $450 million investment in MSNBC, the 24-hour news channel it launched in mid-1996. Another example is found in its 2,000-employee Interactive Media Division, which is compiling a library of brand-name, mass-market interactive media assets (such as *Encarta*, the largest selling print or electronic encyclopedia in the world, and *Cinemania*, a movie guide). In addition, Microsoft is making high-profile investments with large, traditional media and entertainment companies—including DreamWorks SKG, the studio founded by Hollywood moguls Jeffrey Katzenberg, Steven Spielberg, and David Geffen—and forging joint ventures throughout the creative community for new interactive media properties.

The company has also created The Microsoft Network—which had 1 million subscribers a year after its launch. It has also lined up interactive distribution deals with companies ranging from national Internet service providers (UUNet) to direct broadcast satellite companies (DirecTV). Over the past few years, Microsoft has also been stockpiling advanced-technology assets that target, with surgical precision, each area where the creation and distribution of media are headed, from visual computing to high-speed, interactive digital video. And while no one knows quite how to go about tapping it, Microsoft sees vast opportunity in interactive media—a business potentially many times the size of the current software market.

Depending on how you tote it up, Microsoft's commitment to these projects over the next five years could be

*continued on page 184*

*continued from page 183*

# GORILLA IN THE PICTURE BUSINESS

well over $1.5 billion. That's serious money, even by Disney or Viacom standards.

As growth in old media such as television, books, movies, and magazines levels off, interactive media is the only realm where analysts are predicting giddy growth rates reminiscent of the early PC business. Founder and CEO Bill Gates has said publicly that by 2000, Microsoft will be spending $250 million per year to promote its efforts via interactive advertising. Gates himself is not one of the customers he hopes to attract—a busy guy, he has been heard to say that his regular media consumption includes CNN and *The Economist*—and now, one imagines, MSNBC—and not much more. (*Wired*)

**DAVID WALKER**

Back in the late 1980s, Bill Gates envisioned the house of the future with PC screens throughout. Built into the walls, the screens would display photos and works of art selected by remote control. Perhaps a Picasso motif in the morning; Matisse in the afternoon.

In 1989, Gates started Interactive Home Systems to build the image database so he could make money "renting" the pictures. Along the way he realized that the future belongs to owners of intellectual property, since computer networks will be able to distribute creative works quickly and easily.

The more intellectual property you own, obviously, the more money you make. So Gates' odd little project has turned into a large image licensing enterprise called Corbis. Corbis will eventually license pictures not only to book, magazine, and newspaper publishers (the traditional market for editorial photos) but to Web publishers, school children, consumers with PCs in their walls, and virtually any other type of nonadvertising user.

Corbis employees have fanned out around the world to buy up copyrights—or at least long-term rights of distribution—to the best photographs and paintings they can find. They are shopping at museums, at photo archives, at the homes of private collectors and the studios of the artists themselves to find pictures of everything known to mankind. And as Citizen Gates, the Microsoft CEO is exercising his right to obtain essentially free copies of pictures from NASA and the Library of Congress, adding those works to Corbis as well. For images he can't find in existing collections, Gates is hiring photographers to shoot for him.

But when Gates dominates the editorial image business, as he clearly intends to do, he'll largely control what works are selected for distribution. Will he choose pictures for their diversity of ideas? Or will he choose them for their mass-market appeal? There's good rea-

## The Incredible Shrinking Media Meets Microsoft

As the manufacturer of the operating systems used by 120 million personal computer users, Microsoft controls the gateway to more than 85 percent of the PCs in the world. —(*New York Times*)

"If you own the operating system that runs the world's PCs, and if you are allowed to leverage that power in entering new businesses, you have an advantage that the great monopolists of the 19th century could only dream of."
—James Gleich, commenting on Microsoft in the company's own online magazine, *Slate*

"Some of [Microsoft's] executives privately believe Microsoft could double both its size and its market valuation within the next five years. This would make it the most valuable firm on the planet."
—Steven Levy, *Newsweek*

son to worry that consolidation of the image business, like consolidation of other media businesses, will narrow choice to the bland center, where all the pictures match the sofas and carpets of middle-class Americans and don't upset the guests.

By the end of 1996, Gates had amassed rights to 17 million pictures.

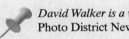 *David Walker is a writer for* Photo District News.

**A few of Microsoft's holdings:**

* MS NBC—$450 million stake

* Bettmann Archives 700,000 images ranging from Delacroix's *Liberty Leading the People* to Einstein sticking his tongue out to Ansel Adams' photographs

* Encarta Encyclopedia

* Gauthier and Gilden, which will write a soap opera for MS NBC

* DreamWorks SKG investment in the Hollywood studio founded by Steven Spielberg, Jeffrey Katzenberg, and David Geffen

* Partnerships or joint ventures with: Viacom's Paramount Television Group, which plans to create an interactive version of Star Trek

* TCI/Time Warner's Black Entertainment Television, with which Micro-soft will produce interactive television and CD-Roms

# 3. The Net

*Plus profiles of* Howard Rheingold, Electronic Frontier Foundation, Voter's Telecommunications Watch, NetAction, and Progressive Networks

## THE NEXT MASS MEDIA?

### FRANK BEACHAM

For the first time, writers can inexpensively publish their work to a worldwide audience without the approval of publishers and editorial boards. But the age-old problem for self-publishers—that of marketing and finding an audience—does not go away with the Internet.

Felix Kramer, an Internet consultant for businesses and organizations, notes that "the biggest mistake people make is just putting up a site and expecting that everyone will come. It's like building a 7-11 in the middle of the desert. Nobody knows about it." A good way to keep people coming back, said Kramer, is to combine a website with a mailing list to encourage return visits.

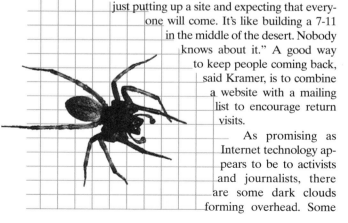

As promising as Internet technology appears to be to activists and journalists, there are some dark clouds forming overhead. Some see an inherent danger lurking in the rapid commercialization of computer networks. "The Web itself is in what I consider to be a real war," said Alfredo Lopez, senior partner in Lopez Communication, a Brooklyn-based marketing and communications firm. "In my opinion the people with money and huge resources are trying to take it away from us."

The mainstream listing directories usually don't include progressive political sites because of bias, said López, who himself maintains an extensive directory of progressive links on his site, People-Link.

Another issue is the technology itself. Dan Levy, founder of Levity Media, worries that big media companies will construct high bandwidth networks for video-on-demand around the Internet and thus render the cheap and open technology of today irrelevant to the mass audience.

"Is there always going to be access for the guy with no money and an unpopular message?" asks Levy. "I hope so but it really depends on whether there continues to be independent Internet access providers and that depends on there being high bandwidth backbones that are not controlled by big media companies." (*AlterNet*)

*Dan Levy's Levity site is at http://www.levity.com. Felix Kramer's Kramer Communications is at: http://www.nlightning.com. Alfredo López's People-Link is at: http://www.people-link.com. The author of this article, Frank Beacham, is at http://www.beacham.com.*

*Frank Beacham is a New York-based writer, producer and director.*

# CYBERSELFISH

**PAULINA BORSOOK**

Silicon Valley, one of the country's biggest recipients of government largesse, would like to bite the hand that feeds it. Although the technologists I've encountered are generally liberal on social issues (prochoice, supportive of domestic partner benefits, inclined to sanction the occasional use of recreational drugs), they are to the last one violently lacking in compassion, ravingly antigovernment, and tremendously opposed to regulation.

These cyberlibertarians are the inheritors of the greatest government subsidy of technology and expansion in technical education the planet has ever seen; and, like the ungrateful adolescent offspring of immigrants who have made it in the new country, they take for granted the richness of the environment in which they have flourished, and resent the hell out of the constraints that bind them.

The convergence between libertarianism and high tech has created the true revenge of the nerds: Those whose greatest strengths have not been the comprehension of social systems, appreciation of the humanities, or acquaintance with history, politics, and economics have started shaping public policy.

*Protecting privacy.* Technolibertarians rightfully worry about Big Bad Government, yet think commerce unfettered can create all things bright and beautiful —and so they disregard the real invader of privacy: Corporate America seeking ever-better ways to exploit the Net, to sell databases of consumer purchases and preferences, to track potential customers however it can.

*Skimping on philanthropy.* In Silicon Valley and its regional outposts (Seattle, Austin), it's not even a joke, not even an embarrassment, that there's so little corporate philanthropy. High tech employees rank among the lowest of any industry sector for giving to charity.

*Gutting the environment.* High tech also has tremendously negative environmental impacts: Manufacturing its plastics and semiconductors is a remarkably toxic and resource-depleting affair.

We make goo-goo eyes over the megabucks that high-tech generates, but we ignore the price. Just as 19th-century timber and cattle and mining robber barons made their fortunes from public

*continued on page 188*

---

### Scary but True...

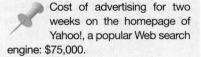 A study by Matrix Information and Directory Services in Austin, Texas, found that as of October 1995, there were about 26.4 million consumers on the Internet, along with 39 million E-mail users and about 10.1 million computers. According to the company, these numbers represent a *100 percent* increase in Internet use since 1988.

An estimated $150–$340 million was spent on Web advertising in 1996, a figure that is expected to grow to $500 million to $1 billion in 1997. Web ad spending is project to reach $5 billion by 2000. *(San Francisco Examiner)*

Cost of advertising for two weeks on the homepage of Yahoo!, a popular Web search engine: $75,000.

---

### Scary but True...

The new information-age companies created a fresh batch of millionaires and billionaires, but you working stiffs shouldn't expect much. Not only do the rank-and-file jobs in this industry offer mediocre-to-miserly pay, very few jobs of any kind are created by these hot new titans. Microsoft and Intel only employ 48,000 people. Ford employs more than three times that, and GM, with 350,000 U.S. employees, seven times.

The new titans' few jobs are a cruel joke on an economy that hires 114 million people and has more than 12 million more unemployed. Indeed, computer-processing and electronics manufacturing combined offer barely two-and-a-half million jobs, and both the number of those jobs and their pay are on the decline.

—Jim Hightower

*continued from page 187*

resources, so are technolibertarians creaming the profits from public resources—from the orderly society that has resulted from the wise use of regulation and public spending. And they have neither the wisdom nor the manners nor the mind set to give anything that's not electronic back. (*Mother Jones*)

Full text of this article is available at http://www.mojones.com/mother jones/JA96/borsook.html.

## Howard Rheingold

Howard Rheingold, an author, columnist, and former editor of the *Whole Earth Review*, finds his website helps keep a connection to his readers. "American journalism has failed in a major and shameful way to live up to its obligation to inform citizens about that which we need to know in order to remain a democracy," Rheingold said. "All this porno on the Internet, all these stupid scare stories about hackers and pedophiles and no explanation of the winners and losers in the telecommunications deregulation. Fundamental rights are at stake with the Communications Decency Act. A real power grab is taking place and the story has not been conveyed to the American people."
—Frank Beacham

*Howard Rheingold's website can be found at http://www.well.com/user/hlr*

# THE VIRTUAL FÜHRER

## CURT GUYETTE

Skinheads. The Ku Klux Klan. Identity Christians. White Supremacists. Patriots. Militiamen. Neo-Nazis.

It is the far-right edge of the World Wide Web, a place where Aryan cybernauts and hyperlinked Klansmen spew their racist views and troll for new recruits.

Type the words "Aryan," "skinhead," or "white power" into your favorite web search engine and stand back. Dozens of sites will appear, many featuring sophisticated designs, compelling graphics, and text that drips bile and fear. It's not just a problem in the United States. Just as the Internet knows no boundaries, neither does the white-supremacy movement. Which is why Montreal resident David Abitol for the past two years has maintained a site dedicated to tracking these groups.

"Our 'Net Hate' page was spurred by the growing use of the web," says Abitol. "There has been a tremendous growth in the number of hate pages we've been coming across."

"This is a perfect medium for [hate groups]," contends Rabbi Abraham Cooper of the Simon Wiesenthal Center in Los Angeles. "Their cultural impact can be enormous. And the fringe groups have been much more adept at realizing the potential of this technology and putting it to use. The real value is the way in which it increases their ability to put their message out, and to recruit new members. Especially young people. It is a fantastic marketing tool."

How best to combat the issue is a matter of great debate. The Wiesenthal Center is calling on access providers to exercise "good corporate citizenship" and banish hate groups and is calling upon the Clinton administration to make the issue a top priority.

Others bristle at any attempt to curtail free-speech rights, no matter how odious that speech may be.

"The best response to bad speech is more speech," contends Barry Steinhardt of the American Civil Liberties Union. "To sweep these groups' speech under the rug where it can't be exposed to counterargument is the most dangerous thing you can do."

Besides, says Steinhardt, effective censorship is virtually impossible, given the international, borderless qualities of the Internet. How great a threat do these groups pose? No one can say for sure. But notorious neo-Nazi Tom Metzger, who operates the White Aryan Resistance Hate Page, offers one piece of advice: "Underestimating the opposition is always a dangerous delusion." (*Detroit Metro Times*)

*Hate Watch can be found at http://hatewatch.org.*

# GRASSROOTS ACTIVISM IN THE ELECTRONIC AGE

### JESSE DREW

The Internet has combined a very old form of technology, the telephone, with a relatively new one, the microcomputer, and thus created the potential for democratic, two-way communications. Thanks to strict regulations imposed on the telephone companies in an era more sympathetic to the public-interest, the phone lines serve as the Internet common carrier to all those who can get their hands on a home computer and a modem.

A dramatic example of this is how the Zapatistas spread news and communiqués of the Chiapas uprising to the world, confounding the traditional Mexican press censors and contributing to building an international support network. Another example of using the net to bypass the media gatekeepers are the documents leaked from the Brown & Williamson tobacco company to health researchers at the University of California at San Francisco (UCSF). While tobacco industry lawyers were conspiring to seize these "Pentagon Papers" of the industry, the people at UCSF scanned the documents and posted them on the Web. While CBS's *60 Minutes* had backed down from airing its investigative report on the tobacco industry, the UCSF researchers were able to help get the story.

The Net has been critical to communication among grassroots activists. I first heard about the case of Mumia Abu Jamal, for example, via the Net, as did many others, helping to generate mass public outcry to stop his slated execution. National networks working for human rights in Burma and East Timor, labor organizers attempting cross-border alliances, students setting up national organizing projects, and many other groups rely on the Net to help them converse, share information, and strategize and coordinate across great distances in a short amount of time.

Contrary to many Internet booster's beliefs, the Net was not designed to promote democracy. In fact, many new communication tools are used for just the opposite, such as expanding global corporate control or infringing on privacy rights. Yet these technologies cannot remain monolithic: As we've learned, there are enough cracks and fissures to exploit them for activism and social justice.

*Jesse Drew is an independent video-maker, writer, media activist, and member of* Paper Tiger Television.

---

### Electronic Frontier Foundation

The Electronic Frontier Foundation (EFF) was founded in July 1990 to ensure that the principles embodied in the Constitution and Bill of Rights are protected as new communications technologies emerge. Along with the ACLU, activist groups, and industry leaders, EFF is leading a court battle against the communication decency provisions of the Telecommunications Act of 1996.

EFF's call to action: Every day decisions are being made that will affect the future of communications.

* Decisions about what sorts of technology you can use to protect the privacy of your communications
* Decisions about what services you will be able to get over the emerging national information infrastructure
* Decisions that are made before you even know that there are choices

*For more information, visit EFF at http://www.eff.org; E-mail: ask@eff.org*

Other Good Guys:
* The Benton Foundation's Communication's Policy Project: http://www.benton.org
* Electronic Privacy Information Center (EPIC): http://epic.org
* Center for Democracy and Technology: http://www.cdt.org
* American Civil Liberties Union: http://www.aclu.org
* Computer Professionals for Social Responsibility: http://cpsr.org/home/

## Voters Telecommunications Watch

Can a couple of guys with modems really make a difference? Voters Telecommunications Watch (VTW) is proof positive of the vast potentiali of online organizing. A volunteer organization concentrating on legislation as it relates to telecommunications and civil liberties, VTW has been behind some of the most visible campaigns in cyberspace to date. As organizers of the December 12, 1995, Internet Day of Protest, VTW helped spur some 50,000 calls to Congress protesting the Communications Decency Act (CDA). The group was also behind the "black out" on the Web, where thousands of web pages turned their background color to black on the day the Telecommunications Act of 1996 was signed.

The organization publishes regular action alerts and announcements and tracks anything and everything related to online civil liberties and privacy, from the CDA's legal status to encryption, copyright, and voter issues. Its "Guide to Internet Parenting" is a must for everyone interested in sane, responsible ways of monitoring their child's activity on the Net.

Voters Telecommunications Head head Shabbir Safdar argues that people who care about Net freedom must organize into a political force. "I formed VTW with many others when I realized that nobody was doing the grassroots work," says Safdar, whose modesty obscures his achievements. "The truth is, anyone can do this stuff. You don't need too much organization, just persistence."
—Christine Triano

Contact: Voters Telecommunications Watch can be found at http://www.vtw.org; E-mail: vtw@vtw.org.

# Net Directory

## Institute for Global Communications (IGC)

*http://www.igc.org*

Institute for Global Communications is an online service provider geared toward activist and grassroots communities. In addition to providing access to the Internet, E-mail, and online conferences, it runs four networks: PeaceNet, EcoNet, WomensNet, and LaborNet. Its greatest resource is its "Progressive Directory," which lists groups by issue, including media.

## People-Link

*http://www.people-link.com/links/index.html*

A directory and links to people, organizations, and companies "involved in building a better world," People-Link is attractive, easy to use, and includes an interesting list of links to other sites. Links are grouped by categories including "Women," "People of Color," and "Labor." Also featured is a strong section of "Right Wing" and "Fight the Right" links and a section called "Good News," which includes a good list of progressive media sites.

## WebActive

*http://www.webactive.com/*

Originally dubbed "What's New in Activism Online?," WebActive is a project of Progressive Networks, the Seattle-based company that developed RealAudio. A well-done and professional digest of activism online, WebActive uses RealAudio to supplement interviews with activists and provide access to progressive media, such as FAIR's radio show, *CounterSpin*, and Hightower Radio. It also features a directory of over 1,250 links to progressive sites on the Web and opportunities to get involved in issues like saving the Headwater's Forest and stopping Internet censorship.

## Media Democracy

*http://www.mediademocracy.org*

The official site of the Media & Democracy Congress, an annual conference bringing together activists, journalists, students, and media makers of all stripes, this site offers up-to-date information on the burgeoning media democracy movement. Also available is the full text of the *Media & Democracy Field Guide* and the cutting edge newsletter, *MediaCulture Review*.

## Znet

*http://www.lbbs.org/*

Znet is *Z* magazine's online presence and home of LBBS (Left Bulletin Board System), the Chomsky Archives, links to other media-related sites, and ShareWorld, a new online service aimed at progressives.

## FAIR
*http://www.igc.apc.org/fair/*
This page is the online home of the media watchdog, FAIR. It contains lots of content, including text of the group's magazine, Extra!, *CounterSpin* scripts, and links to RealAudio of the show on WebActive (described above).

## Email to the Editor
*http://www.armory.com/~leavitt/ medialist.html*
List of E-mail addresses of dozens of papers, national and local TV, radio, and other media.

## Project Vote Smart
*http://vote-smart.org*
A self-described "voter's self-defense system," the nonpartisan Project Vote Smart puts information on thousands of elected officials and candidates at your fingertips. It also offers a Reporter's Resource Center.

## New York Online (NYO)
*http://www.nyo.com*
Part consumer online service, part virtual community, NYO is the first African-American-owned Internet service. Its success is in building online community among people not historically part of the digital frontier. The service attracts an "intellectual and eclectic" crowd.

## Political Research Associates
*http://www.publiceye.org/pra/*
A great research source, this site features an extensive online library of articles, book excerpts, bibliographies, lists, and resource guides concerning the right. These files are loaded with detailed information about right-wing groups, individuals, and trends. This site also includes the full text of the right-wing reader, Eyes Right!

## Democracy Works
*http://www.democracyworks.org*
This site, a project of the Institute for Alternative Journalism, is a magazine featuring information about the far right and efforts to promote democratic values. A mixture of journalism and advocacy news, the site features articles from the alternative press, excerpts from reports and action alerts, and extensive links to groups fighting the right.

## CultureWatch Online
*http://www.igc.org/culturewatch/*
CultureWatch is a monthly annotated bibliography that monitors the religious right's political agenda and strategy. Drawing on almost 400 sources across the political spectrum, it offers news briefs on the world of the right wing.

## Web Surfing Starter Links

In an age where new becomes old in a nanosecond, the net is already being nostalgically compared to the birth of radio and television. But traditional media—newspapers, magazines, radio TV—rely on a gatekeeper model. The Internet has been widely lauded because it eliminates the gatekeeper. The result is a dizzying array of news and information, so much so that, to put it crudely, it can be hard to separate the wheat from the chaff.

A search using Alta Vista, a popular search engine, for example, came up with 75,993 links for "progressive and media." The first 30 or so listings were helpful, pointing to, among others, FAIR, *Mother Jones*, and my own organization, the Institute for Alternative Journalism. But due to the amount of information on the Net, and the way it is organized, most of those 75,000-plus links were useless to my search.

Today, most major progressive non-profits and media outlets have websites, as do many smaller groups. About two thirds of the country's 105 alternative weeklies run websites, and most of the bigger magazines of opinion have some form of online presence. A number of "directory" or "digest" sites have also emerged, making the browsing endless. The trick is knowing where to find them, who provides useful information, and who just blows off steam. To that end, below is a starter guide to some of the best progressive resources on the Net.
—Christine Triano

## NetAction

 Longtime activist Audrie Krause was fed up. Community groups she worked with seemingly knew little about the power of the Internet and the issues surrounding it. At the same time, she realized Net activists could learn a great deal about organizing tactics from those same grassroots organizations. So in July 1996, Krause quit her high-profile job as executive director of Computer Professionals for Social Responsibility (CPSR) to do a little cross-training.

Using her experience in CPSR and as head of Toward Utility Rate Normalization, a California consumer watchdog group, she started NetAction with the intent to link Net activists and community groups and to educate the public about cyberspace issues.

Even someone who never uses a computer has a stake in the cyberspace regulations being bounced around Washington, Krause says. "My 70-year-old mother will be affected by encryption technology," she notes, "because she and most people who see doctors have medical records on computer, and if those records are sent back and forth between doctors or clinics without effective coding, there's no real certainty they'll remain private."
—Michelle V. Rafter, C/Net

*NetAction can be found at http://www.netaction.org. To contact Krause, E-mail: krause@igc.org.*

## Progressive Networks

 In the fall of 1996, Internet broadcasting proved that it wouldn't be merely a witness to history, it would help shape it. Radio B92, an independent broadcaster in Belgrade, Serbia, was briefly shut down by the government of President Slobodan Milosevic. The station was reporting on mass demonstrations by students and others against the government's decision to ignore unfavorable election results. The state-controlled media refused to report on the demonstrations.

Almost as soon as the government shut off B92's transmitter, the staff began converting their audio reports to computer audio files, using RealAudio, made by Progressive Networks of Seattle. When staff at Progressive Networks learned of the station's efforts they offered to help by putting audio news reports in Serbian and English on their servers. With one of the busiest sites on

the Web, Progressive Networks instantly placed B92 before a worldwide audience. Thousands of people listened to B92 newscasts the first day they were available, rendering meaningless the Serbian government's efforts to censor the station.

The technologies for streaming audio over the Internet give broadcasters an unprecedented opportunity to reach global audiences cheaply and efficiently.

The tools are available now; one need only put them to work. At the end of 1996, at least 1,400 websites were using RealAudio, with more added every day.

## Size Matters

When talking about Internet broadcasting, you will hear the word "bandwidth" thrown around. Basically, bandwidth is a measurement of the size of the pipe digital information travels through. The more information you want to send, the bigger bandwidth you need. While you can get a RealAudio signal through a 28.8 connection, the bigger the bandwidth, the better off you are.

*For more information on getting started with RealAudio, visit Progressive Networks at http://www.prognet.com/*

# 4. Feed Your Mind

*The old media deliver the old politics: the insider's game, presented on high, from the elite to the masses. The new technologies break the journalist's monopoly, making some of the new news an unmediated collaboration between the sources and the audience.*
— Ellen Hume, Director, PBS's
Democracy Project

*The problem is how to decide what is significant, relevant information and how to get rid of unwanted information.*
— Neil Postman, author of Amusing
Ourselves to Death

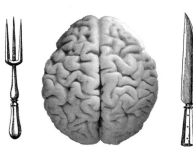

# HTTP://WWW.JOURNALISM.NOW

**KATHERINE FULTON**

Journalism is facing a historic challenge to adapt to a new medium. All journalists—even the most technophobic—need to understand how digital communication systems are challenging both the business models and journalistic conventions we've inherited from other eras.

Most reporters and editors think journalism means covering and uncovering news, but that definition doesn't describe the business of most commercial American journalism, which is selling advertising. And it doesn't incorporate all the things the average American newspaper and some of its broadcast counterparts provide—commodity information (weather reports, sports statistics), community bulletin boards (calendars, obituaries), community forums (letters to the editor), entertainment (comics, crossword puzzles).

Strip away some of the more profitable or popular items under this current umbrella, and you could strip away the means of paying for serious reporting aimed at mass audiences. One very important thing to understand about the new media world is just how easy such unbundling becomes.

What can journalists do to avoid being left behind? The wisest strategy is to remain committed to high-quality reporting and storytelling—and to invest seriously in understanding new media. That doesn't mean you have to take on the near-impossible task of mastering all the changing currents and cross-currents. But we still have to keep our eye on the big picture.

Everything I've learned argues that digital technologies will continue to grow, eventually creating a new medium that will force all previous communications media to redefine themselves, just as radio had to do when television came along.

Of my many fears about the future of journalism, this is the one that scares me the most: That journalists and their companies will keep their eyes on the horizon of the next deadline, the next paycheck, or the next quarterly shareholder report and fail to understand the horizon of history, which could yet yield a journalistic renaissance.

I worry that now-profitable journalism companies will join the online fray, then pull out or cut back too soon when they don't get immediate results or definitive answers. I worry that the profits that now support the great journalism a democracy needs will disappear into niche businesses run by people with little

interest in journalism but more imagination or staying power. I worry that too many of the best journalists will cling to the past. And I worry that the most successful innovators—the ones who will write the rules for the new medium—will be technophiles who don't give a damn about the difference between a news story and an ad and who think the First Amendment is a license to print money.

The horizon may be long, but, actually, time is short. The choice for everyone committed to the future of journalism is simple: Follow, or lead. (*Columbia Journalism Review*)

*Katherine Fulton is founding editor of the North Carolina* Independent Weekly. *She currently works with Global Business Network, a consulting firm that specializes in helping businesses and organizations prepare for the future.*

*Full text of this article is available at http://www.cjr.org/KFulton/journow1.html*

*continued on page 196*

## The Consortium

In a world of compromised news, investigative reporter Robert Parry is an odd man out.

He is perhaps best known for his exposés on the Iran-Contra affair for the Associated Press, where he delved into the activities of an obscure marine officer named Oliver North. Parry later became a reporter at Newsweek, where his persistent efforts to explore the "hidden corners" of the Iran-Contra scandal cost him his job. Relentless in his pursuit of the truth, Parry has since published the books *Fooling America* and *The October Surprise X-Files: The Hidden Origins of the Reagan-Bush Era*. He also helped investigate a *Frontline* documentary on the "October Surprise" that explores a reputed Republican conspiracy in 1980 to cut a secret deal with the Khomeini regime that would have disrupted then-President Carter's negotiations and delayed the captives' release.

# THE CIA, CRACK, AND THE WEB

### CHRISTINE TRIANO

A lot of people think one of the last great hopes for investigative journalism is the Net. With its absence of gatekeepers and 24-hour access to infinite material, the

Web can give added life to stories that might otherwise disappear with the day's recycling. It can also keep the flame burning under a particularly hot story, and generate far-flung debate and discussion. There's probably no better example of this than Gary Webb's now well-known series for the *San Jose Mercury News*, "Dark Alliance."

In his reporting, Webb alleged that the CIA knew about right-wing Nicaraguan exiles bringing crack to Los Angeles in the early 1980s in order to

raise funds to support the Contras. Subsequent reports by other news organizations questioned the story. But the paper's website, the Mercury Center (www.sjmercury.com), not only made available the entire four-part series, it included links to court documents, police reports, and other pieces of evidence.

"Basically, our website pushed Dark Alliance into the national consciousness in two ways," says Webb. "It gave people

*continued on page 196*

*continued from page 195*

all over the U.S. and the world a chance to read a story they otherwise never would have seen, and it created an incredible synergy with other forms of mass communication, particularly talk radio and TV." Within days, over 2,500 sites had linked to the story. The site had its most active day ever following one of Webb's national television appearances, recording more than 850,000 hits.

The Dark Alliance site appeared simultaneously with the print version of the story, taking three months to design and one month to produce. The results are a hypertextbook lesson in the ramifications of new technology on old-school journalism.

Describing the journalistic advantage of the Web, Webb explains, "we finally had the ability to *prove* what we were saying. With just a mouse click, online readers could actually see our supporting documents, actually hear the testimony of the principals for themselves, and then make their own evalua-

*continued from page 195*

"By the early 1990s," writes Parry, "space for serious reporting on such stories had shrunk to almost nothing. Time and again, well-organized cover-ups replaced honest pursuit of the truth, with the Democrats and the Washington media often assisting in the falsification of history." Parry's antidote: Take the story directly to the public. *The Consortium*, a biweekly online `zine and newsletter, was launched by Parry, who also heads the investigative unit at the Nation Institute, to defy the myths that mainstream news was perpetrating. This hard-hitting investigative forum covers topics from former CIA director William Casey's paranoia over Nicaragua to deciphering the magnitude of Bill Clinton's indiscretions. Serious topics are handled with unflinching integrity, and hard-hitting news is handled deftly with the mark of a well-seasoned journalist.
—Julie Winokur

*The Consortium can be found at http:// www.delve.com/consort.html or contacted at 2200 Wilson Blvd., Suite 102-231, Arlington, VA 22201.*

## Self-Made (Media) Man

 In the unwieldy world of cyberspace, Matt Drudge is the excited kid yelling "Extra! Extra!," a throwback to the old days of spreading the news.

With its packed list of wire services, daily papers, magazines, and columnists culled by the 30-year-old CBS-gift-shop-manager-cum-newshound, the *Drudge Report* is one-stop surfing for breaking news and opinion. This no-frills website offers links to national and international news outlets from the AP to the *New York Post*, columnists ranging from Maureen Dowd to Liz Smith, as well as search engines for a number of wires.

"What I had sensed was a lack of provocative news out there," explains Drudge. "You read these newspapers and they are dry—it never was like that in our news history. We used to have these great editions with big, bold headlines. . .and now the papers are boring, they have drained the spice out of life."

Scouring more than 20 daily papers online (usually hours before the newsprint hits the stoop), hacking into wire services, receiving deep-throat-like E-mail missives, he quietly collects items and scooplets, airbrushing them with a stroke of his own style of playful spin. In just a few years, Drudge's E-mailed gossip column of the same name has garnered a serious following among the New York–L.A.–D.C. media axis.

Like many Netizens, Drudge does his job from the privacy of his own apartment, where he operates his media nerve center of three TVs (dish, cable, broadcast), two computers, and three phone lines. His overhead comes in at $200 per month, fees that cover Internet access, occasional lunches, and a lot of periodicals.

Answering to no large corporation and at the mercy of no advertisers, Drudge is free to say whatever he pleases about whomever he pleases. While he's had numerous buyout offers, including one from Microsoft, his desire to remain free means he continues to work with a mean indie streak.

—Larry Smith, P.O.V.

*The Drudge Report can be found at http://www.lainet.com/~drudge*

tion of the evidence."

A committed optimist, Webb believes the new medium can actually *raise* the standards of investigative reporting. "With the unlimited headroom that the Web provides, I don't believe it's journalistically acceptable anymore to use such phrases as 'records show' or 'courtroom testimony revealed'—without providing those documents to your readers," he explains. "The only question now is whether the mainstream media has the balls to expose its reporting to that kind of scrutiny."

*Christine Triano is founder of VoxPop, a progressive PR firm. To see the Dark Alliance series: http://www. sjmercury.com/drugs/.*

# FEED YOUR MIND URLS

## WEB-ONLY PUBLICATIONS

### Salon
*http://www.salon1999.com*
An "interactive magazine of books, arts, and ideas," Salon was voted Best Website of 1996 by Time magazine. It is one of the classier roadshows to set up shop on the Web, with regular contributions from well-known literati. According to their editorial statement, the folks at Salon seek to exploit the democratic potential of the Net "to advance the cause of civic discourse." Right on.

### Word
*http://www.word.com/*
Word is a good example of the proliferation of beautiful, hip online magazines of essays and opinion. Started by three guys in New York (with a $1 million backing from a technology company), Word cannot be described as progressive or political, but it is the type of electronic publication progressive media is competing with.

### Feed
*http://www.feedmag.com*
A Web magazine of culture, politics, and technology especially known for its "Dialogs"—electronic roundtables—where experts, activists, pundits, and professors discuss topics ranging from America's drug policy to wage stagnation to the recent "Heroine Worship" issue of the New York Times Sunday Magazine.

### The Netizen
*http://www.netizen.com/netizen/*
Original political commentary from HotWired, the online arm of Wired magazine. Good, sometimes progressive writing with, of course, a digital focus. Essentially, this is politics for Webheads, mostly drawn to media critic Jon Katz's controversial and entertaining column, "Media Rant."

### Boulevards
*http://www.boulevards.com*
An index of alternative newsweeklies and websites emphasizing travel, arts, entertainment, contemporary culture, and politics, the site features several sections, including AlterNation, which culls some of the best writing from the alternative press.

### @tlas
*http://atlas.organic.com*
One of the more creative magazines on the Web, Atlas truly treats the Internet like a new medium, breaking the boundaries of print through vivid graphics, moving images, and sound. The site features everything from humor to hard-hitting photojournalism on sociopolitical issues around the world.

### Suck
*http://www.suck.com*
Despite its name, this site generally doesn't. Straightforward and brimming with wit, Suck offers a new column of commentary and opinion every day.

### The Consortium
*http://www.delve.com/consort.html*
(see story, p. 195)

### Working Assets Long Distance/Newsbites
*http://www.wald.com*
Despite the fact that the point behind it is to sell long-distance phone service, Working Asset's site is worth visiting. NewsBites, an online newspaper, features regular columns by Mario Cuomo and Jim

Hightower and articles by and about other leading progressive figures.

## Jinn
*http://www.pacificnews.org/jinn/*
This site compiles the essays and op-eds of Pacific News Service (which serves about 150 print dailies). It also features extensive archives and YO! (Youth Outlook), writing by teens about issues that affect them (see chap. 3).

## The Progressive Review
*http://emporium.turnpike.net/P/ProRev/index.htm*
A lot of text is featured in this electronic newsletter, described as "Washington's unofficial source," on a range of issues. The design is basic, but this project of editor Sam Smith is interesting enough to keep reading. This newsletter is also available via E-mail and hard copy.

## America Newspeak
*http://www.scn.org/news/newspeak/*
This satirical weekly e-zine draws attention to those absurd news items that get short-shrafted in the crease fold of your newspaper. From the sublime to the ridiculous, these blurbs make fact the envy of fiction.

## Minding Business
*http://www.igc.org/preamble/*
A newsletter of the Preamble Center for Public Policy, this site focuses on grassroots progressive activism and corporate accountability.

## Free Speech TV
*http://www.freespeech.org/*
Site of the only progressive TV channel in the United States, FsTV uses the site to disseminate information about where to find its programs while making ambitious use of video and audio.

## AlterNet
*http://www.alternet.org*
Site of the news and information service AlterNet, features summaries of the 50 best stories from independent publications around the country each week, advocacy and activist news, job listings, and a full-text database of thousands of stories.

## LINKS

## Hotlinks
*http://www.naa.org/hot/*
Maintained by the Newspaper Association of America, this site is a good place to gain a sense of the range of news organizations that have ventured online.

## Weekly Links
*http://aan.org/*
Site of the Association of Alternative Weeklies, Weekly Links features links to papers across the country.

## Media Watchdog
*http://theory.lcs.mit.edu/~mernst/media/*
An extensive collection of online media watch resources, including specific media-criticism articles and information about media-watch groups. The emphasis is on examining the accuracy and exposing the biases of the media.

## MAGAZINES

## MoJo Wire
*http://www.mojones.com/*
One of the first, and among the best, Mother Jones's site seeks to take advantage of the online medium rather than use it as another place to dump its content. Easy to get around, the site is full of juicy information, including reports not published in the magazine and expanded editions of ones that are.

## The Utne Lens
*http://www.utne.com*
Originally a very ambitious venture, with all-new content and a full-time staff of five, The Utne Lens is now significantly pared down from its earlier incarnation. The content, while interesting, is mostly pulled from the magazine.

## AdBusters
*http://www.adbusters.org/adbusters/*
The site of the Canadian magazine of the same name, this journal of "culture jamming" is very popular and respected. It's site is jazzy, with an ominous, morphing greeting from Marshall McLuhan: "World war three is a guerilla information war, with no division between military and civilian participation."

## The Nation
*http://www.thenation.com*
Weekly contents of this stalwart of the progressive press, plus browsable back issues.

## Columbia Journalism Review
*http://www.cjr.org*
Still an important journal after all these years, the site offers some excellent resources for journalists, including a guide to covering the "culture wars."

# Activist Resources

# IMAGINING A DEMOCRATIC MEDIA

**DON HAZEN**

Just as our physical environment has suffered clearcutting, strip mining, and massive pollution, so our media environment is being despoiled in the interests of profit. Public-interest journalism—the kind of news and information that enlightens and informs us—is moving toward extinction. An infestation of violence, fluff, pompous punditry, and celebrity worship fills its place. This book challenges its readers to confront the threats posed by today's media.

Encouraging informed opinion is not a priority in today's market-driven world. Participation in public life does not generate profit; developing a sense of com-munity does not feed the marketplace. Investigative journalism is not profitable. We're rapidly approaching a time when everything we encounter in the media is designed to get us to buy something, not to help us think, reflect, understand, or appreciate our world.

A lot of people—maybe you—have said no to this overwhelming commercialism by turning their TVs off, or at least off the commercial stations. Each day, more people grow disgusted with the way the media is going. People instinctively mistrust the media monopolies and their tremendous concentration of power. They are appalled by perverse TV violence. They're fed up with celebrity journalists who make $25,000 speeches to organizations they supposedly cover as reporters. And they're infuriated by rising cable rates and poor content.

Media monopoly is destined to become a major issue; already, the public is in the early stages of media rebellion. We can't sit around and wait for the moguls to see the light. We have to fight back, and we have to start now. Call it a movement for the millennium. Call it a Media and Democracy movement.

These days the only movements people hear about all seem to be going in one direction: backward. Movements for so-called welfare reform, against affirmative action, for Draconian spending cuts, and against immigrants and immigration seem to get all the media attention these days.

In large part, all this attention reflects the radical right's effective media organizing.

It's time for some movement in the other direction, movement that will reshape the media. We can learn from the right's reactionary yet successful strategies in our organizing against the big corporations and on behalf of people and their needs.

To effect change, we must recognize the perils of our current media system, accept that they represent a vital social issue, and organize accordingly. Since the media present the information that we and our fellow citizens use to make political decisions, we face a dual task. We must hold the corporate media system accountable, we must create alternative media of our own, and we must teach community activists and advocates how to shape public opinion through the press.

Change rarely comes from isolated efforts or from the top down. In our country's recent history, change has almost always started at the grass roots, with people from different points of view coming together to fight a common enemy. The Media and Democracy movement is no different. It's parents who teach their kids to deconstruct TV commercials; online activists who build Web pages and use listservers to counter distorted coverage; members of community organizations who fight the steady violence on local news shows or block commercials from their schools; unions who fight for fair portrayals of working people; journalists who see a discredited version of objectivity standing in the way of seeking the truth.

How can we envision and create compelling independent media that will offer a true alternative? How can we reach larger audiences with alternative messages? How can we protect and support public-interest journalism? How can we hold the corporate media system more accountable? Contributors to this book light the way by describing some steps they have taken. But it's a long and difficult road, and we'll need to be in for the long haul.

Successful organizing must be complemented with several ancillary efforts: Using think tanks and researchers to document the consequences of media concentration and to translate the findings to legislative strategies and convincing materials; putting dynamic spokespeople on the road to popularize the themes of media democracy; training publicists to influence the mainstream media; and building coalitions across organizational, issue and ethnic lines.

Throughout this book you've read about important efforts toward media reform. In the spring of 1996, for example, the Institute for Alternative Journalism hosted the first-ever Media and Democracy Congress. The congress brought together more than 700 media activists, critics, working journalists, and editors representing print, electronic, and online outlets.

Many participants saw what they have in common despite their different issue areas or mediums. They agreed that people must come to know and care more about the dangers of media monopoly if our participatory democracy is to survive. They agreed to share resources and to collaborate in the future. The congress also developed an Information Bill of Rights for organizers to use as a foundation for moving forward. (The full draft of the bill is in the index.)

What follows are 10 steps toward media reform, organizing campaigns, and garnering better publicity for your issue and your organization.

### 1. Teach Our Children

As Leslie Savan describes, media literacy offers an antidote to a commercial system gone mad. It should be practiced at home and at school, by adults and by children. Advertising seduces us; we need to be on our toes to counter its effects.

### 2. Celebrate Diversity

Moving forward means seeking common ground that draws strength from diversity. The division between the ethnic press and alternative media can be bridged with collaborative efforts. Diversity is as necessary to our media system as it is to any ecosystem. Fighting homogeneity of ideas and media fare may require seeking out new forms of media —whether it's zines, talk radio, the Web, the community press, or anything out of your usual routine. Besides, it's fun.

### 3. Support the Alternative

If we accept even a fraction of the arguments made by the authors in this book, our only logical step is to dramatically strengthen independent, alternative, and advocacy media. Buy it, use it, support it—criticize it. Treat these outlets for what they are: imperfect but often inspired incubators of ideas and opinions. We've been losing the war of ideas for a long time. It's up to us to shift the momentum.

### 4. Do It Yourself
After criticism comes doing it yourself. Never has technology fostered so much do-it-yourself media. It's not just the Web that can reach audiences cheaply. The camcorder and the VCR revolution, microradio and the profusion of zines all hold opportunity.

### 5. Take Advantage of Technology
Sure, new technology can lead to information overload, but it also opens up the potential for democratic, fast, and cheap communications. The Net is no substitute for face-to-face interaction, but it can keep people informed, involved, and on to the message like nothing else. At a minimum, everyone should be able to send E-mail, participate on mailing lists, and access the Web. Minus these skills, you'll find yourself increasingly out of the loop—which is why the argument for universal access is made so strongly in this book.

### 6. Popularize the Message
Progressive media makers must reach a broader audience without compromising the message. We have been perched on the margins of American political discourse for too long. Alternative media has plenty of niche markets, which need support and strengthening. But we also need some broader outreach vehicles. These can be provided by such outlets as the Pacifica Radio network and its many local affiliates, or by efforts like Boom TV, an experiment to bring provocative and humorous programming to public-television stations on Saturday nights.

### 7. Garner Better Press for Our Causes and Our Organizations
Getting good press isn't rocket science, but it does require taking specific steps to reach your goals. Increasingly, skilled trainers are available to grassroots groups and media organizations to help frame the issue and get the message out in a clear fashion. The Institute for Alternative Journalism's Strategic Progressive Information Network (SPIN), headed up by savvy activist trainer Robert Bray, is one place to go. Many other suggestions appear in the following pages.

### 8. Seek Common Ground Between Journalists and Activists
Journalism is at its best when it acts as society's conscience, speaking truth to power. But avenues for this kind of journalism are shrinking. On the other hand, advocacy organizations are increasingly playing the role of investigative journalists, doing the in-depth research required to change policy. The more nonprofits use journalists for their research, the more credible will be their findings.

### 9. Mentor Youth
In conjunction with all of the above-mentioned steps, young people must be included every step of the way. Digging in for the long haul requires supporting the next generation of independent media makers and advocates today. This is both a long- and short-term strategy for success because young people bring savvy ideas and technical skills that will increase the effectiveness of all of our efforts.

### 10. Work Hard at Collaboration
With modest resources, competing in the media marketplace is quite a challenge. Through collaboration—sharing talent, ideas, resources—our chances of enhancing quality and extending reach increase. Of course, many think progressives can't agree on anything and easily become entrenched in unconstructive battles. Collaboration demands much more than cooperation, it requires new habits, flexible styles, parking egos at the door—a substantial list. But in the face of the greater challenge before us, what choice do we have?

# TO TELL THE TRUTH

### MAKANI THEMBA

Anyone who believes their thinking isn't shaped by media has got his or her head in the sand. Stop for a moment and take this simple test. Imagine the following: a manager of a 7-11 store, an urban teenager, and a suburban mother of two. Be honest with yourself about the pictures that come to your mind.

Media activists are truth warriors who fight to ensure that the pictures we see more accurately reflect real life. They work to render the invisible visible and break through the monopoly corporations exercise over information. Media activism requires a diligence and faith in the possibility of media as a force for good—a faith that is getting harder and harder to validate. After all, if we call the important work on crack importation and the Contras done by Gary Webb of the *San Jose Mercury News* "advocacy journalism" and the *New York Times* and *Washington Post's* ballyhoo of it "unmodified journalism," what are we really saying about what journalism is? And whose side it's on?

Perhaps ironically, it was the *Times'* Arthur Hays Sulzbuger who said it best: "Obviously, a man's judgment cannot be better than the information on which he has based it." Organizing for democracy of information can seem a bit esoteric at times, but it is information legitimated as news that drives public judgment and the public agenda. Complex issues like welfare, jobs, and health care are no longer debated. They devolve into comic strips: reduced to an image and a soundbite in a bubble. If poverty-stricken children don't fit within the frame, they are rendered invisible. Under these conditions, informed judgment, much less consent, is impossible—and policymaking reflects this.

Challenging the megacorporations that control most of our news is important. And believe it or not, people are facing Goliath and winning. Communities in New York, Baltimore, and beyond are demanding respectful portrayals and balanced stories. They are artfully framing their efforts in ways that force their local media outlets to tell the whole story in all its rich detail. As one activist said to me, "If they can spend two whole pages on paper versus plastic bags, they damned sure better cover what welfare reform is going to do here."

This activist, an African-American woman like me, is working at the very heart of what media and democracy is all about: who controls the narrative and for what purpose. It is identity politics and we cannot get beyond it, as some may suggest, until those who portray us and politicize us so it is easier to starve, beat, and oppress us "get beyond" identity oppression and suppression.

There is much at stake. Resources are cut, churches are burned, and people are beat and murdered in the night. There are children who have watched television all their lives and have never seen an honorable character who looks like them. How can we work to create a democratic media infrastructure and never address this?

These are the frontline issues for media activists today. And it will take more than reforming corporate media to bring about the change we need. Strong movements require a vital independent media. From civil rights to trade unionism, social movements thrive when they have their own media organs that speak to supporters, interpret the issues, and encourage debate.

Without care and attention to independent media with an agenda—a democratic agenda—we will be forced to articulate our issues soundbite by soundbite, then wonder why no one "gets it." After all, we are attempting to build what few people can imagine and even fewer think possible: a humane and democratic society. Not that a great soundbite won't help, but it's certainly not the panacea.

We need dreaming room and debating room to construct this thing of human liberation. We need places to tell the stories of victory and despair that compel us to rise up so we can effectively do battle. Of course, this is not exclusively a media project or an organizing project. It's both, because in all likelihood, the revolution *will* be televised.

*Makani Themba is co-director of the Praxis Project, a nonprofit organization dedicated to developing community-based approaches to policy development.*

# MAKING MEDIA WORK

### DANNY SCHECHTER

A headline in the *New York Times* noted, "In Centers of Power, Fewer Voices on Left," reporting that liberal advocates admit that they are not skilled in framing issues, using technology, or electronic media. In short, they acknowledge not being sophisticated enough to compete with a far smaller but better-funded opposition.

As a media professional with a unique vantage point, having worked in alternative and mainstream media—print, radio, and television—I am always struck by how the right properly pinpoints media at the top of its strategic plan, while the left thinks about media strategy as a afterthought when it even considers at all.

If we want to promote democracy and challenge vested interests pursuing global economic agendas at the expense of social needs, we have to focus on understanding and explaining how the media fits into this—as both a hegemonic force of domination and an indispensable tool for outreach and organizing.

We cannot even talk about changing America without confronting and remaking media power.

Besides the squeeze of economic threats, the media industry is also feeling political pressures as opinion polls contin-

## Pressuring the Media: Two Success Stories

### Improving Public Television in Chicago

In Chicago, a diverse coalition won greater public input and diversity on a local public-television station. The Coalition for Democracy in Public Television (CDPT) consisted of more than 100 public-interest organizations—including reproductive rights groups, labor unions, civil rights organizations, environmental groups, and independent film organizations. These groups demanded that WTTW fulfill its mandate "to serve as a forum for voices not ordinarily heard on commercial television." The coalition convinced WTTW to air several award-winning documentaries that PBS had excluded from its national feed, to diversify its board, and to add two new weekly series: one by and about working people, and one showcasing independent documentaries.

### Combating Hate Radio In New York City

For years, hate jocks and the accompanying rise in hate violence went virtually unchallenged on America's airwaves. But in 1996, activists drew national attention to New York hate jock Bob Grant's racist remarks and the impact of hate radio. Groups like the Rainbow Coalition, FAIR, and the NAACP generated a firestorm of news coverage. They also organized a call-in and letter-writing campaign to Grant's employer, WABC radio. Callers requested that WABC balance Grant with a program exploring the impact of racism and hate speech. As a result, ABC's new owner, Disney, fired Grant—the most widely listened-to radio talk-show host in New York City.

—Kim Deterline, We Interrupt This Message

ue to register mounting public dissatisfaction with the products of our commercial popular culture as well as much of the news media. More and more people are now complaining, writing letters, feeling distressed and even outraged.

The politicians who play to this sentiment, in effect running against Hollywood and the mainstream news media, have tapped into a growing vein of public sentiment, however demagogic and hypocritical their stance. Progressives must speak out on these issues too and not leave the subject to Bill Bennett

and the Christian Coalition.

We need to move beyond criticism to consciousness raising and creative action. Enough critique. Enough of pointing out what is increasingly obvious. The shallowness, superficiality, and vapidity of so much of our media has to be redefined as a political challenge, as an issue to mobilize around. Media priorities have to be challenged, and themselves become a priority of a more urgent kind on any progressive agenda for change. Alternative journalists have to resist marginalization by becoming adversarial journalists. There's nothing wrong with being both oppositional and proactive.

In the '60s, corporations like Dow Chemical became targets of protest and symbols of corporate greed and irresponsibility; in the '90s, many media companies deserve similar contempt. The same people who would be outraged if toxic waste was dumped on their door step have to be encouraged to express similar rage at the no less toxic junk programs and newsless news being dumped into their living rooms and their brains. Our problem is that there isn't much to view. The Boss is right: 57 channels, nothing on.

The right to information has to be discussed as a human rights issue. Article 19 of the Universal Declaration of Human Rights puts it this way: "Everyone has a right to freedom of opinion and expression. This right includes freedom to hold opinions without interference and to seek, receive and impart information and ideas through any media regardless of frontiers." In the United States, the Carnegie Commission that gave public television its mandate spoke of a "freedom to view."

It is my hope that new visions can speak to growing public anxieties and complaints and help spark a broad-based media reform movement.

## Demand Media Accountability

Once armed with more information—especially information that is collected by people themselves—citizen groups will be in a better position to demand responsiveness and accountability by media cor-porations. When media executives are forced to meet with their consumers, they will become more responsive. Most are sure to resist so called "pressure politics" but they will not be able to ignore it. (You undoubtedly will find that the institutions that do the most to violate the spirit of the First Amendment will be zealous in wrapping themselves in it as an opportunistic shield against criticism.)

## Advocate For New Legislation and Enhanced Regulation

Deregulation has given media companies a free hand to pollute the airwaves. Tougher antimonopoly laws and greater regulation in the public-interest by a revamped Federal Communications Commission is in order. The FCC itself has to be democratized with more public hearings and public votes.

## Transform Public Television

It is time to put the public back into public television with more locally elected community boards and a return to its original mandate to provide a space for alternative voices and broader program choices. Pressure will be needed to democratize and properly finance PBS, which should be funded through a tax on commercial television stations and their advertisers. There needs to be at least one channel in every area that serves the public-interest in the broadest possible way.

*Danny Schechter, co-founder of Globalvision is author of* The More You Watch, The Less You Know .

# HOW TO GET BETTER COVERAGE

### ROBERT BRAY

Two major strategies for changing how the media works and who gets covered are featured in this section. The first requires working directly with the mainstream and independent media by developing messages and packaging your news to maximize coverage of your organization's efforts. The second requires monitoring and pressuring the media from the outside.

Working with the media to shape and influence coverage requires a media plan containing at least three basic components for proactively capturing media attention and garnering coverage for your issue. Too often community activists give media only scant attention, if any at all. The point is, *have a plan*. It's time to seize the media spotlight.

## 1. Identify the News

Don't waste reporters' time with non-news events or press releases. Identify what is newsworthy about your issue and build a media campaign around it. Tips for determining what is newsworthy: new report or survey; new key personnel with exciting new vision; controversy; local hook to national or state story; dramatic human interest; response to new government legislation; special event, protest, rally, vigil scheduled; celebrity angle; calendar hook (same-gender domestic partnership rally on Valentine's Day; protest against welfare cuts for poor children on Mother's Day).

## 2. Form Strategic Key Messages

What are your three main points that must be moved into the media at all costs? Develop your key messages before you make news. Repeat them over and over during every interview. Don't simply answer reporters' questions, *respond* to reporters' questions with your key messages.

The first message should state your advocacy position ("Welfare cuts are disastrous—they will imperil the lives of poor children and tear apart the social fabric of our country").

The second message should be broader in scope and contextualize your first message into a bigger picture of justice ("All citizens, including poor children, deserve the same basic rights, shelter, food, and fair shot at attaining the American dream —these welfare cuts will cut off that dream for America's poor").

The third message should be a call to take action ("Vote no on House Bill XYZ," "Urge the president to veto the bill," "Join our rally against welfare reform").

## 3. Communicate Your Messages

*Media advisories* should be succinct and contain who, what, where, when, and why ("why" is your key message). Don't forget a contact name, phone number, and a date on every release. Fax and/or mail to reporters well in advance of an event (at least one or two weeks), then follow up with a phone call a day or two before the event.

*Speak in soundbites*. You must condense your issue into 12-second "bites" that communicate your key messages. That means you cannot unlearn years of ignorance or explain everything about your issue in 12 seconds, so don't try. No sound banquets, please. Skip lengthy rhetoric, propaganda, manifestos, and dogma. Make your bites pithy and attention-getting.

*Stage events with television in mind.* TV needs pictures, so always design your news events with visuals in mind. Be conscience of location, background, speakers, decorations, and visual aids. Events held outside or with dramatic visual impact will beat boring events held indoors in a conference room any day.

And, *follow up.* "Spin" or push/tweak/nudge the story into a favorable direction that presents your messages in a clear manner. Thank those reporters who covered the news, and contact those who missed it with an invitation to receive your press kit and follow-up news. Finally, monitor coverage to clarify any missed points or factual inaccura-

cies and, if you're lucky, celebrate a job well done.

*Robert Bray is director of Strategic Progressive Information Network [SPIN] media training and organizing project, Institute for Alternative Journalism.*

A useful book on improving coverage of your issues is *Prime-time Activism— Media Strategies for Grassroots Organizing,* by Charlotte Ryan (South End Press, 1991). The book presents an overview of the media, including understanding its role, implications for social movements, and how the news business is organized, plus technical advice for identifying and framing news, creating visual news, forming soundbites, and more.

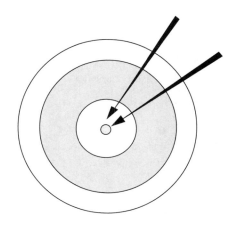

# Building a Media–Monitoring Project

Before criticizing the media, it is important to document your concerns by studying the coverage. Decide on the issues that need better coverage, then develop a study that documents specific examples and patterns of factual error, substantive biases, and a lack of diverse viewpoints.

## How To Study The Media

Choose a period of time (four to six weeks) to survey a particular media outlet. Then, ask yourself these nine questions:

*1. How much coverage does your issue get?* Count the number of times a story on your issue appears in the particular media outlet you're monitoring.

*2. Who are the sources used in the story?* List their names and positions.

*3. Where did the story come from?* For instance, was it from a wire service or a staff reporter?

*4. Is the coverage factual or based on speculation or opinion?*

*5. Are negative terms used to describe sources that might be considered alternative to the "official" sources?* For instance, are environmental groups labeled "radical" while governmental officials are labeled "official"?

*6. How long are the stories that cover your issue?*

*7. Does the coverage reflect actual circumstances?* For instance, does a story on unemployment talk about businesses that move out of the country to take advantage of lower wages and fewer regulations?

*8. Are the root causes of the problem explained?*

*9. Are there places where your issue is being covered better?* If so, who are the sources and how are both sides represented?

Don't forget to document biases or inaccuracies while keeping track of the news that's left out. Make sure your data are accurate and your conclusions are supported.

## Meeting With The Media

Once you've compiled a comprehensive study, you're ready to make your case. Get the names of the editors at the media outlet you've studied and write a letter asking them for a meeting. Explain that you represent a group concerned with their coverage and that you'd like to discuss the findings of your study with the appropriate editor, producer, or news director. Follow up with a phone call about a week later and be persistent. It is best not to bring more than four or five people to the meeting and a good idea to bring a community representative.

Prior to the meeting, prepare an agenda or identify points for discussion. Develop a format for presenting the information.

It is also important to be psychologically prepared. Don't be intimidated. Insist on being treated with courtesy and respect. Avoid making accusations and never lose your temper.

Request that coverage feature expert sources and people who are affected by policy decisions in contrast to the views of policymakers and other spokespeople. Request space for public-service announcements and inquire about expressing your views on the op-ed page or during on-air commentary.

Conclude your meeting with specific requests for better coverage. Offer yourselves or community representatives as sources. Recap any commitments the media representatives may have made and thank them for their time.

## Short-Term Follow Up

About a week after your meeting, send a letter to everyone who attended, summarizing the points and agreements made. As you continue to monitor coverage, look for material that may be a positive response to your concerns, and express thanks for improvements.

## Long-Term Follow Up

If you haven't noticed any changes in the coverage:

1. *Organize letters to the editor campaigns.* Get people in your group and others interested in your issue to write letters asking for more coverage of the issue. Include what's been left out of the coverage and any inaccuracies.

2. *Organize an informational picket.* Take your protest to the streets around the media organization's building and hand out informational flyers. Urge the public to write letters to the editor and boycott that particular outlet until it covers the issue fairly. The organization will feel the threat of public embarrassment as well as the threat of reduced profits.

3. *Write op-ed pieces.* Writers or journalists who are familiar with your issue and willing to align themselves with your cause can write op-ed pieces for the newspaper.

4. *Provide ongoing documentation.* Prove yourself a credible and up-to-date source of information by sending press releases on new developments to the media. Call them immediately with breaking news.

5. *Publish your study.* Try to get local, alternative publications or competing media to publish your study. Avoid being accusatory or hyperbolic. Just state the facts and figures.

**Conclusions**

Don't give up. After a year, begin the process again and note improvements, lapses in coverage and other developments. Think of the media as a tool for change. You can impress the press and impact decisions on what gets covered.

Excerpted from *Impress the Press*, 1997, Media Alliance Latin America/Caribbean Basin Committee. A copy of the full booklet may be purchased for $3 by contacting Rich Yurman, 2516 24th. Ave., San Francisco, CA 94116, (415) 665-8649.

# THE ART OF THE SPIN: A MODEL PROJECT FOR MAKING MEDIA MORE DEMOCRATIC

**ROBERT BRAY**

The American media has become a battleground of symbols, signifiers, and soundbites that collapse controversial political issues into easy-to-digest news stories that have the power to influence public policy. Unfortunately, the soundbite media culture is too powerful to ignore. Consequently, many progressive activists must develop basic skills and resources for shaping media coverage of critical issues. Who has the upper hand in framing news in the media? What

strategic messages are we communicating? And how can progressive activists energize media debate on their issues?

One answer is an innovative new media training and organizing project sponsored by the Institute for Alternative Journalism: the Strategic Progressive Information Network (SPIN). Through SPIN, IAJ makes media skills and resources available to many activists and media makers. SPIN also brings together media activists from different progressive social-change movements and encourages dialogue with journalists.

SPIN is directed by veteran media professional and trainer Robert Bray, most recently Fight the Right Organizer and Media Director at the National Gay and Lesbian Task Force. SPIN develops public-relations and communications skills among community activists and provides ongoing media support. The project was designed to give activists the concrete tools they need to communicate their stories, advocate for their issues, seize the media spotlight, and educate public officials with points of view and information that are too often squelched. SPIN helps activists write press releases, develop strategic messages, stage media events, develop relationships with reporters, and more.

In addition, SPIN fosters collaboration between communications activists and media leaders from progressive communities. Imagine media professionals from labor, the environmental movement, the civil rights community, the women's movement, and the gay and lesbian community among others joined in a network that can respond to the threat of the well-financed public-relations machines of the Far Right and corporate conglomerates.

*Robert Bray is director of SPIN. Contact: SPIN through the Institute for Alternative Journalism, 77 Federal St., San Francisco, CA 94107; Tel: (415) 284-1420; fax: (415) 284-1414.*

# Pressure Pointers

Community activists are by definition people who believe that, through hard work, they can produce change—whether it's influencing elected officials, improving schools, or reducing violence in their community. Yet when local media outlets ignore life-and-death issues or smear communities, we feel helpless to do anything about it.

The truth is, we can change that. Many of the same savvy organizing techniques we use to fight, say, toxic polluters can also be used to change biased news coverage. If there is no pressure on the media to be accurate then those with the most resources devoted to public-relations campaigns can heavily influence public opinion.

What's required for ordinary people to positively impact news coverage? Training, planning, and a well-developed strategy that encompasses traditional public-relations strategies and media activism. Here are three tips for turning up the heat on biased media.

### 1. Identify and apply pressure on the economic interests of media.

Media institutions are corporations that rely on attracting an audience that in turn attract advertisers or other funding. Generally, news-media outlets need to maintain their credibility to maintain an audience, particularly in a competitive market. Coordinated letters, calls, demonstrations, and so on, jeopardize an outlet's credibility with viewers. Boycotts and bad press are not good for business. To make fair coverage in the economic interest of an outlet, media activists can pursue two paths:  (1) directly convince advertisers not to buy air time or ads from the news outlet or (2) discredit the news with viewers, thereby cutting into the outlet's audience share and hurting its ability to deliver a large audience to advertisers.

### 2. Build broad coalitions that represent large numbers of people.

Only a broad coalition has the reach to touch the general public audience of the news media. Many organizations claim to represent constituencies, but unless they can mobilize their members to do something—whether taking part in a boycott or deluging a media outlet with letters and phone calls—those organizations won't have real power and influence. In the long term, being able to mobilize a grassroots base is the key to victory.

### 3. Include people in the communities directly impacted by the biased coverage.

Successful campaigns often involve issue-based groups that can mobilize a grassroots base. People directly impacted by biased coverage can see clear self-interest.

—Kim Deterline, We Interrupt This Message
1086 Shortwell, San Francisco, CA 94110; Tel: (415) 905-4527;
E-mail: mapd@igc.org

# Information Bill of Rights

Endorsed by participants in the first annual media and Democracy Congress, san Francisco, March 3, 1996

## PREAMBLE

Freedom of expression, freedom of the press, debate and dialogue, an informed and active public, a robust public culture: What unites these principles is how central they are to the free flow of information vital to participatory democracy. Despite the many advances of the information age, we as a nation must seek to establish clear policies and programs to move us closer to such ideals or we risk losing them.

Despite the sheer volume of today's media culture, we see before us a greater concentration of the resources necessary to produce and distribute information in the hands of the privileged few. The result is a loss of diversity, quality, accountability, and local voices. Despite the democratic tradition of maintaining checks and balances against centralized power, we see the erosion of the regulatory policies necessary to hold our increasingly corporate media infrastructure accountable to the public good. Despite the potentially democratizing technologies now available, we see a decline in mass participation and a growing gap between information "haves" and "have nots." Despite the emergence of democracy worldwide, we see a one-way flow of information originated in the United States around the globe, posing a threat to local customs and cultures.

There are ways of imagining what a more just, equitable, participatory, and accountable media system can be like. In February 1996, hundreds of media activists, independent producers, critics, journalists, artists, and scholars will come together in San Francisco for a Media & Democracy Congress, with the goal of paving a new road for media culture and ratifying an Information Bill of Rights. The following represents an early draft of that document; we urge you to look it over, make suggestions, offer feedback, and help begin to articulate the values necessary to foster media democracy.

## PRINCIPLES

We, the below signatories, maintain that all people have the universal right to a full range of social and political information, including that which is produced and distributed independently of commercial channels. We believe that the highly concentrated ownership structure of the media and information industry undermines the diversity and quality of information available to the public, and that deregulatory media policies which favor big business over the public good pose a serious threat to democracy. We believe that the public has the right to participate in the production and distribution of media culture as well as in the decisions and policies which shape the flow of information and will determine the media system of the 21st century.

We support the following set of principles as the foundation for a people's Information Bill of Rights:

## I. Diversity

People have the right to a full diversity of social and political information, including that which is produced and distributed independently of commercial channels. Independent, local, and noncommercial modes of media production and distribution are necessary to the health of a democracy and must be protected by public policies. Monopolies of any kind pose a threat to the range of information and viewpoints available and must be controlled.

## II. Accountability

People have the right to hold information providers accountable. The means to widely produce and disseminate information are a valuable resource in democratic societies; commercial entities who profit from the manufacture and sale of information should be held accountable to responsibilities of truth, fairness, and the public good. Such responsibility can range from meeting local and community franchise agreements to reflecting the full spectrum of views necessary for public awareness and debate on social and political issues.

## III. Quality

People have the right to quality media culture geared toward a plurality of tastes, cultures, and interests. Since the profit-oriented structure of the free market emphasizes homogeneity, blandness, and lowest-common denominator appeal over innovation, cultural pluralism, and aesthetic risk-taking, quality must be ensured and nurtured by public subsidies and distribution channels.

## IV. Equity

People have the right to economic, racial, social, cultural, and global equity. People from all races, classes, ethnicities, genders, classes, sexual orientations, nationalities, and abilities deserve fair and equitable representation and access to the information infrastructure. United States dominance in the flow of global information poses a threat to democracy in an international context and must be checked.

## V. Access

People have the right to access opinions, information, and ideas about matters of the public-interest. This requires universal, affordable access to common information delivery services (e.g., the information superhighway) regardless of region or income, as well as free access to information and electronic information services via public libraries and schools. People have the right to access public information (such as government information) free of charge.

## VI. Participation

People have the right to participation. This includes the right to participate in decisions, debates, and regulatory policies pertinent to the flow of information today and in the future, as well as the right to participate in local and community culture. People have the right to produce and distribute media content. An open, two-way information infrastructure should be secured and protected by public policy.

## VII. Literacy

People have the right to information and media literacy. This includes the technical skills necessary to participate in an increasingly computer-dominated information society as well as the knowledge necessary to understand the role of the media and information industry in the democratic process.

## VIII. Expression

People have the right to express information, ideas, and opinions regardless of race, sex, creed, color, status, religious, or political belief. Censorship poses a threat to democracy and must be prevented by public policy. This includes political censorship as well as the economic censorship which can result when the means of expression are concentrated among large corporations.

## IX. Privacy

People have the right to privacy. This includes the right to informed consent in regards to the collection of personal and socioeconomic information for marketing or other purposes as well as well as the right to refuse such practices. People have the right to protection from illegal invasions of privacy in the sphere of media and information.

## X. Protection

People have the right to fair use and intellectual property protection. Public policies governing copyright must be extended to electronic information delivery systems in ways which secure an appropriate balance of rights between individual content providers (such as journalists, information users, and others who secure their living producing information of any kind) and commercial information providers (such as magazines and computer networks).
—Compiled by Laurie Ouellette who is a graduate student in Media Studies at the University of Massachusetts.

*References and Assistance: Herb Schiller, DeeDee Halleck, Nolan Bowie, Martha Wallner, Julian Low, People's Communication Charter, Aspen Institute, Telecommunications Policy Roundtable, American Library Association, Taxpayers Assets Project, Media Consortium, National Alliance for Media Arts and Culture.*

# Resource Rolodex

## News Services

AlterNet
77 Federal Street, 2nd floor
San Francisco, CA 94107
Tel: (415) 284-1420; Fax: (415) 284-1414
alternet@alternet.org
http://www.alternet.org/

American Forum
1250 National Press Building
Washington, DC 20045
Tel: (202) 638-1431; Fax: (202)638-1434
forum@forum-media.org
http://www.forum-media.org

American News Service
RR1 Black Fox Road
Brattleboro, VT 05301
Tel: (800) 654-6397
ans@americannews.com
http://www.americannews.com

National Student News Service
116 New Montgomery, Suite 530
San Francisco, CA 94105
Tel: (415) 543-2089; Fax: (415) 543-1480
nsns@igc.apc.org

Pacific News Service
450 Mission Street, Room 204
San Francisco, CA 94105
Tel: (415) 243-4364
pacificnews@pacificnews.org
http://www.pacificnews.org/

The Progressive Media Project
409 East Main Street
Madison, WI 53703
Tel: (608) 257-4626;
Fax: (608) 257-3373
project@progressive.org
http://www.progressive.org/

**Find it, Read it, Support it...
contact these umbrella
organizations for information on
alternative print media.**

Association of Alternative Newsweeklies
1001 Connecticut Ave., NW, Suite 822
Washington, DC 20036.
Tel: (202) 822-1955; Fax: (202) 822-0929
http://aan.eline.com/
*for information on weeklies in your area*

Factsheet Five
P.O. Box 170099
San Francisco, CA 94117
Tel: (415) 668-1781
f5seth@sirius.com
http://www.well.com/conf/f5/zines.html
* for information on zines*

Independent Press Association
P.O. Box 191785
San Francisco, CA  94119-1785
Tel/Fax: (415) 896-2456
indypress@igc.org
http://www.hues.net/ipa
*for information on progressive
publications of opinion*

Institute for Alternative Journalism
77 Federal Street, 2nd floor
San Francisco, CA  94107
Tel: (415) 284-1420; Fax: (415) 284-1414
congress@igc.org
http://www.igc.org/an/

**Independent Radio...
contact these organizations for
more information on programming
and airing schedules in your area.**

Alternative Radio
2129 Mapelton
Boulder, CO 80304
Tel: (303) 444-8788; Fax: (303) 546-0592

CounterSpin—FAIR
130 W. 25th Street
New York, NY 10001
Tel: (212) 633-6700; Fax: (212) 727-7668

Free Radio Berkeley
1442 A Walnut Street, #406
Berkeley, CA  94709
Fax: (510) 664-3779
frbspd@crl.com

Hightower Radio
Box 13516
Austin, TX 78711
Tel: (512) 477-5588; Fax: (512) 478-8536
hightower@essential.org

Latino USA
College of Communication
Building B
University of Texas, Austin
Austin, TX  78712
Tel: (512) 471-6178; Fax: (512) 475-6873

National Federation of
Community Broadcasters
Fort Mason Center, Building D
San Francisco, CA 94123
Tel: (415) 771-1160; Fax (415) 771-4343
LCNFCB@aol.com

National Native News
810 East 9th Street
Anchorage, AK  94501
Tel: (907) 258-8895

National Radio Project
830 Los Trancos Road
Portola Valley, CA 94028
Tel: (415) 851-1730; Fax: (415) 851-0731
contact@igc.apc.org

Native America Calling
P.O. Box 40164
Albuquerque, NM  87196
Tel: (505) 277-5201; Fax: (505) 277-4285

Pacifica Network News
702 H Street NW, Suite 3
Washington, DC 20001
Tel: (202) 783-3100; Fax: (202) 393-1841
pnn@igc.apc.org

Prison Radio Project
558 Capp Street
San Francisco, CA  94110
Tel: (415) 648-4505

The Progressive
409 East Main Street
Madison, WI  53703
Tel: (608) 257-4626; Fax: (608) 257-3373
editorial@progressive.org

Radio Bilingue
111 Fulton Mall, Suite 700
Fresno, CA 93721
Tel: (209) 486-5174

Radio For Peace International
P.O. Box 88
Santa Ana, Costa Rica
Tel: (506) 249-1821; Fax: (506) 249-1095
rfpicr@sol.racsa.co.cr

Radio Nation
72 5th Avenue
New York, NY 10011
Tel: (212) 242-8400

We The People
295 Third Street
Oakland, CA  94607
Tel: (510) 836-3272; Fax: (510) 836-8797

WINGS: Women's International News
Gathering Service
P.O. Box 33220
Austin, TX  78764
Tel/Fax: (512) 416-9000
wings@igc.apc.org

**Community Radio...where you
can find progressive shows.**
ALASKA
Anchorage—AIRRES, 91.1 FM
Dillinghan—KRUP, 99.1 FM
Fairbanks—KUAC, 104.7 FM
Ketchikan—KRBD, 105.9 FM
Valdez—KCHU, 770 AM

**ARKANSAS**
Little Rock—KABF, 88.3 FM

**CALIFORNIA**
Arcata—KHSU, 90.5 FM
Berkeley—KPFA, 94.1 FM
Free Radio Berkeley, 104.1 FM
Chico—KZFR, 90.1
Claremont—KSPC, 88.7 FM
Cupertino—KKUP, 91.5 FM
Davis—KDVS, 90.3 FM
Fresno-Free Radio, 102.3 FM
Garberville—KMUD 91.1/88.5/89.9 FM
Grover Bch—Excellent Radio, 88.9
Los Angeles—KPFK, 90.7 FM
Nevada City—KVMR, 89.5 FM
N. Hollywood—KPFK, 90.7 FM
Pacific Grove—KAZU, 90.3 FM
Philo—KZYX, 90.7 FM
Rhonert Park—KRCB, 91.1 FM
Riverside—KUCR, 88.3 FM
Sacramento—KVIE (cable 6), 89.9
Santa Barbara—KCSB, 91.9 FM
Santa Cruz—KZSC, 88.1 FM
   Free Radio SC, 96.3 FM
San Francisco—KALW, 91.7 FM
   Liberation Radio, 93.7 FM
San Luis Obispo—KCBX, 90.1 FM
Ukiah—KBUD, 88.1 FM
Watsonville—KPIG, 107.5 FM

**COLORADO**
Alamosa—KRZA, 88.7 FM
Boulder—KGNU, 88.5 FM
Carbondale—KDNK, 90.5 FM
Crested Butte—KBUT, 90.3 FM
Durango—KDUR, 91.9/93.9 FM
Paonia—KVNF, 90.9 FM

**CONNECTICUT**
Bridgeport—WPKN, 89.5 FM

New Britain—WFCS, 107.7 FM
Storrs—WHUS, 91.7 FM
Wallingford—WWEB, 89.9 FM
West Hartford—WWUH, 91.3 FM

**D.C.**
Washington—WPFW, 84.3 FM

**FLORIDA**
Tallahassee—WRER, 88.5 FM
Tampa—WMNF, 88.5 FM
Winter Park—WPRK, 91.5 FM

**GEORGIA**
Atlanta—WRFG, 89.3 FM
   WREK, 91.1 FM

**IDAHO**
Moscow—KUOI, 89.3 FM

**ILLINOIS**
Champaign—WEFT, 90.1 FM
   WILL, 580 AM
Chicago—WLUW, 88.7 FM
   WZRD, 88.3 FM

**INDIANA**
Bloomington—WFHB, 91.3 FM
Columbia City—WJHS, 91.5 FM
N. Manchester—WBKE, 89.5 FM

**KANSAS**
Concordia—KVCO, 88.3 FM

**KENTUCKY**
Lexington—WRFL, 88.1 FM
Whitesburg—WMMT, 88.7 FM

**MAINE**
Blue Hills—WERU, 89.9 FM
Portland—WMPG, 90.9 FM

**MASSACHUSETTS**
Amherst—WMUA, 91.1 FM
Medford—WMFO, 91.5 FM

N. Dartmouth—WSMU, 91.1 FM
Provincetown—WOMR, 91.9 FM
Salem—WMWM, 91.7 FM
Worcester—WCUW, 91.3 FM

**MICHIGAN**
Ann Arbor—WCBN, 91.7 FM
Grand Rapids—WGVU, 88.5 FM
Traverse City—WNMC, 90.9 FM

**MINNESOTA**
Duluth—KUMD, 103.3 FM
Minneapolis—KFAI, 90.3 FM
Saint Cloud—KVSC, 88.1 FM
Saint Paul—KFAN, 106.7 FM

**MISSOURI**
Kansas City—KKFI, 90.1 FM

**MONTANA**
Great Falls—KGPR, 89.9 FM
Missoula—KUFM, 89.1 FM

**NEW HAMPSHIRE**
Keene—WKNH, 91.3 FM
New London—WSCS, 90.9 FM

**NEW JERSEY**
Hackettstown—WNTI, 91.9 FM

**NEW MEXICO**
Albuquerque—KUMN, 89.9 FM
Gallup—KGLP, 91.7 FM
Santa Fe—KSFR, 90.7 FM
Zuni—KSHI, 90.9 FM

**NEW YORK**
Brooklyn—WNYE, 91.5 FM
Geneva—WEOS, 89.7 FM
Ithaca—WICB, 91.7 FM
Jeffersonville—WJFF, 90.5 FM
New York City—WBAI, 99.5 FM
Poughkeepsie—WVKR, 91.3 FM
Staten Island—WSIA, 88.9 FM

Stony Brook—WUSB, 90.1 FM
Troy—WRPI, 91.5 FM

NORTH CAROLINA
Asheville—R.A.I.S.E., 105.1 FM

OHIO
Cleveland—WCSB, 89.3 FM

OREGON
Astoria—KMUN, 91.9 FM
Eugene—KWVA, 88.1 FM
Portland—KBOO, 90.7 FM

PENNSYLVANIA
Allentown—WMUH, 91.7 FM
Philadelphia—WKDU, 91.7 FM
    WPEB, 88.1 FM
Pittsburgh—WYEP, 91.3 FM

TENNESSEE
Knoxville—WUTK, 90.3 FM

TEXAS
Austin—KOOP, 91.7 FM
College Station—KEOS, 89.1 FM
Houston—KPFT, 90.1 FM

UTAH
Salt Lake City—KRCL, 90.9 FM

VERMONT
Plainfield—WGDR, 91.1 FM

WASHINGTON
Bellingham—KUGS, 89.3 FM
Mount Vernon—KSVR, 90.1 FM
Olympia—KAOS, 89.3 FM
Seattle—KCMU, 90.3 FM

WISCONSIN
Hayward—WOBJ, 88.9 FM
Madison—WORT, 89.9 FM
Milwaukee—WMSE, 91.7 FM

## Alternative Television/Film/Video

Advocate Films
3514 Emerson Street
Palo Alto, CA 94306
Tel: (415) 493-7955; Fax: (415) 493-7955
70404.3052@compuserve.com

American Documentary, Inc. [POV]
220 19th Street, 11th flr.
New York, NY 10011
Tel: (212) 989-8121; Fax: (212) 989-8230

Appalshop
306 Madison street
Whitesburg, KY 41858
Tel: (606) 633-0108; Fax: (606)633-1009

Association of Independent
Video & Filmmakers
304 Hudson Street
New York, NY 10013
Tel: (212) 807-1400; Fax: (212) 463-8519
aivffivf@aol.com
http://www.virtualfilm.com/AIVF/
*publishes The Independent Film &
Video Monthly*

Black Planet Productions/
Not Channel Zero
P.O. Box 435, Cooper Station
New York, NY 10003-0435
Tel: (212) 886-3701; Fax: (212) 420-8223

Blackside Productions
486 Shawmut Ave.
Boston, MA 02118
Tel: (617) 536-6900; Fax: (617) 536-1732

California Newsreel
149 Ninth Street, Suite 420
San Francisco, CA 94103
Tel: (415) 621-6196; Fax: (415) 621-6522
newsreel@ix.netcom.com
http://www.newsreel.org

Chicago Video Project
700 N. Green Street, Suite 100
Chicago, IL 60622
Tel: (312) 666-0195; Fax: (312) 666-0197
cvp@interaccess.com

Citizen Vagrom
1111 E. Madison, Suite 428
Seattle, WA 98104
Tel: (206) 344-6434
citizen@speakeasy.org

Deep Dish TV
339 Lafayette Street
New York, NY 10012
Tel: (212) 473-8933
deepdish@igc.apc.org

Downtown Community TV Center
87 Lafayette Street
New York, NY 10013
Tel: (212) 966-4510; Fax (212) 219-0248

Dyke TV
P.O. Box 55
Prince St. Station
New York, NY 10012
Tel: (212) 343-9335; Fax: (212) 343-9337

Educational Video Center
60 E. 13th Street, 4th floor
New York, NY 10003
Tel: (212) 254-2848

Environmental Video/ECO-TV
P.O. Box 1680
Sag Harbor, NY  11963
Tel: 516/725-2858

Free Speech TV
P.O. Box 6060
Boulder, CO 80306
Tel: (303) 442-2707; Fax: (303) 442-6472
http://www.freespeech.org/

Flying Focus Video
2305 NW Kearney #231
Portland, OR 97210
Tel: (503) 234-2538

Global Action Project
61 Eighth Avenue
Brooklyn, NY 11217
Tel: (718) 230-8448

Globalvision
1600 Broadway, Suite 700
New York, NY 10016
Tel: (212) 246-0202; Fax: (212) 246-2677
http://www.igc.org/globalvision/

Independent Television Service (ITVS)
51 Federal Street, Suite 200
San Francisco, CA 94107
itvs@itvs.org

Internews
750 Mission Avenue
San Rafael, CA  94901
Tel: (415) 457-5222; Fax: (415) 457-6810

Latino Consortium
3171 Los Feliz Blvd., Suite 210
Los Angeles, CA   90030
Tel: (213) 663-8294
*funds/publicizes/distributes film and
video about Latinos

National Asian American
Telecommunications Association
346 Ninth Street, 2nd floor
San Francisco, CA  94103
Tel: (415) 863-0814; Fax: (415) 863-7428
naata@sirius.com

Native American Public
Telecommunications
800 North 33rd Street
Lincoln, NE  68583
Tel: (402) 472-3522
http://indian.monterey.edu/napt/

National Black Programming Consortium
1266 E Broad Street, #1-East
Columbus, OH   43205
Tel: (614) 252-0921
*funds/publicizes/distributes film and
video about African-Americans

National Video Resources
73 Spring Street, Suite 606
New York, NY  10012
Tel: (212) 274-8080; Fax: (212) 274-8081
NVRinfo@nvr.org
*publishes NV Reports

Paper Tiger Television
339 Lafayette Street #6
New York, NY 10012
Tel: (212) 420-9045; Fax: (212) 420-8223

People's Video Network
237 E 18th Street
New York, NY 10003
Tel: (212) 780-9484; Fax: (212) 260-4404

Signal to Noise
594 Broadway #410
New York, NY 10012
Tel: (212) 219-3102; Fax: (212) 219-2645
signalcm@aol.com

Third World Newsreel
79-10 34th Ave. #3L
Jackson Heights, NY 11372
Tel: (718) 397-5174 ; Fax: (212) 947-9277

Woman Vision Production
3570 Clay Street
San Francisco, CA  94118
Tel: (415) 346-2336; Fax: (415) 346-1047

Working Group Inc.
5867 Ocean View Dr.
Oakland, CA 94618
Tel: (510) 547-8484; Fax: (510) 547-8844
wedothework@igc.apc.org
*makers of Not In Our Town and
We Do the Work

## Journalism and Writer Organizations

American Society of Newspaper Editors
P.O. Box 4090
Reston, VA  22090-1700
Tel: (703) 648-1144; Fax: (703) 476-6125
asne@aol.com
http://www.asne.org/
*maintains demographics of
United States newsrooms

Asian American Journalists Association
1765 Sutter Street, Room 1000
San Francisco, CA  94115
Tel: (415) 346-2051; Fax: (415) 931-4671
aaja1@aol.com
http://www.aaja.org/

Center for Investigative Reporting
500 Howard St., Suite 206
San Francisco, CA  94105
Tel: (415) 542-1200; Fax: (415) 542-8211

Center for Public Integrity
1634 I Street NW, Suite 902
Washington, DC 20006
Tel: (202) 783-3900; Fax: (202) 783-3906

National Association of Black
Journalists
3100 Taliaferro Hall
University of Maryland
College Park, MD 20742
Tel: (301) 405-8500; Fax: (301) 405-8555
nabj01@aol.com
http://www.nabj.org/

National Association of Hispanic
Journalists
National Press Building, Suite 1193
Washington, DC 20045
Tel: (202) 662-7145; Fax: (202) 662-7144
http://www.nahj.org/

Native American Journalists
Association
1433 E. Franklin Avenue, Suite 11
Minneapolis, MN 55404-2135
Tel: (612) 874-8833; Fax: (612) 874-9007
najanut@aol.com
http://www.medill.nwu.edu/naja

National Lesbian & Gay
Journalists Assn.
874 Gravenstein Hwy. South, Suite 4
Sebastopol, CA 95472
Tel: (707) 829-3330; Fax: (707) 829-3365
nlgja@aol.com
http://www.journalism.sfsu.edu/www/nlgj
a/index.html

National Writers Union
873 Broadway, Room 203
New York, NY 10003
Tel: (212) 254-0279
http://www.nwu.org/nwu/

Newspaper Guild
8611 2nd Avenue
Silver Springs, MD 20901
Tel: (301) 585-2990
http://www.wsg.org/222/

Society of Professional Journalists
16 South Jackson Street
Greencastle, IN 46135
Tel: (317) 653-3333; Fax: (317) 653-4631
spj@internetmci.com
http://www.town.hall.org/places/spj/
spj.html

UNITY '99
428 10th Avenue NE, #E-201
Kirkland, WA 98033
Tel: (206) 828-4293; Fax: (206) 828-6417
*A special project of AAJA, NABJ,
NAHJ, and NAJA. Unity '94 published
Newswatch: A Critical Look at Coverage
of People of Color*

## Progressive Publicists

Communication Works
2017 Mission Street, Suite 303
San Francisco, CA 94110
Tel: (415) 255-1946; Fax: (415) 255-1947

Fenton Communications
1606 20th Street, N.W.
Washington, DC 20009
Tel: (202) 745-0707; Fax: (202) 332-1915
fenton@fenton.com

Kent Communications
Route 1, Box 9A
Garrison, NY 10524
Tel: (914) 424-8382; Fax: (914) 424-4849
kentcom@highlands.com

The Mainstream Media Project
101 H Street, Suite E
Arcata, CA 95521
Tel: (707) 826-9111; Fax: (707) 826-9112
msommer@igc.apc.org

McKinney & McDowell Associates
1730 Rhode Island Ave, N.W., Suite 717
Washington, DC 20036
Tel: (202) 833-9771; Fax: (202) 833-9770
mckmcd@ix.netcom.com

Millenium Commications Group
1150 18th Street NW 8th Flr.
Washington, DC 20036
Tel: (202) 778-1466; Fax: (202) 872-8845

Pro Media
225 West 57th, Suite 801
New York, NY 10019
Tel: (212) 245-0510; Fax: (212) 245-1889

Public Policy Communications
73 Trowbridge Street
Belmont, MA 02178
Tel: (617) 489-0461; Fax: (617) 489-6841

Riptide Communications
666 Broadway, Rm 625
New York, NY 10012
Tel: (212) 260-5000; Fax: (212) 260-5191

Valerie Denney Communications
407 S. Dearborn, #1150
Chicago, IL 60605

VoxPop
77 Federal Street, 2nd floor
San Francisco, CA 94107
Tel: (415) 543-7770; Fax: (415) 284-1414
voxpop@igc.org

Miriam Zoll
P.O. Box 1014
Brookline, MA 02147
Tel: (617) 566-7876; Fax: (617) 739-5066
mzoll11481@aol.com

**In the Name of the Public Interest...campaigns with a mission.**

Advocacy Institute
1730 Rhode Island Ave. NW
Washington, DC 20036
Tel: (202) 659-8475; Fax: (202) 659-8484

Public Media Center
466 Green Street
San Francisco, CA 94133
Tel: (415) 434-1403; Fax: (415) 986-6779

## Media Activist Training

SPIN (Strategic Progressive Information Network)
77 Federal Street
San Francisco, CA 94107
Tel: (415) 284-1412; Fax: (415) 284-1414

We Interrupt This Message
1086 Shotwell
San Francisco, CA 94110
Tel: (415) 905-4527
mapd@igc.org

## Media Literacy Organizations

CAMEO (Canadian Association of Media Education Organizations)
60 St. Claire Avenue, Suite 1002
Toronto, Ontario M4T1NF Canada
Tel: (416) 515-0466; Fax: (416) 515-0467
http://interact.uoregon.edu/MediaLit/FE/CAMEOHomePage

CME (Center for Media Education)
1511 K Street NW, Suite 518
Washington, DC 20005
Tel: (202) 628-2620; Fax: (202) 628-2554
cme@cme.org; http://www.cme.org/~cme

Center for Media Literacy
4727 Wilshire Blvd. #403
Los Angeles, CA 90010
Tel: (213) 931-4177; Fax: (213) 931-4177
cml@earthlink.net
http://www.earthlink.net/~cml

Citizens for Media Literacy
34 Wall Street, Suite 407
Asheville, NC 28801
Tel: (704) 255-0182; Fax: (704) 254-2286
cml@unca.edu
http://interact.uoregon.edu/MediaLit/FA/MLCitizens/HomePage

Just Think Foundation
221 Caledonia Street
Sausalito CA 94965
Tel: (415) 289-0122; Fax: (415) 289-0123
think@justthink.org
http://www.justthink.org

Media Education Foundation
26 Center Street
Northampton, MA 01060
Tel: (413) 586-4170; Fax: (413) 586-8398
http://www.igc.apc.org/mef

Media Literacy On-line Project
Center for Advanced Technology in Education
College of Education
University of Oregon
Eugene, OR 97403
Tel: (541) 346-3469
http://interact.uoregon.edu

National Telemedia Council
120 E. Wilson Street
Madison, WI 53703
Tel: (608) 257-7712; Fax: (608) 257-7714
ntelemedia@aol.com
New Mexico Media Literacy Project
6400 Wyoming Blvd. NE
Albuquerque, NM 87109
Tel: (505) 828-3129; Fax: (505) 828-3320
http://www.aa.edu

## Youth Groups

As We Are
P.O. Box 380048
Cambridge, MA 02238
Tel: (617) 492-2462
*A quarterly for young working people*

Bent TV
Hetrick-Martin Institute
2 Astor Place
New York, NY 10013
Tel: (212) 274-9782
*Gay/lesbian/transgendered youth producing videos

Campus Alternative Journalism Project
Center for Campus Organizing
Box 748
Cambridge, MA 02142
Tel/Fax: (617) 354-9363
cco@igc.apc.org

Educational Video Center
55 East 25th Street, Suite 407
New York, NY 10010
Tel: (212) 725-3534
*A nonprofit arts center empowering
inner-city youth through their use
of media.

El Centro de Juventud
3209 Galindo Street
Oakland, CA 94601
Tel: (510) 532-5995

New Youth Connections
*For and by NYC public high school
students.
144 W. 27th Street
New York, NY 10001
Tel: (212) 242-3270

The P.E.R.S.O.N. Project
*For fair portrayals of lesbian, gay,
bisexual and transgendered culture
in public education
586 62nd Street
Oakland, CA 94609-1245
Tel/Fax: (510) 601-8883
richter@eecs.berkeley.edu

Rise & Shine Productions
300 West 43rd Street
New York, NY 10036
Tel: (212) 265-5909
*Produces The Real Deal, a program
showcasing videos by NYC teens about
the social issues that affect them.

UNPLUG
360 Grand Avenue
P.O. Box 385
Oakland, CA 94610
Tel: (510) 268-1100; Fax:(510) 268-1277
*A group opposed to Channel One
and other forms of commercialism
in education.

Youth Action
1830 Connecticut Ave. NW
Washington, DC 20009
Tel: (202) 483-1432
*Provides training, information and
internships for young people working for
social change.

YouthArts Project
c/o Wildcat Press
8306 Wilshire Blvd. Box 8306
Beverly Hills, CA 90211
Tel: (213) 966-2466; Fax: (213) 966-2467
*An online zine for young
gay/lesbian artists
http://queer.qcc.org/yap/

Youth Media
4188 Montgomery Street
Oakland, CA 94611
Fax: (510) 530-4109

YO!—Youth Outlook
450 Mission Street, Room 506
San Francisco, CA 94105
Tel: (415) 243-4364
*"Ask the unsafe questions and
raise unheard voices."

Youth Radio
1925 Martin Luther King Jr. Way
Berkeley, CA 94704
Tel: (510) 841-5123 ; Fax: (510) 841-9804

## Media Watchdogs and Advocacy Groups

Adbusters Media Foundation
1243d West 7th Avenue
Vancouver, BC V6H1B7 Canada
Tel: (604) 736-9401; Fax: (604) 737-6021
adbusters@adbusters.org
http://www.adbusters.org/adbusters/
*publishes Adbusters quarterly

American Newspeak
2002 S. Dearborn
Seattle, WA 98114
Tel: (206) 324-5037
http://www.scn.org/news/newspeak/
*satirical weekly e-zine

Applied Research Center
25 Embarcadero Cove
Oakland, CA 94606
Tel: (510) 534-1769; Fax: (510) 534-9680
*publishes RACEFILE

Berkeley Media Studies Group
2140 Shattuck Ave., Suite 804
Berkeley, CA 94704
Tel: (510) 204-9700; Fax: (510) 204-9710

CEMOTAP
P.O. Box 120340
St. Albans, NY 11412
Tel: (718) 322-8454

Center for the Integration &
  Improvement of Journalism
San Francisco State University
1600 Holloway Avenue
San Francisco, CA 94132
Tel: (415) 338-2083; Fax: (415) 338-3111
*organizes the Community Press
Consortium

Center for Media & the Black Experience
(CMBE)
4357 Luxembourg Drive
Decatur, GA 30034
Tel: (770) 808-9082; Fax: (770) 322-6653
ytoure@mindspring.com
http://www.webcom.com/nattyreb/hype

Center on Alcohol Advertising
2140 Shattuck Avenue, Suite 1206
Berkeley, CA 94704
Tel: (510) 649-8942; Fax: (510) 649-8970

CounterPunch
P.O. Box 18675
Washington, DC 20036
Tel: (202) 986-3665

Cultural Environment Movement
P.O. Box 31847
Philadelphia, PA 19104
Tel: (215) 387-1560

Fairness and Accuracy in Reporting
(FAIR)
130 West 25th St.
New York, NY 10001
Tel: (2120 633-6700; Fax: (212) 727-7668
fair@igc.apc.org
*publishes EXTRA!*

Gay & Lesbian Alliance Against
Defamation
150 W. 26th St., Suite 503
New York, NY 10001
Tel: (212) 807-1700; Fax: (212) 807-1806
glaad@glaad.org
http://www.glaad.org
*produces GLAADLines and
GLAADAlert*

Index on Censorship
29 Cherry St.
Somerville, MA 02144
Tel: (617) 666-1863; Fax: (617) 627-3606

INFACT
256 Hanover St.
Boston, MA 02113
Tel: 617/742-4583; Fax: (617) 367-0191
infact@igc.org

Media Alliance
356 West 58th Street
New York, NY 10019
Tel: (212) 560-2919; Fax: (212) 560-6866
mediaall@tmn.com

Media Alliance
814 Mission Street, Suite 205
San Francisco, CA 94103
Tel: (415) 546-6334; Fax: (415) 546-6218
mapd@igc.org
*publishes MediaFile*

Media Network
39 W. 14th Street #403
New York, NY 10011
Tel: (212) 929-2663; Fax: (212) 929-2732
medianetwk@aol.com

National Center for Tobacco-Free Kids
1707 L Street, NW, Suite 800
Washington, DC 20036
Tel: (202) 296-5469; Fax: (202) 296-5427

Project Censored
Sonoma State University
Rohnert Park, CA 94931
Tel: 707/664-2893; Fax: (707) 664-2108

Project Censored Canada
Department of Communication
Simon Fraser University
Burnaby, BC V5A1S6 Canada
Tel: (604) 291-3687; Fax: (604) 291-4024

PR Watch
Center for Media and Democracy
3318 Gregory Street
Madison, WI 53711
Tel: (608) 233-3346; Fax: (608) 238-2236

Rock the Vote
1460 4th St, Suite 200
Santa Monica, CA 90401
Tel: (310) 656-2464; Fax: (310) 656-2474
rockthevote@aol.com
http://www.rockthevote.org

Rocky Mountain Media Watch
P.O. Box 18858
Denver, CA 80218
Tel/Fax: (303) 832-7558

TV-Free America
1611 Connecticut Avenue, NW,
Suite 3A
Washington, DC 20009
Tel: 202/887-0436; Fax: (202) 887-0436
tvfa@essential.org.
http://www.essential.org/orgs/tvfa

UNPLUG
360 Grand Avenue, Suite 385
Oakland, CA 94610
Tel: (510) 268-1100; Fax: (510) 268-1277
unplug@igc.apc.org

## They Watch the Right...
## A few of the many organizations and publications with information on the right wing

Americans United for the
Separation of Church and State
1816 Jefferson Place, NW
Washington, DC   20036
Tel: (202) 466-2587
*publishes Church & State magazine*

Artists for a Hate-Free America
P.O. Box 40146
Portland, OR  97240
Tel: (503) 335-5982; Fax: (503) 335-5953
ahfa@aol.com

Center for Democratic Renewal
P.O. Box 50469
Atlanta, GA   30302
Tel: 404/221-0025;
Fax: (404) 221-0048
*national clearinghouse of information with focus on hate groups/crimes*

Citizens Project
P.O. Box 2085
Colorado Springs, CO  80901
Tel: (719) 520-9899
*grassroots organization opposing the religious right in Colorado Springs*

CultureWatch/Data Center
464 19th Street
Oakland, CA 94612-2297
Tel: (510) 835-4692; Fax: (510) 835-3017
datactr@tmn.com
http://www.igc.org/culturewatch/

Institute for the Study of the
Religious Right
P.O. Box 26656
Los Angeles, CA  90026
Tel: (213) 243-7598
*supports grassroots organization against the right*

Institute for First Amendment Studies
P.O. Box 589
Great Barrington, MA   01230
Tel: (413) 528-3800
*publishes Freedom Writer*

National Campaign for
Freedom of Expression
1402 3rd. Avenue Suite 421
Seattle, WA 98101
Tel: (206) 340-9301; Fax: (206) 340-4303

National Gay and Lesbian Task Force
2320 17th St., NW
Washington, CD   20009
Tel: 202/332-6483
*sponsors a "Fight the Right" project opposing antigay initiates*

People for the American Way
2000 M St., NW
Washington, DC   20036
Tel: (202) 467-4999
*monitors and opposes efforts to suppress free expression*

Planned Parenthood Federation
of America
810 7th Avenue
New York, NY   10019
Tel: (212) 261-4721
http://www.igc.org/ppfa/

Political Research Associates
678 Massachusetts Ave., #205
Cambridge, MA   02139
Tel: (617) 661-9313; Fax: (617) 661-0059
PublicEye@igc.apc.org
http://www.publiceye.org/pra/
*leading clearinghouse for information on the far right*

## Media Policy and Universal Access

Access for All
368 14th Street
Brooklyn, NY 11215
Tel: (718) 768-1829; Fax: (212) 677-8732

Alliance for Community Media
666 11th Street NW, Suite  806
Washington, DC 20001
Tel: (202) 393-2650; Fax: (202) 393-2653
alliancecm@aol.com

American Civil Liberties Union
132 West 43rd Street
New York, NY   10036
Tel: (212) 944-9800; Fax 212/944-9065
aclu@aclu.org
http://www.aclu.org

Benton Foundation
1634 Eye Street NW, 12th Floor
Washington, DC  20006
Tel: (202) 638-5770; Fax: (202) 638-5771
http://www.benton.org

Center for Civic Networking
91 Baldwin Street
Charlestown, MA 02129
Tel: (617) 241-9205; Fax: (617) 241-5064
http://civic.net/ccn.html

Center for Democracy and Technology
1001 G Street NW Suite 700 East
Washington, DC 20001
Tel: (202) 637-9800; Fax: (202) 637-0968
http://www.cdt.org/

Center for Media Education
1511 K Street NW, Suite 518
Washington, DC 20005
Tel: (202) 628-2620; Fax: (202) 628-2554
cme@access.digex.net

Computer Professionals for Social
Responsibility
P.O. Box 717
Palo Alto, CA 94301
Tel: (415) 322-3778; Fax: (415) 322-4748
cpsr@csli.stanford.edu
http://cpsr.org/home/

Consumer Federation of America
1424 16th Street NW #604
Washington, DC 20036
Tel: (202) 387-6121; Fax: (202) 265-7989

Electronic Frontier Foundation
1550 Bryant Street, Suite 725
San Francisco CA 94103 USA
Tel: (415) 436-9333; Fax: (415) 436-9993
ask@eff.org
http://www.eff.org/

Electronic Privacy Information Center
666 Pennsylvania Ave. SE, Suite 301
Washington, DC 20003
info@epic.org
http://epic.org

Libraries for the Future
121 W. 27th Street, Suite 1102
New York, NY 10001
Tel: 212/352-2330; Fax 212/352-2342
lff@lff.org; http://www.lff.org

Media Access Project
1707 L Street, NW, Suite 400
Washington, DC 20036
Tel: 202/232-4300; Fax 202/466-7656

National Citizens Communications Lobby
Box 1976
Iowa City, IA 52244
Tel: 319/337-5555
1035393@mcimail.com

Voters Telecommunications Watch
vtw@vtw.org
http://www.vtw.org

## Sources for the Web-Hungry

Columbia Journalism Review
101 Journalism Building
Columbia University
New York, NY 10027
Tel: 212/854-1881; Fax 212/854-8580
cjr@columbia.edu
http://www.cjr.org

Cyberwire Dispatch
http://www.cyberwerks.com/cyberwire/

The Drudge Report
http://www.lainet.com/~drudge

Email to the Editor
P.O. Box 7095
Santa Cruz, CA 95060
Tel: 408/457-9671, x101;
Fax 408/457-6316
leavitt@webcom.com
http://www.armory.com/~
leavitt/ medialist.html

HateWatch
http://hatewatch.org

Institute for Global Communications (IGC)
Presidio Building 1012, 1st floor
Torney Ave., P.O. Box 29904
San Francisco, CA 94129-0904
Tel: 415/561-6100; Fax 415/561-6101
http://www.igc.org

Kramer Communications
310 Riverside Drive, Suite 1519
New York, NY 10025
Tel: 212/866-4864; Fax 212/866-5527
felixk@panix.com
http://www.nlightning.com

LatinoLink
410 Townsend, Suite 107
San Francisco, CA 94107
Tel: 415/357-1172
http://www.latinolink.com

Levity
P.O. Box 1013
Cooper Station
New York, NY 10276-1013
Tel: 212/505-5389
danlevy@panix.com
http://www.levity.com

Media Consortium
2200 Wilson Blvd, Suite 102-231
Arlington, VA 22201-9887
Tel: 703/920-7521; Fax 703/920-0946
rparry@ix.netcom.com
http://www.delve.com/consort.html

Media Democracy
77 Federal Street
San Francisco, CA 94107
Tel: 415/284-1420; Fax 415/284-1414
congress@igc.org
http://www.mediademocracy.org

NetAction
601 Van Ness Ave., #631
San Francisco, CA 94102
Tel: 415/775-8674
akrause@igc.org
http://www.netaction.org

NY Online
549 Pacific St.
Brooklyn, NY 11217
Tel: 718/596-6000; Fax 718/596-4607
http://www.nyo.com/

PeopleLink—Lopez Communications
423 54th St.
Brooklyn, NY 11220
Tel: 718/238-8883; Fax 718/492-7389
people@people-link.com
http://www.people-link.com/

Project Vote Smart
129 NW Fourth Street, Suite 204
Corvallis, OR 97330
http://vote-smart.org

Real Audio/Progressive Networks, Inc.
616 First Avenue, Suite 701
Seattle, WA 98104
Tel: 206/447-0567; Fax 206/223-8221
http://www.prognet.com/

WebActive
1111 Third Avenue, Suite 2900
Seattle, WA 98101
Tel: 206/674-2700; Fax 206/674-2699
webactive@prognet.com
http://www.webactive.com/

Women Leaders Online
276 Chatterton Pkwy.
White Plains, NY 10606
Tel: 914/285-9761; Fax 914/285-9763
polwoman@aol.com
http://worcester.lm.com/comen/
women.html

ZNet
18 Millfield Street
Woods Hole, MA 02543
Tel: 508/548-9064
zsysop@zbbs.com
http://www.lbbs.org/